Praise for *Counter Mentor Leadership*

"This is a fantastic book, one of the very few I would call a 'MUST read.' Superb advice, actionable ideas, and fun to read. I will be strongly recommending this book to all of my clients and colleagues."

John Spence, Author, *Awesomely Simple*, and a Top 100
Business Thought Leader in America

"As a leader, one of your greatest challenges is connecting multiple generations within your workforce and getting them to work together effectively. In this immensely helpful book, Kelly and Robby Riggs lay out a set of arguments and a blueprint for success that will sharpen your perspective and give you actionable advice."

Tim Sanders, New York Times bestselling author of
Love Is the Killer App and *Dealstorming*

"*Counter Mentor Leadership* is motivational, thought-provoking, entertaining, and certainly challenging for all leaders! Although extensively researched, the book is an easy read on 'new leadership' - using basic proven methods while adjusting to a new work force that is incredibly driven, motivated, and tech-savvy."

James P. Kellogg, Vice President, Colorado Rockies

"Leveraging the skills and talents of the multi-generational workforce is a leadership imperative in the 21st century, and Kelly and Robby Riggs provide you with the tools, resources, and wisdom to tackle this job head on. Reading this book is just like having a conversation with Kelly and Robby – engaging, fast-paced, lots of laughs, and peppered with practical leadership insights. Put their ideas into practice and watch your leadership rise to the next level."

Randy Conley, V.P. Client Services & Trust Practice
Leader, The Ken Blanchard Companies

"Finally, a book on multiple generations in the workplace written by multiple generations. *Counter Mentor Leadership* will get you thinking, but more importantly it will get you listening to those older and younger than you."

David Burkus, Associate Professor of Leadership and
Innovation, and Author, *Under New Management*

"Shamelessly funny and brilliantly written; just don't let the laughs get in the way of the many important leadership lessons—for every generation!"

Tom Koulopoulos, Author, *The Gen Z Effect: The
6 Forces Shaping the Future of Business*

"Kelly and Robby do a masterful job of transcending 'the way we've always done it,' while distilling the enduring principles of great relationships and effective leadership."

Nate Regier, PhD, CEO of Next Element Consulting,
Author, *Conflict Without Casualties*

"I highly recommend this book to anyone who wants to improve their own leadership skills, or the skills of leaders within their company. The focus on the 1-on-1 meetings has been a game-changer for me and for other leaders, and it has led to a significant increase in our employee engagement scores."

Mary Kay Gribbons, EVP, Human Resources, Animal Supply Company

"GREAT book! *Counter Mentor Leadership* is a reality check for anyone in leadership (young or old). It gives actionable leadership strategies using humor and wit to keep you highly engaged the whole way through."

Jack Kosakowski, CEO (US Division), Creation Agency

"When it comes to pinpointing the real issues facing the modern workplace, Kelly and Robby are spot on. What most have labeled simply as technology gaps or generational differences, they have identified rightly as communication and leadership challenges. The winsome *Counter Mentor Leadership* will help us coach up the right kinds of leaders for decades to come. You and I will be better leaders because of it, too."

Curt Steinhorst, Founder & CEO of Focuswise, Author, *Can I Have
Your Attention? Inspiring Better Work Habits, Focusing Your Team,
and Getting Stuff Done in the Constantly Connected Workplace*

"Insightful, bold and cleverly written, this book addresses the complex dynamics of multi-generational workforce engagement, and describes what effective leaders MUST do to achieve extraordinary results"

Dana Birkes, VP, Business Strategies, Crossland Construction Company, Inc.

"*Counter Mentor Leadership* moves beyond tired management clichés and platitudes, and gives practical advice on how to bridge the divide between Boomers and Millennials in the workplace."

Ryan Williams, Managing Director, FP1 Strategies

"*Counter Mentor Leadership* offers a truly insightful perspective on the modern workplace in an extremely entertaining, often hysterical, read. Kelly and Robby teach the leadership skills and tactics you need to maneuver through this challenging situation and become a legit Counter Mentor Leader. It is an intuitive and easy-to-read format - you won't be able to put it down!"

J.R. Stewart, National Sales Manager, Filtrexx International

"Bridging across the span of generations is not an easy task to do, much less do well. Kelly and Robby provide a plan that any organization can apply today to stop the decline of productivity."

Teri Aulph, Sr. Vice President and Chief HR Officer, Tulsa Federal Credit Union

"The Riggs boys have written a brilliant and timely leadership book. They've written a killer, How To, prescriptive, humorous, engaging and funny book with one purpose, to get everyone playing well in the sandbox. If you've ever even uttered the words "management effectiveness" then this book is for you."

Jim Keenan, CEO of A Sales Guy Consulting, Author, *Not Taught: What It Takes to Be Successful in the 21st Century That Nobody's Teaching You*

"If you are in a leadership role today or want to be in one in the future, give yourself an unfair advantage in the marketplace by immediately buying this book. Not only do both authors have deep experience and credentials in this area, but they are also father and son. That creates a raw, honest, back-and-forth set of perspectives that is unique in a business book."

Miles Austin, President and Founder of FilltheFunnel.com

Counter Mentor Leadership

How to Unlock the Potential of
the 4-Generation Workplace

Kelly Riggs and Robby Riggs

NICHOLAS BREALEY
PUBLISHING

BOSTON · LONDON

First published in 2018 by Nicholas Brealey Publishing
An imprint of John Murray Press

An Hachette UK company

23 22 21 20 19 18   1 2 3 4 5 6 7 8 9 10

A CIP catalogue record for this title is available from the British Library.

Library of Congress Cataloging-in-Publication Data

Names: Riggs, Kelly, author. | Riggs, Robby, author.Title: Counter mentor leadership : how to unlock the potential of the 4-generation workplace / Kelly Riggs, Robby Riggs. Description: 1 Edition. | Boston : Nicholas Brealey, 2018. Identifiers: LCCN 2017040741 (print) | LCCN 2017050558 (ebook) | ISBN 9781473657250 (ebook) | ISBN 9781473658790 (library ebook) | ISBN 9781473657236 (hardback) | ISBN 9781473657243 (ebook)Subjects: LCSH: Leadership. | Executives--Training of. | Mentoring in business. | BISAC: BUSINESS & ECONOMICS / Leadership.Classification: LCC HD57.7 (ebook) | LCC HD57.7 .R537 2018 (print) | DDC 658.4/092--dc23LC record available at HYPERLINK "https://protect-us.mimecast.com/s/dqpKBqhGxdRJfQ?domain=lccn.loc.gov" https://lccn.loc.gov/2017040741

ISBN 978-1-47365-723-6
U.S. eBook ISBN 978-1-47365-725-0
U.K. eBook ISBN 978-1-47365-724-3

Printed and bound in the United States of America.

John Murray Press policy is to use papers that are natural, renewable, and recyclable products and made from wood grown in sustainable forests. The logging and manufacturing processes are expected to conform to the environmental regulations of the country of origin.

John Murray Press Ltd
Carmelite House
50 Victoria Embankment
London EC4Y 0DZ
Tel: 020 3122 6000

Nicholas Brealey Publishing
Hachette Book Group
Market Place Center, 53 State Street
Boston, MA 02109, USA
Tel: (617) 263 1834

www.nicholasbrealey.com
www.countermentors.com

Contents

Acknowledgments

ANYONE WHO HAS EVER WRITTEN A BOOK will tell you how tough the process is, and we are no exception. However, it is not so daunting a task when you have the incredible support team we have been blessed with.

A word of gratitude, first of all, to the brilliant author and professor Tom Koulopoulos, for introducing us to the publishing world and to our outstanding literary agent, John Willig. Thanks to you both for believing in the project and helping us turn our concept into a tangible proposal. We are also deeply indebted to our editor, Alison Hankey, who bought into our vision, sold it to the incredible group at Nicholas Brealey, and helped us transform the book into something truly special. Finally, we'd like to thank Alyssa Connell and Renee Nicholls for their ability to turn our typos and run-on sentences into a coherent message, and Michelle Morgan for her insights and help with design and layout—we never could have produced something this visually compelling on our own.

We want to thank all our consulting partners and clients over the past decade. Your insights, unique challenges, and lessons-learned brought this book to life! Special thanks to Ken Wilkins, Miles Austin, Greg Kach, Eric Winton, Willi Graef, Mary Kay Gribbons, and the entire team at Slalom Boston.

We're fortunate to have a very close family. They have encouraged our work and tolerated our absences the last two years as we transitioned from ideation to outline to manuscript. Kristina, Scott, Greg, Camden, Evelyn, and Cora—someday we will go on a vacation that doesn't include us locked in a room yelling and screaming about the importance of leadership, communication, and alignment. *Maybe.*

A very, very special thanks to our wives, Cassie and Rhonda. There are no words that could ever adequately describe how important, encouraging, loving, and magical you are to each of us! We would never be where we are today without you.

Finally, we want to thank all the Millennials. We're not *really* sure why, but we felt compelled to give you "a special shout out"—whatever that means—since we can't afford trophies for all of you.

Introduction

ALTHOUGH IT'S TYPICALLY BETTER to start a new relationship with good news or encouragement, we actually have some bad news.

You are giving away your company's money.

Actually, to put a fine point on it, you're not really *giving* it to anyone. What you're doing is taking a significant amount of what your company earns every year and tossing it in the trash. Evidently, you take some kind of sadistic pleasure in taking a big pile of your company's money, dousing it in gasoline, and watching it burn.

Hopefully, we've gotten your attention.

You see, most companies believe that when you promote an individual to the ranks of management, that person *miraculously* becomes an *amazing* leader. We expect him or her to become the Queen of Inspiration, the Dean of Workplace Insights, *and* the Emperor of Employee Engagement. Which makes you, unfortunately, the King or Queen of Delusional Thinking, because (spoiler alert) a competent, gets-stuff-done (GSD) employee does not automatically make the transition from rock star individual contributor (we call them *doers*) to a competent, much less *transformational*, leader of other people.

Sorry. Does not happen. #truth (Boomers, refer to Millennials for guidance on those number signs commonly called hashtags.)

Of course, if you're making more money than you know what to do with, you probably couldn't care less. However, for most of us mere mortals, finding a way to add to the bottom line is always a topic of interest and, frankly, a constant struggle.

Oh, and to answer your next question—yes, there is plenty of empirical evidence to support our bold, bordering-on-offensive claim. The good news is that you can recover truckloads of cash by following the advice and tactics in this book. Is that just Millennial daydreaming? We don't think so. Boomer and Millennial, we are on the same page.

One thing you need to know is this book is NOT hypothetical or academic. It is a result of well over twenty-five years of experiences and observations in organizations with multigenerational conflict: a fifty-something entrepreneur and former executive (Baby Boomer) and a thirty-something MBA consultant turned entrepreneur (Millennial) who still thinks he's twenty-nine. We represent two totally different perspectives, but we have seen the same problems over and over:

1. A shocking lack of leadership skills in the workplace
2. The stunning, often unrecognized impact of technology on the workplace
3. The culture-killing generational divide that is demolishing many companies

Surprisingly, despite our very different perspectives as a Millennial and a Boomer, we see the solution exactly the same way.

The fundamental question—the thing we just don't get—is this: Why haven't more companies addressed this modern leadership dilemma? Here is a perfect example of the problem, taken from *New York Times* bestselling author Simon Sinek:

A couple months ago, I stayed at the Four Seasons in Las Vegas. Now that is a beautiful hotel, and the reason it is a beautiful hotel is not because of the fancy beds; any hotel can simply buy a fancy bed. The reason it's a great hotel is because of the people who work there . . . The people who work there, when they walk past you, will say hello and you get the feeling they actually want to say hello, not that someone told them they have to say hello . . .

They have a coffee stand in the lobby and I went down one afternoon to buy a coffee . . . The barista behind the counter, his name was Noah. Noah was fantastic. He was funny. He was engaging . . . this kid was amazing.

As is my nature, I asked Noah, "Do you like your job?" Without skipping a beat, Noah said, "I love my job."

So, I followed up, "What is it that the Four Seasons is doing that you would say to me, 'I love my job'?"

And without skipping a beat, Noah said, "Throughout the day, managers will walk past me and ask me how I'm doing, ask me if there is anything I need to do my job better. Not just my manager. Any manager."

And then, he said something magical. "I also work at Caesar's Palace. There, the managers walk past to make sure that I'm doing everything right. They walk past and catch me if I am doing something wrong. There, I keep my head down. I just want to get through the day and get my paycheck."

Same person. Different leadership.[1]

Some leaders get it, but the vast majority do not. Your people are not the problem; they are not the cause of the typical workplace issues. In most cases, the real problem is you, the leader. It is your inability to adapt to the leadership demands of the chaotic, four-generation workplace, and it is costing you an incredible amount of money.

You do, however, have a decent excuse. The management practices you learned, usually by watching other bad managers flail away, are a remnant of a workplace long forgotten. Those "Taylorian

Management" practices (our label for the methods espoused by nineteenth-century management expert Frederick Winslow Taylor), which are typically manifested in dictatorial, micromanaging behavior, also breed employee disillusionment, cultural complacency, and mediocre performance.

The sad reality, however, is that most of today's leaders have been exposed to little else, and they have been taught even less! The result is a workplace in which two-thirds of employees are disengaged, disinterested in the company's objectives, and cynical about corporate leaders.

As you can see, we place little stock in the premise that the conflict between leaders and employees is about generational differences. Instead, we believe the workplace conflict that exists is not really generational; it's *relational*.

That fundamental difference in perspective has enormous ramifications for leaders, for employees, and for the bottom line.

Yes, we think you will have fun reading this book, but that's not our *only* intention. We will show you two things:

1. The many aspects of the modern leadership dilemma (and the challenges that shape it)
2. A proven, repeatable, seven-step framework to overcome the workplace challenges

Our goal is to ignite the flames of change, compelling you to transform your behavior and make your company an incredible place to work. We will give you theory, research, stories, and actionable tactics that you can use to change your leadership behavior *immediately*.

This isn't your father's leadership book. We are going to push you and make you uncomfortable, because that's where personal growth begins.

Our first tip? Instead of burning that money, you should invest it in teaching yourself and your people Counter Mentor Leadership.

A Short Guide to This Book

1. This is not another #boringleadershipbook. Which is to say, this book isn't a dissertation about some new management theory supported by a regression analysis of relevant research data. Ugh. We stay away from TLAs (three-letter acronyms) and promise you'll laugh and learn at the same time (or curse and throw things at the wall, which we will take as a good sign).

2. This book is for two different groups of people. Generally, they are referred to as Boomers and Millennials, but we will call them the **BOSS (Boomer, Old-School Supervisors)** and the **KIDS (Know-It-All Digital Self-Promoters)**. Clever, huh? (Our acronyms have four letters. You should be impressed.)

3. Okay, so we just offended Gen X (the group after Boomers but older than Millennials) and the Digital Natives (the generation after Millennials). Yes, this book is still relevant for you! In our experience, Gen X typically has Boomer tendencies but is more comfortable with technology, and Digital Natives typically identify with Millennials since they were born with an iDevice in their hands. Confusing? Don't worry, we'll sort it out soon enough.

4. As far as tendencies and how you relate, you are likely one or the other (the BOSS, or one of the KIDS), although you could be

that new species: a Millennial Manager with Boomer Employees. Wherever you fit, blending the two together in the workplace (the BOSS and the KIDS), one as manager and one as employee, creates a recipe for potential disaster. How long did it take for you to understand that you have fundamentally different perspectives on life and work: somewhere around five minutes?

5. If you are, in fact, an "Old School" Boomer Manager, and you're reading this book to learn how to "manage" Millennials you've come to the wrong place. Learning to "manage" a Millennial is like trying to "manage" the relationship with your significant other. It's going to end badly, and you'll be starting over with a different one soon enough. This is about LEADERSHIP, not manipulation.

6. We think you will enjoy the book, but at one point or another, we may actually step on your toes. Hopefully, it will hurt enough that you'll want to change, but make no mistake: our intent is to challenge you to think and to question the status quo of current leadership practices.

7. We've written this book in one voice, but that doesn't mean we will always agree. So, you'll get two perspectives—and you'll always know which is which. Just look for the hats.

 The classy, stylish hat belongs to the perspective of the BOSS (Kelly, aka the Pops).

 The fashion-forward, ecofriendly, socially conscious hat (yeah, it's a baseball cap) belongs to the perspective of the KIDS (Robby).

8. You should find this book to be easy-to-read (Robby says it's "consumable," which is some kind of special MBA word that he

borrowed $100K to learn). Short-ish chapters. Practical advice. Actionable content.

9. We will include **The Key Points to Remember** at the end of each chapter. These quick summaries should be written down and/or tweeted immediately. Don't forget the hashtag #countermentorleadership!

10. No participation trophies were awarded in the writing of this book. #fakenews

Today's
Workplace

TODAY'S WORKPLACE is like Saturday at noon in a suburban mall food court. It's chaotic, diverse, loud, annoying, and frustrating. It is a full frontal assault on the senses. If you're overly shy, reserved, or introverted or have problems with sensory overload, we would highly suggest you avoid it at all costs. That being said, the current workplace is also full of opportunity for the leader who can learn how to navigate it effectively!

To solve its challenges, the leader must first understand the complexities of the current workplace. If you can't define or understand this chaotic environment, there is no possible way you can solve its problems.

This is exactly what many leaders are guilty of: trying to solve a *systemic* problem with a variety of tactical solutions.

In many cases, they only manage to address the symptoms and never get anywhere near the root causes.

The first section of the book explores the workplace—its players, its challenges, and its opportunities.

Chapter 1

What We Figured Out Over Thanksgiving Dinner

"Each generation imagines itself to be more intelligent than the one that went before it, and wiser than the one that comes after it."[1]

George Orwell

THANKSGIVING at our house is an epic event.

Nona, the loving matriarch, makes more food than could possibly be consumed over the long weekend. This results in constantly eating and watching football; eating and *pretending* to watch football; or, when Nona demands, eating all together, engaged in a meaningful conversation.

Unlike many families, we don't have the "no religion or politics at the table" rule at our house. Which means, every once in a while, it can be a touch uncomfortable.

"Because kids these days have no respect!"

 "Actually, it's because the Pops is getting senile and has lost his filter."

Thanksgiving 2014 was no different: seven people trying to catch up on a thousand things, all at the same time. As she often does, Nona reeled everyone back in with a question, this time directed at Robby: "Son," she said, "how are things going in Boston?"

"It's actually going really well," Robby replied. "The client I'm working with is finally starting to understand that our team, though *much* younger than the gray-haired, pleated-khakis executives they would normally 'take direction' from, has a great perspective and a ton of value to offer."

"Rob," Pops interjected, "how did you get them to see the value of your team? Typically, Boomers whine and complain about how terrible Millennials are, and they would *never* listen to their point of view!"

Unfortunately, this is the truth. Even the Pops has been known to get in a few shots about the KIDS. (Don't all older generations complain about the younger?)

"Kids these days with their pants hanging below their waists, with their iSomethings and selfies and apps-for-everything. All about themselves. They can't they read and write like normal people, but they want to come in to work on Monday in flip-flops and be CEO by Friday!"

Nothing like throwing an entire generation under the bus.

 "Hard to ignore when it's so common!"

The challenge for the Pops is a tough one. He hears these same complaints day in and day out from clients who continue to struggle with these new, "high-maintenance" KIDS. And we can't really blame him, can we? This is the popular belief of almost every BOSS. Even Robby experienced it as a brand-new consultant, fresh out of business school. This is a story he loves to tell.

Robby's Stereotypical BOSS Encounter

My first client was an electric utility cooperative in a sleepy little town in North Texas, the kind of place where people have lived a long time and the company picnic is basically a family reunion.

The truth is, I learned more in the first six months with that client than I did in all of business school—about leadership, being a professional, setting expectations, taking initiative, and—sadly—the television show *Lost*. (Why did everyone love that show so much?! Time travel and multiple dimensions? I still don't get it.)

I was working on a project that was to replace the client's paper-based ticketing system. Technicians drove into the corporate office from all over North Texas every morning, picked up their tickets (repair orders), and then returned to the field to complete the work. Once completed, the techs would drive all the way back to HQ to turn in their tickets, resulting in thousands of miles driven each day. (Hopefully, you are starting to see the inefficiencies!)

I quickly realized we weren't so much doing a technology project as we were helping the client transform their thinking.

The solution was to arm field technicians with electronic tablets, eliminating manual data entry by back-office staff and dramatically reducing drive time for each technician. Although the techs were generally reluctant to adopt the new technology, most were curious enough about the tablets that they were engaged in the process.

The supporting departments, however, were a much different story.

Most notable was the company's billing department. Their work-flow process was painful, requiring employees to duplicate their effort over and over, manually inserting the same comments and notes on multiple screens. As I began to document the process, I asked why the notes had to be entered and re-entered that way. I was promptly introduced to that most famous of corporate justifications: "We've always done it this way."

It is that one short sentence that holds most organizations pris-oner, and once that door slams shut, it becomes the equivalent of Alcatraz, seemingly inescapable.

We completed our "current state" documentation and moved on to designing the future state: the process that would support the new tablets. Clearly, one of the prime opportunities for improvement was the process within the billing department, which required me to meet with the director of billing. To say she wasn't excited to see me is an understatement, and she made it perfectly clear that she wasn't happy about me "messing up" her department. #perspective

However, I carefully explained the benefits of the changes: the elimination of the need to enter data on multiple screens, the ability to auto-fill comments from the tablets, and the opportunity to push meter readings into the system automatically from the field. A huge win, right?!

After showing her all the great things the new process would do, I wasn't exactly prepared for her response: "Who do you think you are? I have children older than you! What do you know about running a billing department?!"

After I pulled my chin up off the table (I was early in my career and hadn't developed a great "ARE YOU FREAKING KIDDING ME?" poker face), I asked her to explain to me why this wasn't good for her and her department. "Well," she replied, "that's just not how we do things here!"

Wow. Just . . .
Wow.

Finding Our Middle Ground

Much has been written about the clash between generations in the workplace. The challenges and the issues are undeniable, but we believe the key to success in this chaotic, four-generation workplace is completely dependent upon a change in leadership approach.

So, before we go any further, it's important that you understand how we define leadership. No, it's not the same thing as *management*.

The fact is, the majority of "leaders" are still trying to manage people using the same techniques that were developed in the late 1800s by Frederick Winslow Taylor, the godfather of modern management. He was the pioneer, and he quite literally wrote the book on it: his 1911 work entitled *The Principles of Scientific Management*. His ideas were all about enforcing standards and controlling workers (what is referred to as "management").

Here is a summary of his core principles:

1. Corporations are wildly inefficient in production processes.

2. The remedy for this inefficiency lies in systematic management rather than in searching for some unusual or extraordinary leader.

3. The best management is a true science, resting upon clearly defined laws, rules, and principles as a foundation.[2]

Management, according to Taylor, is all about the *system*. The people are simply part of the system; they are meant to serve it.

Taylor said, "In the past, the man has been first; in the future, the system must be first."[3] Furthermore, his approach was built on the premise that the "workman" was considerably less capable (and by *capable*, we mean smart, savvy, talented, educated, and innovative) than the "manager." Taylor says,

> It is only through **enforced** standardization of methods, **enforced** adoption of the best implements and working conditions, and **enforced** cooperation that this faster work can be assured and the duty of **enforcing** the adoption of standards and **enforcing** this cooperation rests with the *MANAGEMENT* alone.[4]

To summarize: Taylorian Management is all about forcing workers to do it "my way." (Every BOSS just did a little fist pump and let out an audible "YES!")

The problem here is obvious. Taylor wrote and tested his methods in a working environment that is *slightly* different from a *collaboration workspace* in the twenty-first century. He developed his philosophy in railroad yards, on factory floors, and alongside pig-iron handlers. We're talking about the tail end of the Industrial Revolution, not exactly a Silicon Valley cube farm with a shuffleboard table in the break room.

Taylor, showing proof of his methods, adds this:

> This work is so crude and elementary in its nature that [Taylor] firmly believes that it would be possible to train an intelligent gorilla so as to become a more efficient pig-iron handler than any man can be.[5]

To be fair, Taylor's ideas, in the environment in which he lived and studied, really worked. Industrial America became more efficient. But, just because they worked *then*, we've allowed this philosophy of management to permeate our workplace *today*, more than a hundred years later. Successive generations of "leaders" have watched and soaked up command-and-control management, forcing and enforcing employees for over a century.

We shake our heads in shame and disgust. We aren't pig-iron handlers anymore! We are connected, distracted, educated, and innovative knowledge workers. It is only because of a lack of education in *leadership* that we are STILL trying to employ the Taylorian Management model today.

Do you get how ridiculously and offensively preposterous this is?! We've seen our world transform in basically every way, yet we think we can continue to utilize an out-of-touch and out-of-date management philosophy that was developed, more or less, to create indentured servitude.

Driving Transformation: Counter Mentor Leadership

For the first time in history, the younger generation has something more to offer an employer than enthusiasm and a fresh canvas. In the past, a new employee was instructed to "pay your dues," and promotion and advancement were dependent upon years of service and "working your way up the corporate ladder." But the workplace has been evolving quite rapidly since the Internet crashed the party. Now, the younger generation brings much more to the table than the ability to fetch coffee and make copies.

The KIDS have both the knowledge and the practical experience to navigate the rapidly evolving landscape of social media and digital tools. As technology infects the workplace, the value of the innovative, tech-savvy, so-called "junior" employee has increased a hundredfold.

Today's leaders must adapt! Any model of leadership that doesn't embrace intentional inclusion and collaboration with the KIDS is ultimately a death sentence to the organization and a ceiling for a manager's career.

After working with clients all over the world, from start-up to Fortune 100, our perspective is that leadership is **the art and science of getting things done through other people**, and *Counter Mentor Leadership* is the playbook to bring it to life. The transformational leader is a leader who coaches and develops the high-potential employee and simultaneously taps into the wealth of knowledge available from the younger generations and grows from below. Mentoring, reverse mentoring, and building a trusting relationship—these are the critical elements of Counter Mentor Leadership.

Most importantly, these new leaders have learned how to use every resource available. They are taking the best of the wisdom and experience of the "older" generation (the BOSS) and mixing it with the innovation and technology savvy of the "newer" generation (the KIDS) to bridge the generational divide and drive their organization to new and higher levels of performance and success.

These leaders put the following steps into action:

- Communicate the desired outcomes and constantly seek to be transparent
- Own the relationship with their employees
- Understand their people's perspective
- Negotiate the obstacles that threaten success
- Teach their employees the essential skills
- Evaluate and course correct as needed
- Review constantly with their people—seeking feedback, new ideas, and engagement in the form of a very specific type of one-on-one meeting

Are you ready for this?

Key Points to Remember

1. If you ever hear "we've always done it that way" in the workplace, you should immediately investigate the process or task. We'll wager big money there is an opportunity to improve!

2. Taylorian Management—the micromanagement style you see every day in the workplace—is dead and will not enable you to reach your true potential in the workplace.

3. Leadership is the art and science of getting things done through other people.

 Check out this related *Counter Mentors* podcast episode: "I'm the Leader. Now Sit Down and Shut Up!" Visit cmtr.co/ep9.

Chapter 2

Technology: The Good, the Bad, and the Truly Scary

"I don't have any of the modern electronics at all.
I know the Internet would be a distraction. I would see things
that interested me and never get back to writing."[1]

Elmore Leonard

THE POPS purchased his first "mobile" device in 1988.

Back then, a mobile device was actually a car phone, which is really the only thing that made it mobile. It had an antenna for the roof of the car and a black box that went under the seat—very James Bond-ish (the Sean Connery version). They did make a portable version of the car phone, affectionately referred to as a "bag phone." The problem was that it bore little resemblance to a bag, unless you're referring to a twenty-two-inch roll-aboard.

This *innovation* did exactly one thing, and one thing only: phone calls. No texting. No browsing. No pictures of your food. No videos of screaming goats. Just phone calls.

The monthly investment for using that phone, using about thirty-five minutes a day, was well over $400—about $820 per month in today's dollar. Today, of course, you can pay around $60 a month for a miniature supercomputer, a truly *mobile* device that will do everything short of teleporting you to another time zone. Streaming video. Instant communication. GPS. Online banking. Information on demand. And hipster food pictures by the billions.

 "The KIDS and their food pics. I'm pretty sure pictures are the new trophies."

This radical transformation took less than twenty years. By comparison, the time between the invention of radio and the first black-and-white television was over forty years, and it was another quarter century before flat-screen technology was invented.

Most importantly, for our purposes, technology has radically transformed the workplace in just about every way that you can imagine. Information is now available in the cloud, allowing every device in the building to connect and sync autonomously. Automation is possible in every part of the company, from manufacturing and operations to sales and marketing. Communication is instantaneous, around the world, across multiple platforms. We're always on, always connected.

Technology has crushed the barriers to entry in dozens of industries previously occupied only by large companies. Smaller companies—even solopreneurs—can look and sound much larger and more sophisticated than they may actually be. Furthermore, today's technology provides access not only to information, but also to customers, their habits, and their immediate feedback, creating an incredibly cost-effective platform for marketing and promoting a brand while providing the opportunity to personalize and individualize those products and services.

So, what's not to like about technology?

We heard you laugh! Or was that gasping for air? Quite obviously, technology, for all the incredible benefits it provides, also presents some serious challenges.

First, just keeping up with technology is a battle all its own. The newest version (hardware or software) is basically out of date by the time you get comfortable with it. Then, the time required to train on any new technology is always a significant drain on productivity. Worse still, technology issues, from hardware malfunctions to password changes to software patches, are a persistent source of friction and frustration in the workplace.

Yes, indeed, IT is the department we all love to hate. Nir Eyal, a contributor to *Forbes*, presented the truth of that statement in his article entitled "Why Everyone Hates IT People."

> Quick: what's the biggest bottleneck in your company? Yup, we both know it's the Information Technology department. Let's face it, nobody likes IT people. For all of their technical wizardry, IT is where good ideas go to die. We follow their onerous documentation requirements and patiently wait in line through endless backlogs, yet somehow IT still can't seem to get their work done.[2]

Truth or tongue-in-cheek, most people understand the frustration of technology. However, we typically chalk it up to the small price we have to pay for progress—a whole new world, brimming with possibilities, propelled by a tidal wave of new and advancing technology solutions. Onward and upward!

Right?

Unfortunately, there's more to technology problems than a bit of inconvenience. For many, there is a real belief that technology has created as many problems in the workplace as it may have solved. In an *MIT Sloan Management Review* article entitled "The Dark Side of Information Technology," the authors describe some of the more common issues:

> Pervasive and near-continual use of organizational IT systems is now beginning to take a toll on some employees' health. Individuals experience "IT use-induced stress" or "technostress" for a number of reasons. They feel forced to multitask rapidly on simultaneous streams of information from different devices simply because information feeds come at them in real time; remote work and flextime tether them round the clock to their devices and workplaces; and short technology cycles and pressures from IT vendors mean constantly changing interfaces, screens and functionalities, often without sufficient FAQs and help-desk support. We also found in a survey of about 600 computer-using professionals that 73% worried that refraining from constant connectivity and instantaneous information-feed response would place them at a disadvantage at work.[3]

Stress? Pressure? Health issues? Maybe there is more to the price of progress in the workplace than we anticipated.

We're not even close to finished yet.

The Scary Parts of Technology

One of the most pernicious workplace challenges presented by technology is *distraction*.

From Internet access and text messaging to social media and YouTube videos, technology provides constant and persistent diversions to workplace productivity.

A Harris poll, conducted on behalf of CareerBuilder, surveyed 2,138 hiring managers and HR professionals and 3,022 full-time workers to determine how employees waste time in the workplace.[4]

Twenty-four percent of workers *self-reported* that they spend at least an hour of a typical workday on personal email, texts, and personal calls. Twenty-one percent estimated that they waste an hour or more searching the Internet for non-work-related information.

According to that poll, these are the top four time-wasters in the workplace:

1. Talking on the cell phone and texting—50%
2. Gossiping—42%
3. Time on the Internet—39%
4. Time engaged with social media—38%

If you're a BOSS, you probably have a hard time believing these numbers. You likely think they are *way too low*. After all, the one consistent complaint from the BOSS is how much time those KIDS spend on their phones when they should be working! Unfortunately, the BOSS might be right. A 2014 Salary.com survey revealed that employees admit to wasting a significant amount of time at work:

- 31% admitted to wasting as much as 30 minutes daily
- 31% admitted to wasting as much as 1 hour daily
- 16% admitted to wasting as much as 2 hours daily[5]

That's right, roughly one out of every six employees (16%) *admit* they waste as much as a quarter of the workday!

But that's not the worst of it.

- 6% admitted to wasting as much as 3 hours daily
- 2% admitted to wasting as much as 4 hours daily
- 2% admitted to wasting as much as 5 hours daily[6]

One out of every ten employees admitted to wasting away 3 or more hours every day!

EVERY SINGLE DAY.

And we don't even have to guess what employees are doing to waste that time; the employees themselves told us. The biggest culprits? Google (24%), followed by Facebook (23%) and LinkedIn (14%).

Ah, yes, social media—*the gift that keeps on taking.*

That one problem—distraction—is bad enough to make any BOSS want to throw something, but there is even more danger lurking out there. Mobile technology and social media create a volatile weapon capable of inflicting great harm on your business.

Can You Say, "United Breaks Guitars?"

In 2008, David Carroll and his fellow band members from the Canadian band Sons of Maxwell were traveling from Halifax, Nova Scotia, to Omaha, Nebraska, to play a gig. Bad news for the band: upon arrival in Omaha, Carroll discovered that one of his Taylor guitars, valued at $3,500, had been badly damaged.[7]

Carroll immediately filed a claim with United Airlines, but nine months of rejections and denials from the airline led Carroll to do what any self-respecting songwriter would do. He wrote a song about the incident. And then he posted it on YouTube.

Released in July 2009, the song, "United Breaks Guitars," needed only sixty days to garner a whopping 5 million views. With more than 16 million views at the time of this writing, the song, and its two subsequent follow-up songs, made Carroll a bit of a star. He published a book (*United Breaks Guitars: The Power of One Voice in the Age of Social Media*), testified on Capitol Hill, was featured in major news shows and publications, and delivered keynote speeches at events all over the country.[8]

The point of the story, however, is the negative impact these events had on the image and reputation of United Airlines (much more about this phenomenon in chapter 9). Most importantly, little, *if anything*, would have happened to United Airlines without the incredible reach of technology and social media.

See the problem? Not only is technology an *internal* threat to employee productivity, it poses a significant *external* threat should companies screw over, anger, or simply miscalculate with customers. Social media can make you famous, and it can make your company infamous.

In his November 2010 Harvard Business School case, marketing professor John Deighton offered the following observation:

> "[United Breaks Guitars] is a good case for getting a glimpse into a new world of communication, vs. the old world of Super Bowl ads and prime-time audiences," says Deighton. "The new world doesn't necessarily play by the rules of the old. One of the points we debate in class is whether social media are better at destroying value than creating it. In social media, an entity's size and brand recognition make it more vulnerable to parody and attack, not safer. As we accumulate experience with these media, perhaps we will find that they tend to favor the insurgent over the incumbent."[9]

The truth is, technology presents enormous benefits while creating significant hazards. It has completely advanced the business landscape while dramatically altering the workplace. It has made it so much easier to connect to customers, but it has also created a platform that empowers customers to destroy a brand.

Technology has created a love-hate relationship in the workplace which, for some borders on the extreme. Regardless of how you may feel about it, the impact of technology requires leaders to adapt or to be swept aside—assuming your objective is to grow revenues, attract talent, and keep more of your money.

Unfortunately, technology isn't the only challenge you face in the chaotic, four-generation workplace.

Key Points to Remember

1. Technology has enabled us to do incredible things, but it isn't without some *potentially devastating* side effects.

2. Seventy-eight percent of employees self-reported they waste between thirty minutes and two hours throughout the workday on the Internet! Yes, distractions are a huge problem.

3. Your customers are more connected and have more power than ever before. Thank you, social media. *The gift that keeps on taking.*

Chapter **3**

The Fight We
Should've Seen Coming

"Creativity involves breaking out of established patterns in order to look at things in a different way."[1]

Edward de Bono

BEFORE WE GET INTO THE DETAILS of the current generational disconnect—which has shaped up to be an Ali–Frazier-esque title fight—let's define the two opponents in the workplace.

Please understand that, despite the common usage, we're not necessarily fans of the terms *Boomer* and *Millennial*. Gen X winds up getting ignored, and the Digital Natives are barely even in the picture at this point. On top of that, some Boomers have adapted well to Millennials, and vice versa. So, as we mentioned in the introduction, when talking about the workplace, we will simply call them the BOSS and the KIDS.

BOSS: the **B**oomer, **O**ld-**S**chool **S**upervisors

KIDS: the **K**now-**I**t-All, **D**igital **S**elf-Promoters

"And entitled, and lazy, and a lot of other things that don't fit into the acronym."

"'S' is actually for *Superstars*, but Pops is too stubborn to admit it."

Dig in to this chapter! We're going to give you a quick overview of the BOSS and the KIDS (the facts and figures) and throw in all of our favorite stereotypes.

The BOSS: Pagers, Pay Phones, and Pensions

We like to describe the BOSS as anyone who still balances a checkbook or has no idea how to use PayPal. This group is counting on a pension and still believes their union rep has their best interest at heart (haven't they seen *The Wire*?). They are primarily Baby Boomers in their fifties and sixties, the ones who are now retiring en masse, but also includes some older Gen Xers (the ones who don't do change).

Here are the key facts and stereotypes you need to know:

- **The BOSS demands respect.** When this generation started their careers, they arrived fifteen minutes early and sat in the office chair until 5:05 P.M., come hell or high water. They did exactly as they were told and never questioned anything. They were "good soldiers" and paid their dues. They simply cannot understand why these KIDS would even think about, much less actually consider, asking WHY something needs to be done. That is completely *disrespectful*.

- **The BOSS expects loyalty.** This generation, unlike their parents, grew up mostly in a time of security and predictability (notwithstanding their early days with the Vietnam War and the *crazy* hippies). They were raised, however, by parents and grandparents who survived the Great Depression and WWII. As such, there was a premium placed on *loyalty*—to country, family, and the job.

- **The BOSS places enormous value on work ethic, probably more than efficiency.** This generation manages, tracks, and thinks about time as the metric for work. They care about work ethic—time at work—more than just about anything. They place an enormous value on grit and the ability to persevere at work over the course of many years. The fact that these KIDS want to "take breaks" and "get more done with less" is vexing. Don't they understand the value of work?

- **The BOSS prefers a real conversation, not a text message.** Psychologists, psychiatrists, and parents have proven it over and over—the most effective way to communicate is face-to-face. Period. So, obviously, this generation always seeks to leverage the *best* form of communication in each and every interaction. *They* don't bother with Snaps or Facebook Live. After all, how do you communicate if you can't look someone in the eye?

- **The BOSS typically values "the way we've always done it."** If you want something done right, you have to do it yourself. This generation has been taught this and experienced it in real life for decades! Naturally, then, they see the way they've *always done it* as the *right* way. The *only* way. Why do these KIDS constantly rebel and want to do things differently? Don't they understand if it ain't broke, you don't need to fix it?

- **The BOSS craves the comfort of the hierarchical organization chart.** When this generation started a new job, they were usually given the Organizational Chart. This sacred document enabled them to understand whom they could interact with, what the path to the top of the corporate ladder looked like, and whom they needed to buy a drink for. It allowed them to figure out who the most important people were (those at the top, obviously), and whom they should avoid (anyone with "Assistant" or "Marketing" in their title).

- **The BOSS covets the gold watch and the retirement pension.** You show up every day, you work hard, and the company will take care of you. The older generation grew up believing in the company from the time they were old enough to pour their own Wheaties. Success at work—and thus, at home—comes from working hard for thirty years. Respect, loyalty, work ethic, and results (if we're in a good economy)—that is success. And nothing says success like the gold watch and a monthly retirement check.

The KIDS: Snapchat, Smartphones, and Slack

The KIDS are a bit different. #understatementoftheyear

They are made up of people who don't write checks. Ever. They use digital apps like Apple Pay, Venmo, Cash, and PayPal. They believe they can show up at noon and get more work done before happy hour than the BOSS can accomplish during his five-days-a-week, eight-to-five nonsense.

This group is made up of younger Gen Xers, Millennials, and the fresh Digital Natives who are beginning to enter the workforce. Here are the key facts and stereotypes you need to know.

- **The KIDS demand respect.** No, they won't give it out automatically, but they definitely demand it immediately. They've been *experiencing* the new ways of the world since they learned to crawl. They know how to swipe, tap, cache, code, and debug. They have followers, friends, and #swag. They have more to offer the BOSS than she can even imagine. They don't understand why the BOSS is so condescending when they have a *better* way of doing it. In their minds, the KIDS don't get the respect they *deserve*.

- **The KIDS need to know "Why?"** Not once in their lives have they had to settle for the one-word answer "No." Not ever. They have negotiated, complained, whined, and used temper tantrums to get that question answered for two or three decades! "What is the BOSS thinking? He wants to just *tell me* what to do? Unacceptable! Doesn't he understand that if I know *why*, I'll be able to find a better way to do it?"

 "Two bullet points in and already my head hurts."

 "Classic BOSS. Someone get the Pops his medication and a bottle of Ensure."

- **The KIDS want collaboration and coaching, not demands and directions.** This generation grew up learning that "everyone's input matters" and "there are no bad ideas!" This was modeled at home, at school, and in extracurricular activities. They were rarely given directions, much less demands. Instead, they've always been coddled and catered to. (Mr. and Ms. Helicopter Parent, we blame you for this!) They want to brainstorm, ideate, collaborate, and think through potential solutions—not have the answer dictated to them. How dare the BOSS try to tell them what they *must* do each day, or (worse) what time they *have to* be in the office?

- **The KIDS value autonomy through flexibility *and* options.** Let's be perfectly clear. This generation values flexibility because they've had it every single day of their lives. They got to choose whether they wanted to watch TV before or after dinner (both, of course). They chose to take a transitional year between high school and college to work on their apps and journals and adjust to the stresses of life after high school. They got to choose between online, in-person, and "at your own pace" classes, which they attended at their leisure, wherever they wanted.

- **The KIDS will just text or snap you.** The KIDS check their phones a ridiculous 150 times per day![2] *Obvi.* SMH—you don't know? LOL—try n keep up! #winning TTYL. (If you're a BOSS, you'll need a translation.)

- **The KIDS crave new and different.** "The Next Big Thing" is basically the tagline for this generation. They've been seeing bigger (or smaller), faster, more powerful, and just *better* "stuff" every single day. From hardware and software to clothes and accessories, they've helped to build a new standard of industry and innovation. Even *The Tonight Show* is way more hip now (sorry, Johnny, it's true). They want you to know, "You're welcome."

- **Many of the KIDS are "work martyrs." Just ask them!** According to a study done by Project: Time Off and GfK, 43 percent of the KIDS self-report as "work martyrs" (vs. 29 percent of the more than 5,000 survey respondents).[3] They were much more likely to agree with key statements like "I feel guilty for using my paid time off" and "I want to show complete dedication to my company and job." They are so ridiculously important—they couldn't possibly take a day off.

- **The KIDS *will* save the world.** Al Gore was right. Immediately after he invented the Internet, he figured out that the older generation has been killing our planet. Now the KIDS believe their job is to save the world that the BOSS has been destroying with her SUVs and his gas-powered golf carts. They would rather go broke working for a company that makes a difference than make a fortune working on Wall Street.

What Drives the Conflict?

If you're one of those people we've labeled as the BOSS, you may be a little irritated by now. You might think our descriptions about you are all slanted negatively, while the stereotypes for the KIDS sound much more positive. (That may be because Robby wrote the first draft of this chapter, and it explains why he was so quick to volunteer.) You're used to throwing around the negative stereotypes about the KIDS—entitled, lazy, undisciplined—and you tend to forget that there are two perspectives in this conflict.

While there have been many blog posts, articles, and books written on *what* causes the extreme conflict between the BOSS and the KIDS, we believe that there are simply three key issues. We've read about these issues and, more importantly, we've observed them firsthand with our clients.

From start-up to Fortune 100, these are the three components of this conflict:

1. **Attitude.** There is a distinct difference between the way the BOSS was raised and taught to act in the workplace (and social settings) and how the KIDS were raised and taught. The KIDS

have been tremendously influenced by several things the BOSS never had to be concerned with—technology, information access, social media, and helicopter parents. Yes, that's right, BOSS, it will dawn on you at some point that YOU were a huge part of creating this monster!

2. **Workplace Expectations.** This one is incredibly easy to understand, yet researchers tend to confound our understanding with academic jargon. Simply put, the BOSS expects the KIDS to "pay their dues" and "show respect." The BOSS *requires* the KIDS to show up on time, do what they're told, work hard, and (try to) add value. That's it. They are not expected to question *everything* and play on their phones *all day*. Is it really that hard?

   Conversely, the KIDS expect the BOSS to understand the amazing life experiences and skills they have, to be thrilled to work with them, and to value everything they have to offer. The KIDS expect—no, *demand*—the opportunity to give their opinion. Plus, they expect to have the flexibility to work from home whenever they want to. Is it really that hard?

3. **Skills.** The KIDS bring a specific set of game-changing technology skills to the workplace, including the ability to leverage apps like Pocket, Basecamp, Slack, Hootsuite, Canva, Wufoo, Box, Trello, Evernote, Calendly, Nimble, and CheckIn (yes, we made at least one of those up). The BOSS often has no idea what these tools are, what they do, or how they have changed the business landscape. Remember, KIDS were taught differently, raised differently, and they have a very different definition of the status quo.

   The KIDS were taught the value of "teaming" and put a premium on learning to operate in an autonomous team. Roles were constantly changed—note taker one day and team leader the next. Their ability to flex and adapt, while always adding value, is what defines success. The KIDS have *very* different skills.

Even 007 Has Challenges with Millennials

In the opening scene of the twenty-third James Bond movie (*Skyfall*), 007 is shot and appears to be dead. Bond, of course, never stays dead, so when Queen and Country are under attack, he immediately comes back to life. Although he's only been away a short time, there is the sense in the movie that an entire lifetime has come and gone while he was "dead." (Somewhere, Daniel Craig is mildly irritated that we summarized forty-five minutes of his brilliant cinema in one short paragraph.)

After returning to 007-type duties, Bond meets his new quartermaster: the person responsible for supplying him with everything from transportation to his beloved Walther PPK. Q needs to finalize operational details, impress Bond with some cool new spy gear, and generally prepare him to get back in the game. Now, if you've ever seen a Bond film, you know that Q has always been an old, white-haired gentleman in a lab coat. The new Q, however, is one of the KIDS; a snarky young Brit who makes Bond very uncomfortable (cue sarcastic, dramatic eye roll).

Their first meeting perfectly sums up the conflict between the BOSS and the KIDS. Bond is in London's National Gallery, deep in thought, contemplating Joseph Turner's 1839 oil painting of the HMS *Temeraire*. *The Fighting Temeraire*, as the painting is known, is a beautiful work of art showing a once-grand, 98-gun ship being towed into the sunset, presumably to be torn apart and her scraps repurposed. This once-magnificent, lethal ship had played a key role in the British win over the combined French and Spanish navies in the 1908 Battle of Trafalgar. She used to be needed.

Bond's temperament is a bit prickly. The metaphor of an old warship no longer fit for battle in the modern world is uncomfortably accurate for where he is and how he's feeling. Then, a young stranger takes a seat on the bench next to Bond. Smugly, he offers his observation of the painting, a thinly veiled comparison with Bond: "Always makes me feel a bit melancholy. A grand old warship being ignominiously hauled away for scrap . . . The inevitability of time, don't you think? What do you see?"

Bond, irritated and presumably offended, gets up to leave, before learning that the young stranger is Q, his new quartermaster. Their awkward first meeting ends with the perfect example of the conflict between the BOSS and the KIDS:

> Q: 007, I'm your new quartermaster.
>
> BOND: You must be joking.
>
> Q: Why, because I'm not wearing a lab coat?

Referring to Q's relative youth and inexperience Bond quips that, no, it's because he still has pimples.

> Q: My complexion is hardly relevant.
>
> BOND: Well, your competence is . . . and youth is no guarantee of innovation.[4]

In response, Q implies that he can "do more damage" on his computer while in his pajamas than Bond can hope to do "in a year in the field."

In one short scene, you have the perfect contrast between the BOSS and the KIDS—between two completely different worlds and two radically different perspectives.

These differences are real, and they are potentially lethal in *your* business. This is especially true when companies fail to prepare their leaders (supervisors, middle managers, and executives) to be successful in the chaotic, four-generation workplace. How much do you think it's costing you in terms of innovation? Or talent acquisition? Most important, how is it affecting your bottom line?

As you will see, you can capitalize on this tremendous *opportunity*, or you can eventually fade into irrelevance. We're betting you want to leverage the power of both generations but are just a bit unsure of how to proceed. So, our objective is to show you a path away from the problem.

We don't have a bulletproof Aston Martin to offer, but we do have some tools that will serve you best when you need them most.

First, however, we need to brief you on some important details. The problem is probably worse than you think.

How's that for a pep talk?

Key Points to Remember

1. The BOSS and the KIDS have radically different points of view. They were raised differently, taught differently, and (generally) think differently.

2. These differences drive an extreme disconnect on expectations inside the workplace.

3. There are three primary drivers of the generational conflict that you need to understand: attitude, expectations, and skills.

Check out this related *Counter Mentors* video podcast episode: "Why Can't You Act Like Adults?!" Visit cmtr.co/ep19.

Chapter **4**

How Did
We Get Here?

"We always put ourselves at the end of history. It's what
humanity does best, repeatedly. Each generation sees itself as
the pinnacle of civilization."[1]

Tom Koulopoulos and Dan Keldsen

A RE OUR EXPERIENCES somehow different today? Is the chaos
of the current four-generation workplace radically different from
the workplace of four decades ago?

Yes . . . And no. First and foremost, older generations throughout history have always had a problem with the younger generation.
Consider this quote:

Children now love luxury. They have bad manners, contempt
for authority, disrespect their elders, and love talking instead
of exercise. Children are now tyrants, not the servants of their
households. They no longer rise when elders enter the room.
They contradict their parents, chatter before company, gobble

up dainties at the table, cross their legs, and tyrannize their teachers.[2]

Taken out of context, this sounds much like the things people say about the KIDS today! However, this quote (often erroneously attributed to Socrates) was actually penned in 1907!

#somethingsneverchange

We're certain that every older generation has historically considered the younger generation to be frivolous, irresponsible, and the reason the world will soon end. The perception of the KIDS today is no different.

Did we mention selfish? A 2014 public opinion survey revealed that 71 percent of Americans think Millennials are "selfish," and nearly two out of three (65 percent) think they're "entitled."[3] Clearly, where there is smoke, there is bound to be some fire, but concluding that an entire generation is made up of arsonists is a bit of a stretch. Unfortunately, that's what happens—people make sweeping generalizations about each and every one of the KIDS.

If people made sweeping generalizations about any other group of people that share a specific character trait ("all Hispanics" or "all women," for example) they would be labeled as bigots. Why is it, then, that it's not similarly frowned upon to make these statements about a group of people who were born in the same era?

How is this okay?

Debunking the Millennial Myth

You would think "the Millennial problem" came out of nowhere, without warning. The reality is, how we got here is simple, logical, and predictable. First, let's take a very brief look at each generation—what they experienced and what they considered to be important.

1. **Greatest Generation (born 1901–1924)**
   Survived the Depression and fought two world wars. Won
   them both. Absolutely anti-debt (you would be too if you lost
   everything overnight) and embodied the definition of "extreme
   national pride."

2. **Traditionalist (born 1925–1946)**
   Also known as the "silent generation" because they were expected
   to be "seen and not heard." They sought lifelong employment with
   little to no risk since they heard their parents talk of the Depression and saw the sacrifices they made during the wars. They paid
   cash or they didn't make the purchase.

3. **Baby Boomers (born 1946–1964)**
   The first "me" generation. (They love to call the KIDS that!) Self-
   proclaimed revolutionaries and yuppies, they experienced most
   everything in the shadow of the Vietnam War: fighting, drugs,
   protests, and hippies. They were the first generation to really use
   (and abuse) credit cards. They wanted to give their kids everything (both physical and emotional) since they rarely, if ever,
   received anything from their parents.

4. **Generation X (born 1961–1981)**
   The rarely-talked-about, somewhere-in-between, lost generation.
   Cynical, and often anti-establishment, they grew up during the
   dot-com boom and witnessed the digital revolution. Note: Many
   Gen Xers harbor a bit of resentment against Millennials, as evi-
   denced by this online rant:

   > What about us Gen Xers? We were the ones to really work
   > in life to get what we wanted. No trophies for all, no certifi-
   > cates of participation, no soft parenting. These spoiled Ins-
   > tagramming, Snapchatting, Facebooking, IM-ing younger
   > people are taking over the world, while Baby Boomers are
   > getting ready for their retirement, and us Gen-Xers are in

the shadow, confused at what the heck happened to what
was supposed to be the best years of our life.[4]

Ouch.

5. **Millennials (born 1982–1997)**
The most talked-about, hypothesized-about, and Googled generation ever. NPR has interviewed "experts" to try to understand
them, and there has been more content created about them than
any other social issue in history. (Okay, we made that last part
up, but that what's it feels like.) Millennials are the new "me-
me-me" generation, the iGeneration, the ATM generation, that
wants it "my way, right now!" **They spent their formative years
being shaped by technology and have always been the center
of their parents' attention. Always.**

So, why do people (especially the BOSS) wonder what happened?
They raised these KIDS. They spoon-fed them participation trophies
and seventh-place ribbons. They gave them everything they ever asked
for and told the school principal their child "would never do that."
They never let their kids fail, let them do whatever they wanted, and
let them live at home until they were thirty. Really? You're surprised
they are who they are?

No, of course it's not true of EVERY one of the KIDS. That's why
it's outright stupid to place them all in one bucket. One of the most
ridiculous stereotypes voiced about the KIDS is "they don't work
hard," or "they aren't willing to do what it takes to be successful."

Ridiculous. Ryan Williams, a "stereotypical" Millennial, is a perfect example of the fallacy of this rhetoric. Here's a quick look at his
story.[5]

The "Stereotypical" Millennial

Ryan grew up in New England with his life laid out in front of him like the proverbial red carpet. His father, a partner at PricewaterhouseCoopers (PWC) for more than thirty years, had it all mapped out—a degree in accounting followed by an internship at one of the best firms in Boston. Ryan could see the next thirty years of *his* life stretched out in front of him. And it terrified him.

So, he did something about it.

As a high school senior, he showed up, uninvited, at the newly formed Romney for Governor 2002 headquarters in Cambridge, Massachusetts, and wouldn't leave until they made him an intern. His job? "Envelope licker" (his words, not ours). Still, he was committed to getting into the communications side of the campaign, an area that truly fascinated him. He started hanging around the pressroom during his breaks from stuffing envelopes. He waited until, finally, opportunity arrived in the form of driving all over Massachusetts, tracking Romney's opponents.

In his Washington, D.C., office, amidst the incessant buzzing of his iPhone and the dinging of his email, with a TV on in the background, Ryan shared his experiences. (We said "stereotypical" Millennial, didn't we?)

> I started doing it and I loved it. I would catch the opponent doing something stupid—like screaming at someone or giving someone the finger—and I would drive to all the different TV stations in Boston to drop off the tapes. It was awesome for an eighteen-year-old. I felt I was really making a difference.

Wearing the label "Mitt Kid" with pride, Ryan continued to grind out the campaign in the video pits, doing anything and everything to add value. In a huge win, Romney won the election for governor, and Ryan continued his unpaid internship right into the governor's press office. He also started his freshman year at Boston College, where he quickly confirmed he hated both school and accounting.

What he loved was politics.

Selected to be a White House intern to arrange travel for the White House press charter, Ryan ditched college. After twice getting an extension to the internship—something that rarely happens—he had the opportunity to spend election day 2004 with the White House team.

> That was incredible, being with the Bush team on election night. It was too close to call until well after 2:00 A.M., and then Kerry wouldn't concede. So we all went home. The next morning, the press announced Kerry was finally going to concede. So I threw on clothes and ran back down to the Reagan Building to experience what I hoped to experience the night before—victory.
>
> Unfortunately, the Reagan Building isn't big, and it was already completely packed when we got back. There was a line around the building. I called my boss, and she brought three Secret Service agents to grab me and escort me into the building. At that point, I knew I was doing something right.

Ryan had participated in two historic political wins—Romney and Bush—before he could *legally* toast a glass of celebratory champagne.

After the inauguration, he left D.C. to return to Boston and finish school. However, he quickly resumed his role as an intern in the governor's office, so he dropped out of school. Again.

> I had the opportunity to take over the Director of Media Services job at the Governor's Office. I walked in and told them I was going to drop out of college. I wasn't taking no for an answer.

When Romney decided to run for president in 2008, his campaign team was committed to assembling a new group of people, different from the one that ran the Commonwealth of Massachusetts. They were certain they needed a different kind of force made up of different individuals if Romney was to capture the presidency. Ryan got wind of it and quickly showed he was willing to do whatever it took to be part of it.

I pushed hard to stay on to be part of Romney's presidential campaign. I just kept showing up at the campaign headquarters, hounding the IT guy to give me a BlackBerry and an email address. After trolling them for weeks, I was finally hired on as the Director of Television and Radio. It was a great experience. I still use all of those skills today, skills I never would have had if I had waited for someone to just give me a position.

After completing Romney's 2008 campaign and serving as the New Hampshire Republican Party Communications Director (and *finally* finishing his degree doing night school), Ryan joined the Romney team for the final time during the 2012 presidential campaign—this time as the Deputy National Press Secretary—becoming a mainstay on cable news as a campaign spokesman at just twenty-seven years old.

Ryan's experience of doing whatever it takes to get the job done has propelled him to a Managing Director role at a FP1 Strategies, a public relations, marketing, and strategy firm based in D.C., where he counsels clients from Lyft to Philip Morris in the "art of the Press." He's been able to overcome the stigma of youth and, in many cases, a lack of experience, time and time again.

I've just jumped into it. I've had confidence. If you make valid points and provide relevant insights, you are listened to—so that's what I learned to do. I watched those in line ahead of me and did what I saw the next level doing.

Ryan's story isn't at all unusual. It's silly to assume all of the KIDS are lazy and entitled! They're not. They want to change the world. They just need you to mentor and develop them.

We aren't attempting to convince you that there aren't challenges with the KIDS. Of course there are! However, you need to understand that those challenges—what the BOSS usually describes as "entitled" or "lazy"—are actually a result of how they were raised.

In the perfectly titled article "How to Land Your Kid in Therapy," author Lori Gottlieb of Stanford University summarizes the challenges facing Millennials: "Today, it's not enough to be happy, if you can be happier . . . The American dream and pursuit of happiness has morphed from contentment to 'must be happy at all times in every way'!"[6] UCLA psychiatrist Paul Bohn, Gottlieb explains, "believes many parents will do anything to avoid having their kids experience even mild discomfort, anxiety, or disappointment—'anything less than pleasant,' as he puts it—with the result that when, as adults, they experience normal frustrations of life"—conflict at work, no promotion, only a 3 percent raise, etc.—"they think something must be terribly wrong."[7]

Gottlieb also cites child psychologist and Harvard lecturer Dan Kindlon: "If kids can't experience painful feelings" in their youth, they can't and "won't develop 'psychological immunity'"—the ability to adapt, cope, react to discomfort, failures, and struggles. "Civilization is about adapting to less-than-perfect situations, yet parents often have this instantaneous reaction to unpleasantness, which is 'I can fix this.'"[8] The point, Kindlon says, is that parents have created a problem that is leading to a "burgeoning generational narcissism that's hurting our kids."[9] Those "kids" are the Millennials of today! Finally, Gottlieb cites professor of psychology at San Diego State University and co-author of *The Narcissism Epidemic* Jean Twenge: "'[Millennials] don't know how to work on teams as well or deal with limits. They get into the workplace and expect to be stimulated all the time . . . They don't like being told by a boss that their work might need improvement, and they feel insecure if they don't get a constant stream of praise.'"[10]

No doubt. The KIDS are clearly toting around some very real baggage, but inside that baggage lies some very big opportunities. The fact is, there are a whole bunch of powerhouse high-potential KIDS out there, like Ryan Williams, just waiting for a real leader to transform that potential into performance.

Key Points to Remember

1. The "Millennial Problem" didn't happen overnight, and it didn't happen by accident.

2. No, this isn't the first time the older generation hasn't gotten along with the younger generation.

3. Using a blanket stereotype to label an ENTIRE generation is nuts. There is an incredible opportunity here if you'll get your biases out of the way!

 Check out this related *Counter Mentors* podcast episode: "I Didn't Win, but I Got a Trophy!" Visit cmtr.co/ep2.

Chapter **5**

Old-School Is Dead (Somebody Please Tell the BOSS)

"I do no social media," said Hall of Famer Charles Barkley. "I feel no need to talk to all these fools," he continued. "I don't feel the need to talk to every idiot out there. Everybody's opinion is not important so I stay 100 percent away from social media."

"I love new technology. I'm not like Chuck," said announcer Ernie Johnson. "I'm not going to refuse to get on Twitter [just] because he feels like if he gets on Twitter they're going to know what he ate for dinner. I see some valid reasons for a lot of the new technology."[1]

DESPITE WHAT SUPERSTARS, movie stars, and business legends want to believe, old-school has left the building. Old-school is dead.

Especially old-school management. Along with 8-track tapes, cassettes, VHS, and the compact disc, it's just a memory. Can you name anything that you would consider old-school in the workplace that is still hanging around, remaining relevant?

Before you rattle off things like leadership, teams, training, or something similar, note that those things are not old-school at all; they are constant. Some leadership *approaches* are old-school, but leadership is always critical. Some team-building *ideas* are old-school, but teams are always needed. Training *methods* have radically changed, but the need for training is more important than ever.

The point is that ideas or principles remain constant but methods change, and most old-school methods are demonstrably—some might say "laughably"—out of date. However, it appears that the BOSS missed the memo about the demise of old-school management (KIDS, old-school communication was printed on real paper, called "memos," and they were put in an actual, physical "in" box).

We know that to be true, because the classic BOSS is still out there in the workplace using some (or all) of these priceless gems:

"Because I said so."

"That's the way we've always done it."

"If you don't like it, don't let the door hit you on the way out."

"If I want your opinion, I'll ask for it."

"I don't have time to babysit you."

Remember those good old days? The days when managers told employees what to do and they just did it? When employees didn't really like their jobs, but they quietly endured their manager because they needed that job? The KIDS don't realize how much *fun* they missed out on!

Well, wait a minute. Maybe they do.

According to research, there are still plenty of those kinds of managers in the workplace, and they are one of the primary reasons people quit their jobs. According to a 2015 Gallup survey, 50 percent of the employees who reported leaving their companies did so to escape a manager!

> A Gallup study of 7,272 U.S. adults revealed that one in two had
> left their job to get away from their manager to improve their
> overall life at some point in their career.[2]

That number was actually pegged at a staggering 70 percent in Leigh Branham's landmark book, *The 7 Hidden Reasons Employees Leave* (more on that in chapter 7).[3]

There's more: Something very interesting happens at the HR exit interview when those employees leave. They typically tell the HR manager the reason for leaving is to pursue "a better opportunity." We're betting that sounds very familiar. Here's the problem: it's usually not true.

We can reasonably make that assumption because of another piece of research data from the Saratoga Institute reported in Branham's book:

- 89 percent of managers believe employees leave their jobs for more money.

- 88 percent of employees reported they left for reasons *other* than money![4]

Didn't see that one coming, did you? That is what is generally referred to as being *completely* out of touch.

Both anecdotally and empirically, it's quite common to bump into an old-school management practitioner. However, as we strongly warned about stereotyping the KIDS, it's unfair to conclude that every BOSS leads that way. That said, those methods are still recognizable today because they still exist and have been the most common approach to "leadership" for decades.

Enter the KIDS, now the largest percentage of the workforce— brazen, fearless, and won't take "no" for an answer. That outdated, top-down, command-and-control, because-I-said-so leadership style has become a far more dangerous practice in the workplace since they arrived, because the KIDS want no part of it. If that means more than six jobs in ten years, so be it.

Typically, when the KIDS flee a job, they are leaving because the manager is terrible, the culture that manager has created is terrible, or there is no opportunity to grow or contribute in a meaningful way. You can hate it all you want, but the KIDS have proven they are more than willing to check out in a hurry if you are determined to cling to your old-school management practices.

Are You Old-School?

So, what exactly is old-school management? It is a generic term, but we use it to communicate an approach to management that is directive and autocratic, or, as we like to say, *Taylorian* (as in, a product of Frederick Winslow Taylor's turn-of-the-twentieth-century approach to managing employees, which we discussed earlier).

Here's how it has manifested itself in corporate managers:

- They rarely encourage employee input or feedback.
- They are focused on the task far more than the employee.
- They can be stern, even harsh, and in many cases intimidating in an effort to get *their* way.
- They may be given to excessive criticism.
- They tend to be impatient, and they may not listen very well (if at all).
- They often seek power or authority far more passionately than results.
- They believe every employee should have to endure what previous employees have endured.

- They may dislike new ideas—especially from younger employees (thus, it's not *their* idea).
- They have typically lagged behind (sometimes *far* behind) in technology adoption.
- They really don't understand "KIDS these days . . ."
- They struggle with the radical changes in workplace attitudes.

There is one additional item that would be a huge indicator that you are probably old-school. If you just read that list and you don't understand why some of those items represent a problem in the workplace, it's incredibly likely you're a BOSS. On the other hand, if you just read that list and took a picture of it for Twitter, you're most likely one of the KIDS who wants to validate the way you feel about the workplace (just make sure you add @kellyriggs and @robbyriggs to the tweet).

Why Should You Care?

Despite all the obvious challenges of working with the KIDS, the consequences of remaining tied to an outdated leadership style are quite expensive.

Let's talk about employee turnover.

BOSS, in the time it took you to confirm that the *Wall Street Journal* did not have any articles on employee turnover today, the KIDS have already found the 2012 Center for American Progress research paper that provides baseline data. (Yes, we know, that's really infuriating.) Here it is:

> For jobs paying less than $75,000 (in 2012 dollars) the average cost of employee turnover was 20 percent of annual compensation. For higher paying jobs (managers, executives, etc.), the estimated cost of employee turnover ranged to 213 percent of annual compensation.[5]

Warning! Those numbers are conservative, considering only what it costs to replace the employee. It is much more difficult to quantify what is lost in terms of knowledge, relationships, opportunity costs, and much more.

Regardless, a considerable portion of those losses—money that comes directly off the bottom line—can be directly attributed to the BOSS who clings tenaciously to "old-school."

The decision is yours, BOSS. You can refuse to change. Or, you can choose to make the warp-speed jump to effective leadership. The results? Less turnover. Higher engagement. Better performance. A productive culture. And, most likely, a gold watch as a bonus.

Let's be clear, we aren't saying this is going to be easy. Frankly, the transformation will require a ton of effort. As a sign of your intent, you might go ahead and get rid of those cassette tapes and learn how to use iTunes.

And don't worry, we'll help get the KIDS in line as well.

Key Points to Remember

1. Old-school, the management style pioneered by Frederick Winslow Taylor, will not enable you to attract—or retain—high-potential KIDS.

2. Old-school is a set of practices, not a generation.

3. The first step toward changing your old-school management practices is self-awareness.

Check out this related *Counter Mentors* podcast episode: "Old School Is Definitely Dead!" Visit cmtr. co/ep1.

Leadership Is Freaking Hard

BEFORE WE GET INTO THE TACTICS of how to successfully navigate this new workplace reality, it's critical to discuss the big picture. Yes, the new generational dynamics in the workplace are challenging, but there are other, perhaps even scarier, challenges present for the modern leader!

Let's go.

Chapter 6

Leadership Was Tough Enough
before the KIDS

"Anyone can hold the helm when the sea is calm."[1]

Publilius Syrus

HOW TOUGH IS IT to be a great, transformational leader? According to the research, it's nowhere near a sure thing. Not as unlikely as winning the lottery, but, from all appearances, it's a losing proposition.

In 2005, a Conference Board report stated that less than one-third of all supervisors and managers were perceived to be strong leaders.[2] One in three might be a stellar Major League Baseball batting average, but it's not very good in the workplace. The bad news: It might be even worse than that.

In the 2013 article entitled "Should Leaders Focus on Results, or on People?" author Matthew Lieberman reported on two significant pieces of research.[3] The first was a survey taken of 60,000 employees. It was designed to determine how two characteristics, results focus and social skills, impact employees' perception of leadership ability.

A *results focus*, Lieberman says, "combines strong analytical skills with an intense motivation to move forward and solve problems," while *social skills* "combine attributes like communication and empathy." According to the results of the survey, if a leader was considered to be strong in social skills, that person was seen as a great leader only 12 percent of the time. Perhaps surprisingly, if a leader was perceived to be strong in focusing on results, that number increased to only 14 percent!

You might see that as some minor justification for promoting people to management based on the results they create, but that's not the end of the story.

> However, for leaders who were strong in both results focus and in social skills, the likelihood of being seen as a great leader **skyrocketed to 72%**.[4]

That number is, as the number geeks like to say, statistically significant! You are five times more likely to be considered a great leader if you focus on results AND you connect well with your employees.

So, the real question is, how many managers are like that? The second piece of research cited in Lieberman's article gives us the answer:

> David Rock, director of the Neuroleadership Institute, and Management Research Group recently conducted a survey to find out the answer. They asked thousands of employees to rate their bosses on goal focus (similar to results focus) and social skills to examine how often a leader scored high on both. The results are astonishing. **Less than 1% of leaders were rated high on both goal focus and social skills.**[5]

Turns out we were slightly underestimating what it takes to be an effective leader. Apparently, it is *really freaking hard!* To be fair, the leader is not *solely* to blame for being so ineffective. In fact, we will let the BOSS (briefly) steal a catchphrase from the KIDS: "It's not my fault!"

Why? The truth is the vast majority of individuals who get promoted to a "leadership" role get promoted for reasons having absolutely nothing to do with leadership. Instead, most often, people are promoted for knowledge, skill, or performance in their current job. There is little, if any, consideration of their ability to communicate, set strategy and direction, create a plan, or develop people.

Did you catch that?

Almost ALL individuals who progress from individual contributor roles to supervisory—*leadership*—roles are promoted because of their technical competence or skill at their *previous* job! People don't get promoted to leadership because of their potential to be great leaders. Instead, promotion decisions are typically based on the candidate's ability to react to the most pressing emergencies of the day (the tactical), to get things done (the technical), and to manage administrative details (the trivial).

Yes, today's "leader" is generally a highly skilled firefighter in casual business attire. #truth

How Companies Make the Problem Worse

So, the scarcity of effective leadership is largely a self-inflicted wound. According to more research from Gallup, when companies select a new manager, they "fail to choose the candidate with the right talent for the job" 82 percent of the time.[6]

Seriously? Eight times out of ten? You'd think a company would be at least as good as a coin flip, wouldn't you? Sadly, however, they are not, and upon closer inspection, we uncover three critical *systemic* issues that explain the problem.

1. Assuming that "Doing" is the Same as "Leading"

Companies promote individuals almost exclusively for their technical competence or their ability to produce *individual* results without any assessment of their ability to lead a *team*. See the problem? Doing is *not* leading. An individual may be great at getting things done and be an absolutely *terrible* leader of people. This individual may have little idea of *how* to communicate, teach, coach, manage conflict, set strategy, create a performance culture, or any of several other critical leadership skills.

But it doesn't seem to matter. Organizations that seek to fill a management position almost always look first to knowledge, skill, or performance as the primary requisites for the position. Clearly, a level of technical competence is important in a management position, but, it is just one piece of the leadership puzzle. That's one of the primary findings of Gallup's research: companies wind up with the wrong people in management roles because they use the wrong criteria.

> Conventional selection processes are a big contributor to inefficiency in management practices; they apply little science or research to find the right person for the managerial role. When Gallup asked U.S. managers why they believed they were hired for their current role, they commonly cited their success in a previous non-managerial role or their tenure in their company or field.[7]

We hire or promote technical competence and we're surprised why our managers are taskmasters instead of leaders.

2. Neglecting to Train and Develop the Leaders

Companies rarely train and develop their leaders. Instead, most companies simply identify their top performers, move them into a new office, provide updated business cards, and prepare them for their new role with the two ever-so-popular, not-so-helpful words: "Good luck."

You're gonna need it.

This particular mistake takes on a special significance when you realize that leadership is a set of skills that can be learned. The great NFL coach Vince Lombardi said, "Leaders are made, they are not born. They are made by hard effort, which is the price which all of us must pay to achieve any goal that is worthwhile."[8]

That sentiment ("leaders are made") is reinforced in a 2013 scientific study published in *The Leadership Quarterly*. The article concludes that, while there are some innate characteristics needed to become an effective leader, most of what makes someone a great leader is *learned*. Researchers estimate the "heritability of leadership role occupancy at 24 percent," meaning an individual's learning and development accounts for 76 percent of leadership capability.[9]

So, while some natural ability is needed to become an effective leader, don't lose sight of the fact that leadership is a *set of skills that can be acquired and developed* over time. Yes, leadership can be *learned*. As Mike Myatt so eloquently wrote in *Forbes*: "You don't train leaders, you develop them."[10] A subtle distinction perhaps, but training is typically perceived as occurring in a classroom, while development happens as a result of repetition and practice.

No matter what you call it, if you don't equip your managers with the skills that make for great leadership, it's *highly* unlikely you will get a manager who is perceived to be an effective leader.

3. Failing to Incentivize Managers to Be Great Leaders

Managers are rarely incentivized to be great leaders. Typically, managers are paid to "get results." On the surface, that would actually seem to make sense, but a problem arises when companies see performance results and talent development as two mutually exclusive ideas. Companies can be guilty of focusing on results, while overlooking cultural and morale issues, high employee turnover, systemic conflict avoidance, and a lack of talent development.

Which is a bit silly.

It should be self-evident that great people create those performance results we all crave. And strong performance cannot last if people disengage or fail to develop their potential. Did we mention turnover is extremely costly?!

It is the very rare organization that includes people development as a component of compensation. In fact, it is difficult to find a company that has more than just a superficial approach to intentionally developing the talent of its employees, much less making it a part of the incentive compensation.

Again, this is a systemic problem. The "system" is one that is designed to pay leaders for results rather than paying them to develop the people who create those results. Worse, paying for results encourages decisions that reward short-term behavior while ignoring the long-term consequences.

It's a bit like killing the golden goose. (KIDS, if you're not familiar with this common analogy, consider the thought of moving out of your parents' house before you have to—it captures the idea perfectly!)

So, companies promote the wrong people to leadership positions, they fail to develop a methodology for training and developing their leaders, and they reward the wrong management behaviors. No wonder leadership is tough.

The good news is, systemic leadership failure is just that—a system failure.

And systems can be fixed.

Key Points to Remember

1. It's freaking hard to be a great, transformational leader.
2. Typically, promotion is based on your ability to execute the tactical, the technical, and the trivial in your current role, not on your potential to do the transformational.
3. Leadership is a set of skills that can be learned and developed.

Check out this related *Counter Mentors* video podcast episode: "You Want a Raise Already?!" Visit cmtr.co/ep17.

Chapter 7

Why Leadership Matters

"People buy into the leader before they buy into the vision."[1]

John Maxwell

OKAY, big deal.

So, leadership is no walk in the park. Whatever. Why should you care?

The answer to this question is *very* simple: it's costing you a ton of money.

We can easily see that *most* "leaders" are irritatingly ineffective (not you, of course!), but when it comes to quantifying the monstrous impact of that below-average group, we tend to consciously or subconsciously paint a picture of sunshine and rainbows and just blame it on things we can't control. The things that always make for great excuses: the KIDS, the economy, competitors, a short month, daylight saving time, brochure color changes. Something. Anything!

Here is the reality: Nothing impacts the organization's results as much as leadership. Absolutely nothing. Leadership touches EVERY-THING, and we can easily prove our point.

Let's talk about employee engagement.

Employee engagement is defined as the level of an employee's emotional commitment to the organization—its purpose, vision, values, people, leadership, and goals. The Gallup organization defines engaged employees as "those who are involved in, enthusiastic about, and committed to their work and workplace." Simply put, engaged employees are motivated to do their best work and go the extra mile for the company every day. *Not-engaged* employees, on the other hand, typically "[do] the minimum required with little extra effort to go out of their way for customers."[2]

The most important question is, how does engagement, or the *lack* of engagement, impact your company? Data is plentiful, but a 2015 report in *Harvard Business Review* provides all the information you need to know about the impact employee disengagement has on your bottom line:

> Disengagement is costly. In studies by the Queens School of Business and by the Gallup Organization, disengaged workers had 37% higher absenteeism, 49% more accidents, and 60% more errors and defects. In organizations with low employee engagement scores, they experienced 18% lower productivity, 16% lower profitability, 37% lower job growth, and 65% lower share price over time.[3]

This and other research draws a straight line from your engaged or disengaged employees to all of the critical financial metrics you care about—not just in terms of profit and productivity, but also in terms of safety, turnover, mistakes, and more. Which, if you think about it a bit, is actually a bit of good news: once you figure out how to improve employee engagement, you figure out how to improve just about everything, from culture to performance. #realtalk

Allow us to give you a hint to the solution: It has absolutely nothing to do with "Blue Jeans Fridays" (that's such a painful, out-of-touch BOSS phrase), or flextime, or foosball tables in the break room.

It does, however, have *everything* to do with leadership.

The System Is Broken

Leigh Branham's book, *The 7 Hidden Reasons Employees Leave*, shares groundbreaking research done by the Saratoga Institute. From that research, we gain tremendous insight into employee engagement and how it is created.

In data collected from a survey of over 19,700 employees, Branham discovered that "more than 70 percent of the reasons [employees leave] are related to factors that are controllable by the direct supervisor." Branham explained,

> This conforms to what most of us already know—that the employee's direct supervisor has the major share of control or influence to prevent or correct those issues. As the saying goes, "people join companies, but they leave managers."[4]

It's time to connect the dots: Your employee joins the company and is very excited. (We all love the energy of a new job, right?) Engagement on Day One is off the charts because your employee feels valued and the future looks bright. Now, fast-forward one year. The technically competent BOSS struggles as a leader and the once-happy employee begins the transformation from engaged to disengaged. The employee gets restless, jumps on LinkedIn during an "important staff meeting," and eventually accepts another position elsewhere.

The sad truth is, 70 percent of the time, employees head for the door because of their direct manager or supervisor. You've got a great company, but a poor manager is killing you. Or, *you* are that manager, and you've convinced yourself you just can't find good people, and you prove it by citing excess turnover. Bad news, BOSS! The odds are very good that *you* are the problem.

Have things changed much since Branham published his findings in 2005? Apparently not. In 2015, research by the Gallup organization

indicated that "managers account for at least 70% of the varian\
employee engagement scores across business units."[5]

The similarity in those two findings, a full decade apart, is uncanny. It validates what researchers have suspected for some time—the practices of an employee's direct supervisor are the primary drivers of his or her engagement (or disengagement).

Let's hammer this critical point home: **People join companies, but they quit managers.**

But, think about what is typically said about employees when they leave your company. "They don't get it," or, "They just didn't fit," or, "I didn't have time to hold his hand on every project." Do you look carefully at the leadership skills of the manager or are you willing to accept those lame excuses without further inspection?

That light you're seeing in the tunnel is getting closer, and it's coming incredibly fast. Let's get directly to the point before the head-on collision:

1. Who hires the employee?
2. Who trains the employee?
3. Who is responsible to *lead* the employee?

This is about to get #uncomfortable ... because *you* do these things. You hire the employees. You train them. And you're their leader.

So, if that employee underperforms or is disengaged, whose fault is it again? Yes, it is that person's failure, but you hired the wrong person. Or you trained the employee poorly. Or you're an ineffective leader who failed to develop the worker. In all three cases, the root cause of the problem is you, the leader.

Yes, we know. Occasionally, a potentially good employee does not perform up to his or her potential. Everyone agreed it was a good hire. The person had the skills. You're known to be a good leader. Yet, the person failed. The pressing question is this: How did you deal with the performance issue? Who is responsible to make whatever changes are needed to preserve the team?

You are.

So please don't blame the employees if you're allowing them to stick around and underperform.

Cause and Effect: Leadership and Performance

How bad is ineffective leadership hurting you or your company?

It depends. It might be a small problem, or it might be sucking the life out of you. Either way, chances are good that you're not getting the performance results you *should* be getting. You see the evidence—disengagement, turnover, marginal performance—but you can't quite put your finger on what's wrong.

In the last chapter, we talked about why leaders are often set up for failure—*condemned* to be ineffective. Companies use the wrong criteria for promotion, they don't train and prepare managers to lead effectively, and they rarely, if ever, incentivize managers to excel in leadership responsibilities.

So we get the wrong people into leadership positions. Again, according to Gallup, it happens 82 percent of the time![6] In fact, when was the last time you heard someone say about a new manager, "He has incredible leadership potential. No question, he exhibits all the right behaviors that will definitely make him a great leader!"

Never heard that? Neither have we.

We promote people almost exclusively for past performance. If someone is exceptional at a job, we assume that person will make a great manager. Since Susie was a great accountant, she will be a great manager of accountants!

The reality: You lost a great accountant and set Susie up for failure. Your team of accountants will disengage and get their resumes ready. You've *produced* an ineffective manager. The cost of turnover is about to go up. Again, this is a systemic problem, one that creates FOUR HUGE performance problems for the company.

1. Bad Hires

Ineffective leaders hire the wrong people. In a 2015 study conducted by Brandon Hall Group, "95% of organizations of all sizes admit to making bad hires every year."[7] Ninety-five percent?! Really? Tweet that with this hashtag: #epicfail.

As a leader, hiring the wrong employees makes the already difficult job of leadership that much more difficult. While this isn't a book about hiring, having the wrong people on your team is like paddling upstream in whitewater rapids. Good luck.

 We *strongly* recommend the book *Who*, by Geoff Smart and Randy Street, as a guide for interviewing and hiring.[8] We use it. Our home runs increased significantly when we began using it as our guide.

Not only do managers receive minimal leadership training; they hardly ever receive training on how to identify, interview, and hire A-Players. What's worse, very few A-Players will go to work for B-Managers. Why? Because great players want to play on great teams.

The old-school hiring practice that is based on help-wanted ads, resumes, and job descriptions is not only outdated, it's fatally flawed. And looking for new talent ONLY when you desperately need someone is a surefire way to end up with the wrong employee. Every middle manager, at some point in his or her career, has said, "A warm body is better than nothing." Which is about one of the dumbest things a leader can possibly say.

To improve performance, you *must* dramatically change the way you identify and acquire talent.

2. Lack of Clarity

Ineffective leaders don't create clarity for the team. A successful team doesn't just happen. As we like to say: "No one runs their best race if they don't know where the finish line is." You should think of that "finish line" as the expectations you set for any given employee. These can range from *general* expectations to *performance* expectations to cultural norms, guiding principles, and values.

General expectations are those expectations you won't find in the HR manual or in any standard job description. For example, think about your pet peeves—the things that drive you freaking crazy. Like showing up late to meetings, failing to communicate schedule changes, or never responding to email invites (don't people know how infuriating that is?). Have you communicated these expectations to your employees?

How about *performance* expectations? Do your employees know exactly what results they are expected to produce? Do they know what success looks like? Are those performance expectations measured and reviewed? No? How do you expect to effectively manage performance if you haven't set the bar and know exactly how high it is?

Finally, do people understand the values that define your team— the kind of people you want your team to be? You will never consistently hire the right *type* of person unless, and until, you define what that looks like.

To improve performance, every employee has to be crystal clear in each of these areas.

3. Ineffective Training

Ineffective leaders don't train effectively. More than three decades ago, Zig Ziglar famously said, "The only thing worse than training an employee and having them leave, is to not train them, and have them stay."[9]

We agree.

But there are at least three distinct problems when it comes to training employees:

- Leaders don't train in good times because they "don't have time."
- Leaders don't train in bad times because they "don't have money."
- When leaders provide training, it's often reactionary and done as a stand-alone event, complete with wordy PowerPoint slides and bad coffee.

We're amazed at how often training is an afterthought, especially when it comes to providing training for leaders. If you don't train because you don't have time, and you don't train because you don't have money, you will soon wind up with bad people and no time whatsoever. All of your talented employees will have left the building, leaving you stuck doing everything. *Great* idea.

The one-time training approach to skills improvement (of any kind) is especially silly. It not only costs a lot of time and money, but it is incredibly ineffective. The reason is simple—it's due to something called the "forgetting curve."

In his article in *Learning Solutions Magazine* entitled "Brain Science: The Forgetting Curve—the Dirty Secret of Corporate Training," Art Kohn describes the problem.

Research on the forgetting curve shows that within one hour, people will have forgotten an average of 50 percent of the information you presented. Within 24 hours, they have forgotten an average of 70 percent of new information, and within a week, forgetting claims an average of 90 percent of it.

Still, companies persist in creating one-time training "meetings," with little thought given to learning objectives, changing behaviors, or measuring the effectiveness of the training. Can training like this be useful? Yes. But not as these events are typically planned.[10]

Fantastic! Companies say they "invest" in training, but as much as 90 percent of it is completely lost. And yet it continues, year in and year out. #insanity

> "C'mon, BOSS, admit it—you're starting to get the hang of the hashtag thing. Now, if you just knew where to use them . . ."

To improve performance, you *must* transform the way you approach people development.

4. Lack of Accountability

Ineffective leaders don't create a culture of accountability. Perhaps the biggest issue associated with ineffective leadership is an extreme lack of accountability. Every manager wants it; few actually get it. The reason they don't get it generally fits into one of two buckets:

- The leaders are absolutely petrified of conflict. Really, anything close to a hard conversation is frightening, so avoidance is the theme of the day.
- The leaders are so drunk on power that they skip accountability and proceed directly to confrontation. Oh, yeah. These are the managers who consistently employ yelling and screaming.

The problem is, when there is no accountability in the workplace, it kills morale and erodes trust. Employees know exactly what's going on, and they don't respect you. They don't believe you. They won't follow you.

To improve performance, you absolutely *must* create a culture of accountability.

Conclusion

What makes these things so troubling (and sad, really) is that these wounds are all self-inflicted! Nobody forces a leader or a company to make these mistakes.

We also know you're probably not all that surprised. Very few people are. Most companies (or leaders) just don't know how to solve these strategic problems. They are mired in fighting the fires that arise almost every day.

So what are your options? The enemy here is inertia. The status quo: "I do it this way because this is what I know." Or, just as ridiculous, "This is how we've always done it."

It's time to make a decision. It's time to change. In the next chapter, we'll show you how a junior senator from Illinois pulled it off.

Key Points to Remember

1. If you're losing good people, look first at the manager—not the people.

2. Ineffective leaders hire the wrong people, they don't create clarity, they don't train, and they fail to create a culture of accountability.

3. Investing in the right training is paramount if you ever hope to do more than only what *you* can do!

 Check out this related *Counter Mentors* video podcast episode: "3 Things Millennials Hate About Managers!" Visit cmtr.co/ep18.

Chapter **8**

As if it Wasn't Bad Enough—
The New Leadership Challenges

"The fishermen know that the sea is dangerous and the storm terrible, but they have never found these dangers sufficient reason for remaining ashore."[1]

Vincent van Gogh

IN 2007, when Barack Obama announced his candidacy for president of the United States, he was a junior senator from Illinois with a very limited national track record. He had served as an Illinois state senator, got elected to the U.S. Senate in 2004, and then, in November 2008, won the world's ultimate political prize.

Although not one of the KIDS (he was born in 1961), Obama faced a Millennial-type challenge when he decided to go up against the very definition of "the way we've always done it and we don't plan on changing anytime soon" in the Democratic establishment.

Obama was the newcomer. Hillary Clinton was the establishment.

His team knew that if he was to have any chance of besting Clinton in the Democratic primary, he would have to do things differently. At the time, the new and different approach was to engage potential voters and solicit donations through social media:

> In February 2007, a friend called Marc Andreessen, a founder of Netscape and a board member of Facebook, and asked if he wanted to meet with a man with an idea that sounded preposterous on its face.
>
> Always game for something new, Mr. Andreessen headed to the San Francisco airport late one night to hear the guy out. A junior member of a large and powerful organization with a thin, but impressive, résumé, he was about to take on far more powerful forces in a battle for leadership.
>
> He wondered if social networking, with its tremendous communication capabilities and aggressive database development, might help him beat the overwhelming odds facing him.
>
> "It was like a guy in a garage who was thinking of taking on the biggest names in the business," Mr. Andreessen recalled. "What he was doing shouldn't have been possible, but we see a lot of that out here and then something clicks. He was clearly super smart and very entrepreneurial, a person who saw the world and the status quo as malleable."
>
> And as it turned out, president-elect Barack Obama was right.[2]

Politics aside, Obama's story is a perfect illustration of old-school vs. new-school. As a political newcomer, he was just one of those

KIDS, a youngster who needed to *pay his dues* and *earn his stripes* before he could have a voice, much less make an impact.

But you know how the story ends. Dude straight #crushedit.

 "Translation for the BOSS: he won in convincing fashion."

 "Can we please call him Mr. President instead of *dude*?"

After racing to a surprise win in the Democratic primary, Obama continued the same social media engagement strategy in the general election, with incredible results:

- He received contributions from more than 3 million online donors.
- He received more than 6.5 million online donations, averaging $80 per donation.
- He raised over $409 million—*twice* as much as Republican candidate John McCain.[3]

His team brought technology and social media to the party and showed the BOSS a thing or two about running a campaign:

"I think it is very significant that he was the first post-boomer candidate for president," Mr. Andreessen said. "Other politicians I have met with are always impressed by the Web and surprised by what it could do, but their interest sort of ended in how much money you could raise. *He was the first politician I dealt with who understood that the technology was a given and that it could be used in new ways* [emphasis added].[4]

The Disruptive Force of Technology

It's difficult to stay on top in the world of politics, and it's just as tough to stay on top in business. Just compare the list of Fortune 500 companies in 1955 to the list in 2015. There are only sixty-one companies that appear in both lists. Said differently, only 12 percent of the Fortune 500 in 1955 were still on the list when their grandkids began trading stock!

What happened to building something that will last forever? What happened to legacy?

Acclaimed economist Steven Denning observed that "half a century ago, the life expectancy of a firm in the Fortune 500 was around 75 years. Now it's less than 15 years and declining even further."[5] WHAT IS HAPPENING!?! In sixty years, seven out of every eight Fortune 500 companies have vanished—bankrupt, acquired, merged, or no longer qualifying for the Fortune 500 badge of honor. Who even remembers Armstrong Rubber, or Cone Mills, or Hines Lumber, or Pacific Vegetable Oil (seriously?), or Riegel Textile?

We readily acknowledge that the ever-changing business environment plays a massive role in the decline of an organization's shelf life. In fact, you'll see that the pace of change is one of the bigger challenges leaders face today. However, we believe there are decisions made by corporate leaders that play just as big a role in the demise of many once-powerful companies.

Just think about the organizational posturing that took place at Kodak when digital technology arrived.[6] We all know how Kodak crashed and burned. They filed for bankruptcy in 2012, sold off a ton of assets, and reemerged as a much smaller enterprise called Kodak Alaris. How did Kodak, of all companies, miss the digital camera revolution? According to Steven J. Sasson, the electrical engineer who invented the first digital camera at Kodak, "it was filmless photography, so management's reaction was, 'That's cute—but don't tell anyone about it.'"[7]

Translation: "We've always done it this way."

Or this: There is the story about the Blockbuster board meeting in which the company decided not to join forces with, or acquire, Netflix. Barry McCarthy, Chief Financial Officer of Netflix, remembers the meeting: "Reed [Hastings, Netflix CEO and founder] had the chutzpah to propose to them [Blockbuster] that we run their brand online and that they run [our] brand in the stores and they just about laughed us out of their office."[8]

Imagine the closed-door conversations at Blockbuster: "Hey, we own real estate all across the country! We ARE the home video market! DVDs by mail? Get real. People want to go in, rent a DVD, and take it home right now. They want to get a recommendation from one of our stellar associates and buy some popcorn. They don't want to wait! Streaming on the Internet?! Puh-leaze."

Blockbuster crashed and burned into bankruptcy in 2010, while Netflix recorded $8.8 billion in sales in 2016 and surpassed 100 million subscribers in 2017.[9]

Oops.

 "No hashtag?"

 "You have to pick your spots, keep people guessing."

The NEW Leadership Environment

If you have been out of leadership a while, you may be shocked. Things have changed more than just a bit because of technology, generational discord, and social media. It reminds us of the marketing tagline for the classic movie *Jaws 2*, the first of three sequels to Steven Spielberg's 1975 suspense thriller, *Jaws*.[10]

> "Just when you thought it was safe to go back in the water."

Well, it reminds Pops of that line. Robby has no idea. Pops was in high school when Spielberg's first big-screen movie hit theaters. Pops didn't buy tickets on Fandango. He actually had to wait in a line in front of the theater and pay cash for tickets.

Yes, leadership has always been tough, but today's business environment has doubled or tripled the stakes. Let's take a look at several challenges that have begun to emerge from the waves of change. (Get it?)

 "The Pops loves his cheesy puns! Puns for DAYS."

 "I love it more that I had to explain it to you."

If you're a BOSS, you probably recognize these issues. Basically, they are all of those challenges you like to blame on the KIDS.

- **Generational Conflict.** We've outlined this problem, but, to summarize again, the BOSS was raised a certain way—both in life and in the workplace—and the KIDS were raised quite differently. The older generation thinks the younger group is a bunch of lazy, entitled, know-it-alls who haven't earned the right to be heard (much less the right to a trophy). The KIDS think this is stupid and outdated and lame and wrong and just plain sad. So, they just say bad things about the BOSS on Snapchat (and it's okay, because Boomers usually have no idea what Snapchat is).

- **A NEW Knowledge Gap: Relationships.** The new knowledge gap isn't about keeping up with *Harvard Business Review*. It's not about learning the tactics for becoming a market leader in a global economy. Instead, the new knowledge gap is a people problem: connecting with your people, learning how they communicate, understanding their work preferences, and discovering what motivates them! When you don't know those things, you have a huge knowledge gap.

  It's a gap driven by the generational differences we've discussed, but its complexity is amplified by the diversity of people and the impact of technology.

- **Complexity.** Technology has introduced complexity into every aspect of the workplace: servers, software, databases, cloud storage, "smart" products, and the generally confusing Internet of Things (IoT). It impacts the way companies train and prepare their people while completely changing how they maintain, service, and upgrade their products and services.

  However, technology also creates enormous complexity in the way consumers interact with the company. No matter where the company meets a customer—sales, service, accounting, operations, shipping, or customer service—the customer can immediately access technology to comment or complain. You can thank Yelp, Glassdoor, Twitter, and several others.

  Today, more than ever before, leaders must prepare ALL employees in the company to consider their actions and reactions from the customer's viewpoint. Failure to do so can be disastrous (remember United Airlines?!).

- **Distractions.** Along with complexity, technology brings another set of workplace issues that will drive you crazy. Remember when we told you the KIDS check their mobile devices up to 150 times per day? So it's not shocking to hear the BOSS say the KIDS "waste" enormous amounts of time Googling everything, posting to Facebook, buying things on Amazon, and keeping up with the Kardashians.

 "Personally, I like to keep up with Todd Chrisley."

 "SMH. Now I'm just embarrassed."

So, what is the solution? Ban the Internet at work? Block every website that isn't "relevant"? Outlaw smartphones and tablets in the office? Eliminate Fantasy Football?!

Good luck, BOSS.

- **Pace of Change.** About the time you think you may see some light at the end of tunnel (usually after your latest technology update), you realize things have changed.

Again.

And they will change again in a few months.

How are leaders to prepare themselves and their teams for rapid and consistent change? Especially when most people are absolutely paralyzed by the thought of doing things differently?

This problem is huge, because it's exhausting. Literally.

There it is. A whole host of new problems to deal with in the modern workplace. Leave it to the KIDS to take something great and turn it into a dumpster fire under the bridge by the highway. Okay, that's not exactly true, but leadership today is far more difficult than it once was, and it was plenty freaking hard to begin with!

Change is the word of the day. Senator Obama became Mr. President by leveraging the concept of *change*. He completely sidestepped "the way it's always been done," and ran counter to the establishment. As with any president in history, not everyone agrees with everything #44 did, but his boldness in running a campaign that challenged the status quo is to be respected.

Now it's your turn. It's time to do something COUNTER to the way it's always been done. Different from the way you've always done it.

But first, let's unpack these new challenges a bit more.

Key Points to Remember

1. You likely won't become an effective leader without challenging the status quo.

2. Leadership is tough, but several new challenges—complexity, distractions, and change—have made it much more difficult.

3. Technology, while an incredible enabler of productivity, has brought enormous challenges to the modern workplace.

Chapter 9

Complexity: Why Your Team Is (Almost) Guaranteed to Fail

"The complexity of things—the things within things—just seems to be endless. I mean nothing is easy, nothing is simple."[1]

Alice Munro

TECHNOLOGY has really complicated the workplace today, almost to the point of being impossible to describe. Products and services are more complex, to be sure, but the entire customer service experience has been tremendously complicated by that same technology. Nothing illustrates this better than what Dave Carroll was able to do to United Airlines in 2009 with the help of YouTube.

Yup. YouTube.

This is the Dave Carroll we mentioned briefly when describing the proliferation and power of technology in chapter 3. There's a lot more to his story, and the story communicates a ton about complexity in the workplace.

Dave Carroll is one of those dudes you just want to hang out with. Okay, we've never met him, but we feel like we want to buy him a drink. As the front man for the Canadian band Sons of Maxwell, he was a road warrior, livin' the dream.

In March 2008, Dave was on a flight from Halifax, Nova Scotia, to Omaha, Nebraska, when the fine baggage handlers at United Airlines damaged his guitar. This happened as a result of, shall we say, *intentional negligence*? That's what we call it when baggage handlers unsuccessfully play catch with a guitar case on the tarmac.

 "You think Millennials know where Nova Scotia is?"

 "Nope. Our parents talked the teacher into giving us an 'A' in geography."

As two guys who travel a ton, we are not at all surprised by this outcome. Have you ever looked out and watched your bags being mauled—um, we mean, "handled"? No? Probably a good decision on your part. It's not something you can un-see.

Dave describes his experience, blog-style, on his website:

On March 31, 2008 Sons of Maxwell began our week-long-tour of Nebraska by flying United Airlines from Halifax to Omaha, by way of Chicago. On that first leg of the flight we were seated at the rear of the aircraft and upon landing and waiting to deplane in order to make our connection a woman sitting behind me, not aware that we were musicians cried out: "My god they're throwing guitars out there." Our bass player Mike looked out the window in time to see his bass being heaved without regard by the United baggage handlers. My $3500 710 Taylor had been thrown before his.

I immediately tried to communicate this to the flight attendant who cut me off saying: "Don't talk to me. Talk to the lead agent outside." I found the person she pointed to and that lady was an "acting" lead agent but refused to talk to me and disappeared into the crowd saying "I'm not the lead agent." I spoke to a third employee at the gate and when I told her the baggage handlers were throwing expensive instruments outside she dismissed me saying "but hun, that's why we make you sign the waiver." I explained that I didn't sign a waiver and that no waiver would excuse what was happening outside. She said to take it up with the ground crew in Omaha.[2]

How many WHAT-ARE-YOU-DOING moments did you count? Crazy stuff, right?

Carroll goes on to describe the next nine painful months, battling United Airlines' "Customer Service"—multiple phone calls with reps in both India and the U.S., several emails, and probably (we're going to go out on a limb) the need to consume more than a few stiff drinks.

He ends his description of the saga with an idea to actually do something about it.

So, after nine months it came down to a series of emails with United Arilines' employee Ms. Irlweg and, despite asking to speak to her supervisor, our conversations ended with her saying United would not be taking any responsibility for what had happened and that that would be the last email on the matter. My final offer of a settlement of $1200 in flight vouchers, to cover my salvage costs repairing the Taylor, was rejected.

At that moment, it occurred to me that I had been fighting a losing battle all this time and that fighting over this at all was a waste of time. The system is designed to frustrate affected customers into giving up their claims and United is very good at it but I realized then that as a songwriter and traveling musician I wasn't without options. In my final reply to Ms. Irlweg

I told her that I would be writing three songs about United Airlines and my experience in the whole matter. I would then make videos for these songs and offer them for free download on YouTube and my own website, inviting viewers to vote on their favourite United song. My goal: to get one million hits in one year.

Here's what Ms. Irlweg was probably thinking: "ONE MILLION HITS? On a song about United Airlines' baggage handlers and their terrible customer service? Yeah, that's not gonna happen." Except, this is the age of extreme connectivity, and there is an enormous amount of power in our complex social networks.

Dave uploaded his first video, "United Breaks Guitars," to YouTube on July 6, 2009, with no pomp, fanfare, or "next big thing" commercials. Just a normal video posting, not unlike the other 86,000+ hours of content uploaded on any given day.[3] (Hey, BOSS. If you don't know what YouTube is at this point, put down the book, turn on your desktop computer, go to the world wide web, and spend the next couple of hours exploring *youtube.com*!)

 "Not a good idea."

 "Nope. Probably never see that BOSS again."

By the middle of August, the video had attracted more than 5 million views and hit #1 on iTunes. ON iTUNES!! Next thing you know, Dave Carroll was a minor celebrity, appearing on everything from *Good Morning America* to *Jimmy Kimmel Live*!

United Airlines, on the other hand, wasn't having much fun at all, dealing with a full-fledged "worst nightmare" scenario. Chris Ayres of *The Times Online* perfectly summarized United's nightmare in a column on the paper's website:

> Within four days of the song going online, the gathering thunderclouds of bad PR caused United Airlines' stock price to suffer a mid-flight stall, and it plunged by 10%, costing shareholders $180 million. Which, incidentally, would have bought Carroll more than 51,000 replacement guitars.[4]

#thepowerofsocialmedia
The video has now been viewed more than 16 million times, with not one, but two sequels written and recorded by Carroll. And there are the countless parodies and inevitable spinoffs created by starving artists and *Saturday Night Live* hopefuls.

Did United recover? Of course, but that's not the point. We're quite certain the leadership team at United learned that we live in a new, complex world, with new, complex challenges—like social media and smartphones with cameras.

So, at least they learned from the ordeal, right?

Maybe not.

In 2017, just eight years later, United Airlines lost more than $250 million in shareholder value when multiple videos went viral of them dramatically dragging a doctor off a flight from Chicago to Louisville.[5] Experts are now considering the long-term impact this incident will have in one of United's primary growth markets: China. Why? That story was the #1 trending topic on Weibo—China's version of Twitter—with more than 100 million hits.

Not. Good.

Maybe Carroll will now make his fourth video, "United Beats Their Head Against the Wall!"

What Is "Complexity" in the Workplace?

Complexity is the mean, brooding brother of what techno geeks refer to as *seamless integration*. We love integration—being able to work on a document on the iPad, then tweak it on the train on the iPhone, and then finish it at the office on the Mac. It's freaking awesome. Frankly, it would be a nightmare if we had to deal with the tremendous *complexity* that powers that perfectly seamless user experience.

Once upon a time we cared about one metric, on one report, for one business unit. Now we have multi-layered, real-time dashboards that provide advanced analytics to transform data into actionable information about our hyperconnected global business team. (It is possible that one thing the BOSS and the KIDS have in common in the workplace is that they love jargon, buzzwords, and acronyms.)

Technology, whether centralized in one location in a single package or decentralized in multiple systems in data centers all over the world, results in extreme complexity—complexity that your people are then required to manage. This is the reality of our business environment today: things have gotten so complex that it's difficult, sometimes nearly impossible, to identify the most important thing. How do you make the most important thing the most important thing if you can't even identify the most important thing?

Increasingly, just when we think we have identified the most important thing, we figure out how incredibly difficult it is to train and manage the people who drive, interact with, serve, or manage the most important thing! That's one HUGE reason why leadership is so freaking important.

Today, customers rarely deal with one individual who handles an entire transaction. Someone sells them the product; another person services the product; a different department deals with shipping. Then there is billing and warranty and customer service, and on and on and on. And in each area, the influence of technology is ever present: operations systems, field service systems, customer facing systems, and computer applications for basically everything.

The real truth is, complexity has reared its ugly head in every department in the building. Even your sales team is not exempt. In some cases, it can hit you twice—selling something incredibly complex into an organization rife with complexity. You know, just in case you didn't have enough challenges to deal with.

Tim Sanders is the former Chief Solutions Officer of Yahoo! and the *New York Times* bestselling author of the book *Dealstorming: The Secret Weapon That Can Solve Your Toughest Sales Challenges.* He describes the challenges of dealing with increasing levels of complexity in his sales career:

> As the years went on, selling became more complicated. Instead of selling to an owner or a single decision maker, I had to persuade buying committees or multiple departmental heads. No longer did I sell a single product or service; the customer wanted an entire solution, with a suite of options. Instead of demonstrating product benefits to prospects, I had to calculate their total cost of buying and managing my solutions (aka total cost of ownership). Simple purchase agreements were replaced by lengthy contracts.
>
> Sales complexity, the addition of steps and variables, is rising as a result of four developments: more decision makers and influencers, more information at our prospect's fingertips, **increasingly complex technology in our products and services**, and more competitors to battle in the marketplace.[6]

Yes, complexity is the new normal in business. Even small businesses rely on a variety of technologies to serve customers. In our own work as consultants, we need websites, cloud storage, web-based delivery, a help desk (outsourced, of course), marketing and sales automation, and a host of other web-based tools. Each and every one of those functions becomes a source of potential failure and extreme frustration.

 Especially for the Pops—he and technology don't get along!

Stop and think about the hotel business, for instance. The general manager prides herself on ensuring a positive customer experience for every customer, *every time*. She has worked hard to implement systems that measure everything. She's trained her people. She actively empowers her managers to delight her customers.

There are five key points of contact that hotel customers can have with her staff, and she is proud to report a guest satisfaction rate 92 percent or better in all five areas:

1. Bellman / Valet—94%
2. Front Desk—95%
3. Concierge—97%
4. Restaurant/In-Room Dining—92%
5. Housekeeping—94%

Awesome, right?! Well . . . not really.

This level of customer satisfaction looks pretty good in each *individual* department, but do you know that it means about one out of every four of her beloved guests will have an issue? (Do the math!) Are you listening? Almost 25 percent of guests will leave that hotel less than completely satisfied!

All the KIDS know what this means. The hotel won't be listed on the first page on Yelp or TripAdvisor, so there is no way they would stay there. (They wouldn't even suggest that hotel to the BOSS, who doesn't know how to use the interwebs or those newfangled apps.)

Apps? Meaning "appetizers"? I'm confused.

"Applications." The Pops kinda struggles with tech stuff and is basically always confused without his newspaper.

The workplace is technologically more complex, is cognitively more complex, and is driven by a customer base that is considerably more complex. When you consider that your company's success is highly dependent upon execution, increasing complexity creates HUGE issues.

In a survey conducted by Wharton and SAP, 74 percent of executives said that "process and decision-making complexities have inhibited their ability to reach their business goals."[7] You read that right. It isn't the macroeconomic conditions, or inability to find good people, or vendors, or way-too-demanding customers.

It is *complexity*.

How Complex Is the World Today?

We all intuitively know that people have become more savvy and complex, but have you seen the statistics on technology usage? They're insane. And, frankly, they are the perfect metaphor for how incredibly connected we truly are.

- In 1995, less than 1 percent of the world's population had an Internet connection. Today, more than 40 percent are connected.

- We reached the first billion people with an Internet connection in 2005; the 2 billion mark was surpassed just five years later in 2010. We added another billion in just four years, reaching 3,000,000,000 with Internet access in 2014.

- Facebook went from 100 million users in 2008 to over a billion in 2012. In 2017, there are 1.8 billion *active* users!

- In 2012, there were 8.7 billion connected devices. It is projected there will be more than 50 billion in 2020.[8]

Let's check in with the BOSS: "So what? Why does this matter? The fact that a bunch of people have smartphones and the KIDS waste their time on Facebook doesn't have anything to do with my business."

Brilliant. In case you think we made up that classic BOSS response, we can assure you we didn't. The impact of *complexity* will continue to have huge repercussions on you and how you run your business. Here's why:

- **Your people are connected.** You're right. The fact that your marketing intern has 300 friends on Facebook doesn't really impact you. What *does* impact you is that she *sees* what all 300 of her friends are doing, accomplishing, experiencing, and getting. (Notice we didn't say "earning"—the KIDS always think their Facebook friends are just *lucky* and are *given* promotions *and* new cars *and* fun vacations.) "Keeping up with the Joneses" has never been more overwhelming and scary and emboldening (all at the same time!).

  Why do the KIDS show up on Monday in flip-flops and expect the corner office and a six-figure salary on Friday? Because that's what they "saw" someone post online at lunch.

- **Your people are aware.** From the new dancing cat video to the dynamics of the U.S.–Russia relationship, your people are more aware of what's going on in the world around them than ever before. No, we are not claiming that all people are suddenly Rhodes Scholars and have a well-informed opinion—that would be just plain wrong. What we are boldly claiming is people are much more acutely aware of their worth, what opportunities exist, and what everyone thinks about your company.

- **Your people have a broader understanding.** The obvious next step is for your people to quickly move from aware of the world around them to actually beginning to *understand* it. Forums, groups, and meet-ups are all incredibly motivating and empowering to people, driving them from being simply *informed* to fully *engaged* and empowered to *actually do something*. That includes starting a company that becomes your competition, mobilizing a protest against your current labor actions, or engaging others to do something to make the world a better place. Your people can move from unaware to understanding and ownership quicker than ever before in human history!

Here's the bottom line: people are more savvy and more empowered than ever before. That makes the marketplace far more complex than ever, and the impact on your business is undeniable.

YOU MUST ACT DIFFERENTLY. NOW!

There is some good news for you. Things are changing at a nice, measured, slow pace.

#sarcasmfordays

Key Points to Remember

1. Technology is the great equalizer—providing your customers with more access and insights than ever before.

2. The workplace is technologically more complex, it is cognitively more complex, and it is driven by a customer base that is even more complex.

3. Your people are more connected, aware, and have a broader understanding than ever before.

Chapter **10**

Distractions: It's Even Worse than You Think

"There is time enough for everything in the course of the day, if you do but one thing at once, but there is not time enough in the year, if you will do two things at a time."

Lord Chesterfield[1]

PICTURE THIS TYPICAL OFFICE SCENE: A manager is trying to have a one-on-one conversation with an employee. . .

"The crazy part about technology is the negative impact it's having on the workplace . . . Too many distractions—["Sweet Home Alabama" starts playing on the mobile phone.]

"Hey, sorry, that's my sister calling. Can you give me a second?"

"FaceTime? No, no, no . . . I'm right in the middle of something. Let me call you back . . ."

"Sorry about that. Let me just put my phone on silent. Okay, as I started to say, before all of this technology, my assistant could ensure that I was undisturbed. Today, with the—[A loud *DING!* from the computer.]

"Ugh, my apologies. What is that? Oh, it's my email. I'll get it later . . . wait . . . my order from Madrid is delayed? What the heck? [Types a quick reply.]

"Sorry, dude. What was I saying? Oh, yes. Distractions. So, what happens in the workplace is that distractions cause us to communicate in 'beeps and buzzes.' But even that doesn't do justice to all the challenges we have to contend with when it comes to—[Someone knocks on the door.]

"Seriously? Hang on a sec. Let me grab that. I'll just let them know we're busy."

"Do what? A meeting in five minutes? Oh, of course, I almost forgot. Yeah, yeah, I'll be right there."

"Wow! Just can't seem to get a minute to get something done. Can we get together this afternoon?"

We're thinking that scenario sounds familiar. *Painfully* familiar, in fact.

Distractions have always been a problem in the workplace, but today they have become a performance-robbing, time-sucking, some-body-stop-the-madness kind of problem. Back in the day, the BOSS had to contend with phone calls, meetings, and people dropping in unannounced. In today's workplace, those are the least of your worries.

As we pointed out in chapter 2, technology has created an enormous amount of distractions in the workplace. Google, Facebook, LinkedIn, texting, and email have ushered in a brave new world of nonstop, crush-your-productivity distractions. However, even though you sense the problem, you may not realize how bad it really is.

Dr. Gloria Mark, a professor at the University of California, Irvine, has studied workplace distractions for well over a decade. To say her findings are stunning qualifies as a huge understatement. In fact, we've begun to wonder how employees ever get anything done.

> What we found is that the average amount of time that people spent on any single event before being interrupted or before switching was about three minutes. Actually, three minutes and five seconds, on average. That does not include formal meetings, because we figured if they were in a formal meeting, they were prisoners at the meeting, right? They couldn't leave or switch activities. So, we didn't count that.[2]

In case you breezed by that paragraph, she said employees are interrupted at work every—hang on—*"What? Oh, see if I can call her back, will you?"*

Get the point? Employees are interrupted at work, on average, every **THREE minutes**! #crazy

We're sorry to tell you that was actually the good news. As if getting interrupted every three minutes (we're trying to imprint that on your brain) wasn't enough to make you want to smash your fingers with a hammer, it turns out that little nugget of news is only the hail, high winds, and driving rain—not the actual tornado:

> To have a uniform comparison, we looked at all work that was interrupted and resumed on the same day. The good news is that most interrupted work was resumed on the same day— 81.9 percent—and it was resumed, on average, in 23 minutes and 15 seconds, which I guess is not so long.[3]

Not so long? Are you freaking kidding? Evidently, Dr. Mark is working on her night-club comedy routine. Or, she's got a mean streak. Twenty-three minutes to get back on task? That tidbit of information qualifies as a government-certified, EF5 twister (and we take that stuff very seriously here in Oklahoma).

And she hasn't even gotten to the "bad news" yet?

> But the bad news is, when you're interrupted, you don't imme-
> diately go back to the task you were doing before you were
> interrupted. There are about two intervening tasks before you
> go back to your original task, so it takes more effort to reori-
> ent back to the original task. Also, interruptions change the
> physical environment. For example, someone has asked you for
> information and you have opened new windows on your desk-
> top, or people have given you papers that are now arranged
> on your desk. So often the physical layout of your environment
> has changed, and it's harder to reconstruct where you were.
> So, there's a cognitive cost to an interruption.[4]

Welcome to the NEW leadership environment, my friend! You get to deal with all of the classic leadership issues in a work environment where interruptions are like the levers on a pinball machine. Employees bounce around from one task to the next, and many times things aren't where they expect them to be when they get back.

The real question is, what kind of impact does all of this distraction have on performance? That really is the $64,000 question, isn't it? (KIDS, *The $64,000 Question* was a big-money game show back in the '50s. You don't think we make this stuff up, do you?)

A report by Integrated Research Advisory Services & Employerbility provides some detailed, although not encouraging, answers. According to the *2013 Workplace Productivity Report*, 55 percent of people are frequently distracted throughout the workday, with only 33 percent of those frequently distracted able to effectively get on with work and disregard distractions.[5] According to that report, four in ten employees are "frequently distracted and unable to disregard distractions and get on with the job."

Oh, is that all?! Only 40 percent of employees are unable to disregard distractions?

Yes. There's more! Let this information rattle around in your head a bit:

> Self-assessed respondents of the survey revealed that there are periods throughout the week where they were completely unproductive, and alarmingly:
>
> - 25% of people were completely unproductive 7 or more hours a week
> - 22% of people were completely unproductive 5–6 hours a week
> - On average—this represented approximately 11% of people costs or 2.3 days lost per employee per working month.[6]

So, let's see if we have this straight. About one-fourth of your employees are "completely unproductive" almost 20 percent of the time? And the end result is you're losing as much as 2.3 *days* of productivity PER EMPLOYEE every month?

Call FEMA. Surely that's the worst of it.

Actually, no. It gets even worse. Our friend Curt Steinhorst, author of *Can I Have Your Attention*, is one of the leading authorities in the field of workplace distractions. He shared these scary statistics with us:

- Distractions account for a 40 percent reduction in worker productivity.
- Distractions drive the IQ of a Harvard MBA down to the level of an eight-year old.
- Distractions cost businesses $10,375, per person, ANNUALLY.[7]

On our *Counter Mentor* podcast, we asked Curt to share his understanding of the impact of distractions on different generations.

Specifically, we wanted to know, "are distractions, especially technology, a problem for everyone or just the KIDS?" Here's Curt's reply:

> If you look at Boomers, and you add TV in, they are more disconnected from personal conversation than any generation. They spend more time in front of a screen than anyone . . . It's interesting. What it really indicates is, even though Boomers tend to think differently and use different channels of communication, we are all moving toward this constantly connected, incapable-of-focus world that we live in.[8]

Oops. Not exactly what the BOSS wanted to hear. Turns out, every generation battles distractions, only the sources are a bit different.

 "Pops, you get that? *Your* generation is actually the worst."

 "Actually, we've spent all day explaining things to Millennials. We're exhausted."

The Curse of Email

In some ways technology is a blessing, but in other ways it's a curse of biblical proportions. By now, that probably doesn't seem like an overstatement, since all of this technology has taken your team's productivity and reduced it to never-before-seen levels of mediocrity. But technology isn't quite done jackin' with you just yet. The worst part is that some of the problem is of your own making.

The culprit is email. It's the tool the BOSS cannot live without, and, unfortunately, the tool he loves to make sure his people can't live without either. Yes, as it turns out, the BOSS LOVES technology—as long as that technology is email.

Email even has its own marketing tagline: It's the quicker interrupter (with apologies to *Procter & Gamble*). You see, the BOSS has decided that it is absolutely fine, even preferable, to interrupt employees every hour of the day with email. In some cases, the 1:30 A.M. email has become the proverbial badge of honor for the over-the-top micromanager. #pumpthebrakes

Why is that a problem, you ask? Well, actually, that's the wrong question. The question should be, "How many problems does that create?"

Problems. Plural.

1. You create the expectation that—regardless of the time of day—your employee *must* respond. No—it doesn't matter if you tell your employees they can answer in the morning. Especially for one of the KIDS.

Project: Time Off conducted a survey of more than 5,600 employees to discover attitudes about the way they view the separation between the workplace and their own leisure time. The survey defined the term "work martyrs" as people who believe no one else can do the work they do, "don't want others to think [they are] replaceable," "want to show complete dedication to [their] company and job," and actually "feel guilty for using [their] paid time off." The results were quite revealing:

> Workers who meet the work martyr definition . . . are over-whelmingly Millennials. More than four in ten (43%) work martyrs are Millennials, compared to just 29 percent of overall respondents.[9]

 "Finally! Proof the KIDS DO work harder!"

"Nice try. The survey didn't ask if they ACTUALLY work harder; it just asked if they want people to *think* they work harder."

 "Semantics . . . We work harder! #science."

When you send an email to employees, the last thing most of them want to do is leave the impression they're not all-in for the job. So, despite any instructions to the contrary, they feel compelled to reply. At all hours of the night. On weekends. And on vacation. If they happen to take one.

2. You create a justification for NOT working during actual work hours. The KIDS figure if they have to work all of hours of the night and on weekends, then a few hours on the iPhone, doing yoga, or playing golf each day is a small price to pay. Then you see your hard-working employee on his cell phone in the middle of the day, and you start complaining about "no work ethic" and all that nonsense. What happens? The resentment starts to build, and workplace engagement starts to tank.

3. You add even *more* distractions. As Maura Thomas, founder of *RegainYourTime.com*, notes in her *HBR* article, "Your Late-Night Emails Are Hurting Your Team," you're now responsible for adding to the already massive pile of distractions employees have to deal with. Yes, *distraction* is back with a vengeance:

A frantic environment that includes answering emails at all hours doesn't make your staff more productive. It just makes them busy and distracted. You base your staff hiring decisions on their knowledge, experience, and unique talents, not how many tasks they can seemingly do at once, or how many emails they can answer in a day.[10]

4. You completely miss the point that employees actually do need some downtime. It's not that they deserve it (although they do), or that they would like to have it (although they do), but as Thomas observes, it is that they NEED downtime to function at their best.

> Being "always on" hurts results. When employees are constantly monitoring their email after work hours—whether this is due to a fear of missing something from you, or because they are addicted to their devices—they are missing out on essential downtime that brains need. Experiments have shown that to deliver our best at work, we require downtime.[11]

So, you foster guilt in your employees, set the stage for conflict, multiply their distractions, and make them less productive. And all this time you've had this idea that you're getting tons of work done with your middle-of-the-night electronic missives! What you're really doing is setting your people up for failure.

Isn't that special?

The Distraction You're Not Even Aware Of

So, enough with technology already. Clearly, it's a sign of the apocalypse or the electronic version of the bubonic plague. But, let's keep piling on the BOSS and address another monumental management misstep. You see, all these years, you've demanded that every job description include these magical words: "Must be able to multitask."

This is one of our favorite distraction topics. You've got this "job description" with sixty-two different bullet points outlining tasks for which the employee has to be responsible. At the end of all that misery, you feel compelled to add the catch-all phrase present in *every* job description we've seen: "Any other tasks or responsibilities as your manager may assign." Covered all the bases, didn't you? No litigation loopholes at your company!

And then, there is this:

MUST BE ABLE TO MULTITASK.

As if all of the distractions we've outlined aren't enough of a problem for employees, some genius decided to make "multitasking" an entry requirement into your workplace. Today's employee is fully expected to respond to email, answer calls (or texts, if you hire one of the KIDS), attend all-day meetings, write reports, and handle multiple "business critical" projects—all at the same time!

And that doesn't include Google or Facebook or setting fantasy football lineups. (Note: To be clear, we fully support providing time to set fantasy football lineups and fill out March Madness brackets.) Big data, social media, and digital *everything* have done nothing but empower managers to believe in this mythical notion of multitasking. Yes, *mythical*. As in, makes for a good story but is completely FALSE.

That's right, we now know, without question, that multitasking is a complete and utter myth. John Medina wrote about it in his book *Brain Rules*. In fact, *wrote* isn't strong enough language. Medina *imperatively stated*, "To put it bluntly, research shows that we can't multitask. We are biologically incapable." He went on to say, conclusively, "The brain is a sequential processor, unable to pay attention to two things at the same time."[12]

Unfortunately, that doesn't keep you from making it a job requirement for every new-hire. Why? Because *YOU* are a multitasker. *YOU* have always been a multitasker. So, *YOU* claim an employee can't survive in this day and age without multitasking.

Hey, Ms. Science Deny-er, how many ways can you be wrong? Not only is multitasking a myth, it's a performance-robbing mistake, something researchers have known about since 2001!

According to research in the 1990s led by Joshua Rubinstein and David Meyer, multitasking, or, as academics accurately refer to it, "switch-tasking," can actually *reduce productivity* by as much as 40 percent since the brain cannot focus on two different complex tasks at the same time.[13] A CNN article elaborates on their findings.

> "People in a work setting," says Meyer, "who are banging away on word processors at the same time they have to answer phones and talk to their co-workers or bosses—they're doing switches all the time. Not being able to concentrate for, say, tens of minutes at a time, may mean it's costing a company as much as 20 to 40 percent" in terms of potential efficiency lost, or the "time cost" of switching, as these researchers call it.[14]

 "Word processor? Is that like a typewriter?"

 "More like an alphabet juicer."

But that was back in 2001, right? Like something might have changed? Not so much. It's actually worse than you thought (seems to be a theme in this chapter). University of Utah researchers found that combining two normally simple tasks—driving a car and talking on a mobile phone—is the equivalent of driving drunk![15]

By the way, it doesn't matter at all if you're using a hands-free system in the car.[16] That's why, at the time of this writing, fourteen states have already enacted "distracted driving" laws that prohibit using mobile phones while driving.

Need more? Well, just because we know the BOSS will have a real problem letting go of "the way we've always done it," we will throw in one more nugget. Research has also shown that multitasking or switch-tasking, or whatever term you prefer, actually makes people stupid:

> A study by the University of London found that participants who multitasked during cognitive tasks experienced an IQ score decline similar to those who have stayed up all night. Some of the multitasking men had their IQ drop 15 points, leaving them with the average IQ of an 8-year-old child. The next time you find yourself in a meeting, trying to juggle listening to your boss and reading the day's top stories, know that little information will be stored from either task when all is said and done.[17]

See the problem? Do you want a bunch of eight-year-olds working for you? Well, actually, you might need one to help you with your smartphone, but that's not really our point.

Conclusion

All sarcasm aside—and we've offered up plenty—these are issues that have a dramatic negative impact on your company. It's just that you've grown accustomed to it. It's so common, and so much a part of the work environment, you feel it must be the price of being in business. But it's not. You can change it.

To change it, we've got to get your attention and create a sense of urgency around it. You have to see the magnitude of the problem.

This one single issue—DISTRACTION—is costing you a ton of money. Multitasking, in particular, is not only detrimental to employee productivity, it is a ticking time bomb when it comes to employee engagement and communication. Here's why: As a leader, if you try to have a conversation with an employee while you're working on something else, even something as simple as checking your email, you send that employee a clear message: "You're not important enough for me to focus exclusively on you. I can listen to you and check messages at the same time."

You most likely don't intend it that way, but we can assure you that employees take it that way. If you doubt it, try the same thing at home with your children. Or your spouse. #enjoythecouch

Workplace distractions are a *real* problem—a clear and present danger. However, you can't just get rid of them, and, clearly, you can't bang your head against the wall until the madness stops.

On the other hand, you *could* wait until tonight and send emails to your subordinates just to make them feel as stressed as you do.

Key Points to Remember

1. Distractions are crushing your team's productivity.

2. Distractions, quite literally, make people stupid.

3. Multitasking is a myth!

 Check out this related *Counter Mentors* video podcast episode: "Working While Distracted?!" Visit cmtr.co/ep25.

Chapter 11

Pace of Change:
It's Way Faster than You Think

"Perhaps the greatest challenge business leaders face today is how to stay competitive amid constant turbulence and disruption."[1]

John Kotter

ALTHOUGH IT OFTEN LEADS to bone-crushing complexity and productivity-killing distractions, technology continues to produce innovation and progress. Which means, of course, that new technology also produces another powerful, potentially momentum-stopping problem: change.

Constant, predictably unpredictable change is happening at an unprecedented pace. It's not just the technology that changes—more and more gigabytes and gigawatts (isn't a *Back to the Future* reference perfect here?)—it's also the direct and indirect impacts of technology that produce astounding change. Freaking cool and terrifying all at once.

The impact that technology has had on the newest generations entering the workplace is unprecedented. Like a hurricane coming ashore, it's never just one issue you have to deal with. Hurricanes bring 150 mph winds, a tidal surge, inland flooding, electrical outages, and other problems. Technology brings chaos, complexity, distractions, and change.

Gone are the days when you can "see that coming" and prepare your business for that new technology. You can't prepare for something that is newly announced on Monday and mainstream by Tuesday! What turns this into a Hurricane Katrina kind of problem is that your customers AND employees AND vendors AND shareholders are ALL expecting you to be up to speed. On *everything*. Even if, on occasion, some of those shareholders have no idea what "it" is.

Yes, we can all thank Apple for this behavior!

In an age where your customers and employees can download their iPhone updates immediately, or, when they get a new iPhone, they log-in to iCloud and all their apps and preferences are just "magically" there. How can it take eighteen months to make that systems change? ("Are you kidding me?")

But that's the business environment you operate in today. You have to satisfy short-term-obsessed analysts and shareholders AND constantly respond to the demands of your key customers and partners, all while cultivating a culture of purpose, agility, and transformation to keep your employees engaged.

A recent article in *The Economist* sums up the challenge associated with rapid change:

> A customer downloads an app from Apple every millisec-
> ond. The firm sells 1,000 iPhones, iPads or Macs every couple
> of minutes. It whips through its inventories in four days and
> launches a new product every four weeks. Manic trading by

computers and speculators means the average Apple share changes hands every five months.

Such hyperactivity in the world's biggest company by market value makes it easy to believe that 21st-century business is pushing its pedals ever harder to the metal. On Apple's home turf in Silicon Valley the idea that things are continually speeding up is a commonplace. "The pace of change is accelerating," Eric Schmidt and Jonathan Rosenberg of Google assert in their book *How Google Works*. For evidence look no further than the "unicorns"—highflying startups—which can win billion-dollar valuations within a year or two of coming into being. In a few years they can erode the profits of industries that took many decades to build.[2]

NBD. (That's "no big deal," BOSS.) We suggest you just keep doing what you're doing and watch your once mighty and powerful organization crumble around you. #thesarcasmneverstops

Not convinced?

The *Financial Times* reported recently that the world will spend approximately $1.6 TRILLION on the research and development of cutting-edge technologies, ranging from robotics to social media.[3] The number of global workers pursuing careers in these once-in-a-generation technologies is now more than 7 million! To be clear, this isn't just an American pursuit. Brazil, India, and China are doing everything they can to claw their way to the top of the technology and innovation food chain.

According to international author and futurist Jim Carroll, research suggests that 65 percent of preschool students will do a job that we don't even know about today. He isn't saying they'll work for a company that doesn't yet exist; he means they will be *doing something* that doesn't exist today! Along the same lines, Carroll asserts that "50% of the information taught to first-year science undergraduates will be obsolete by the time they graduate."[4]

Holy. Crap.

It's just as overwhelming when you look at the data related to the business world. Did you know that approximately 60 percent of Apple's top line comes from products that were made after you bought your last computer?[5] Best-in-class organizations are changing the way they do business, source materials, manufacture products, test, teach, lead, and develop their people. If you have any hope of success in this too-fast, chaotic workplace, you must be prepared for change.

Put simply, don't be like the taxi business.

Change Is Crushing Cabbies (Should You Blame Uber?)

There have been more articles written about the often corrupt, sliding-toward-bankruptcy taxicab industry in the past three years than the New England Patriots have won football games. (That's a LOT.)

From Yellow Taxi in San Francisco to the self-proclaimed Taxi King in New York, the industry is getting absolutely hammered.[6] Built on the back of legislation, (alleged) corruption, lobbying, and control, the taxi business was the gold standard of growth for decades. The best example is the cost of a coveted "medallion"—the token required to own a cab—in the most influential city on the planet, New York City. In 1947, the cost was $2,500. After years of litigation, infighting, and growth, that same medallion was worth more than $1.3 million in 2013.

Unsurprisingly, taxi owners and operators turned their noses up at the likes of Uber and Lyft—thinking that the giant could never be slayed. (The phrase "too big to fail" comes to mind.) Since 2013, the value of NYC's medallions has plummeted, with Bloomberg reporting their worth as low as $650,000 in 2015.[7]

We're not mathematicians, but a 50 percent decline in three years can't be good.

This is not just a problem in the Big Apple. Medallion prices in Boston and Chicago have also fallen, according to the *New York Times*.[8] Uber, although not exempt from its own challenges, litigation, and bad press, has expanded its reach to five continents and has a current valuation approaching $70 billion.

Uber is innovating and continues to adapt. Most cabbies, on the other hand, appear to be glued to "the way we've always done it."

Adapt or Die

In the past twenty years, in every major sport, there have been substantive changes in the game.

Just think about the NFL. You've seen significant (sometimes *ridiculous*) rule changes, new offensive and defensive schemes, changes in positions, games on three days each week instead of just Sundays, and much, much more. Every year, teams turns over every rock, looking for an edge, something they can do differently to win the championship *next* year. And every time someone finds success, every other team is forced to respond (except, it appears, the Cleveland Browns, who just keep losing).

 Sorry, Cleveland. On the other hand, no one can take away your 2016 Cavs Championship! #thanksLeBron

Change is simply a given. You can adapt or you can become irrelevant. A coach will never survive playing the game the same way it's always been played, because the game is *always* changing!

And, of course, players have changed. Yes, even the world of sports has not escaped the dramatic change in employees. Perfect example: In the 2017 NFL playoffs, completely unknown to Head Coach Mike Tomlin, a star player on the Pittsburgh Steelers decided to stream his coach's locker room talk on Facebook Live. As he fired up his players, Coach Tomlin had a couple of choice words for his next opponent, the New England Patriots—the kind of stuff we would rather keep just between us teammates, if you know what we mean.

Turns out, not only was Coach Tomlin not thrilled (to say the least), the NFL has a rule against that kind of thing, so it resulted in a $10,000 fine.[9]

Expensive video.

Remember *Moneyball*?[10] It's the true story turned bestselling book turned Hollywood movie about the General Manager of the Oakland As, Billy Beane, and his relentless pursuit to enable his small-market, no-money team into a contender against the always-rich, always-winning New York Yankees. This story is the perfect illustration of the need to ask hard questions and push against the status quo.

In a key scene early in the movie, Beane (played by Brad Pitt) is meeting with his scouts about how they are going to replace their key offensive players, who signed big deals in the off season to go to teams with *real* money. Flanked by baseball newcomer and Ivy League-educated Peter Brand (hysterically portrayed by Jonah Hill), Beane obnoxiously pushes back on every stereotypical comment and textbook idea presented by his group of—how do we say this nicely— "seasoned" scouts.

After the meeting, Grady, Beane's head scout, confronts him about his "wrong way of thinking" and insists he is listening to the wrong guy. "You're discounting what scouts have done for one hundred and fifty years," Grady exclaims.

Beane's response is priceless: "Adapt or die."

There you have it. Our mantra—the mantra of the Counter Mentor Leader: Adapt or die.

If you're a BOSS, you just shake your head and say things like, "KIDS these days!" But you need to know that those KIDS have no idea what the fuss is all about. They have no clue. Why? Because they have been raised in a society whose norms are completely different from the ones you grew up with. To them, Google is the ultimate authority. The neighborhood they live in is called Snapchat. Their currency is Apple Pay, PayPal, and Venmo.

Yes, the KIDS are different, but it DOES NOT mean they can't crush it. It simply means their perspectives are different from yours. By chance, have you completely forgotten how different you were when you stumbled into the workplace thirty years ago (or longer)?

It's called the arrogance of experience. Translation: "MY way must be the BEST (or only) way, because that's the way I did it." This is the BIG change confronting today's manager: you must overcome the arrogance of experience with regard to the KIDS. In our experience, the BOSS is often unwilling to adapt to the monumental changes that technology and the KIDS represent in the workplace.

For example:

- The BOSS refuses to consider different workplace practices because the older generation has always worked eight to five (or some other *ridiculous*, arbitrary rule that drives away top talent).

- The BOSS constantly complains about the KIDS, but make absolutely no effort to understand things from their perspectives since "those little snowflakes wouldn't know a good day's work if it hit them in the head" (or some other choice words).

- The BOSS continues to talk about the way things used to be when she or he was young ("uphill, both ways, in the snow" and all that nonsense) with their bell-bottoms and elbow grease.

You get the idea. Some leaders are arrogant. Some are just stubborn. Some check both boxes.

They refuse to adapt.

DISCLAIMER: This doesn't mean you should hand out trophies for showing up, or that you should allow some novice to "live stream" your next sales meeting. It does mean, however, that you should wake up.

Do you want to do it the way you've always done it, or do you want to learn to thrive and be successful in a state of constant change?

Key Points to Remember

1. The pace and impact of change are staggering.

2. Change isn't limited to technology; it also impacts people and workplace culture.

3. You have two choices: adapt to change or die on the vine.

 Check out this related *Counter Mentors* podcast episode: "Could You Do Change Any Worse?!" Visit cmtr.co/ep7.

Chapter 12

The Four Most Dangerous Words in Your Vocabulary

"Time management is an oxymoron. Time is beyond our control, and the clock keeps ticking regardless of how we lead our lives. Priority management is the answer to maximizing the time we have."[1]

John Maxwell

A S A LEADER, you have more challenges than you know what to do with.

More challenges, but the same amount of time to work with. Well, probably less, now that about half of your workforce is intimately familiar with Google, Facebook, and LinkedIn.

When it's all said and done, time is actually your biggest enemy and your most precious asset.

Success requires the purposeful execution of a number of critical leadership tasks. These are things that employees simply cannot do; only you, the leader, can make them happen. Things like communicating the vision, strategic planning, and people development. Employees are not expected to execute these, nor will they ordinarily take it upon themselves (since the BOSS will likely have a coronary).

So, let's put our cards out on the table. Those critical areas of leadership are both difficult and time consuming. They are reflective of long-term, easy-to-ignore-at-the-moment objectives as compared to the short-term, firefighting tasks typical of the average day in management.

The question is, how long can you afford to ignore these important tasks? Is there a penalty to be paid for putting off the "most important things"? In his seminal book *The 7 Habits of Highly Effective People*, author Stephen Covey outlined a series of seven principles, or habits, that make people "effective."

> The 7 Habits of Highly Effective People embody many of the fundamental principles of human effectiveness. These habits are basic, they are primary. They represent the internalization of correct principles upon which enduring happiness and success are based.[2]

Covey's book, now more than twenty-five years old, has sold more than 25 million copies and has had an enduring influence on business leadership. It has taught millions the value of *seeking first to be understood* (Habit 5) and *sharpening the saw* (Habit 7). It was Covey who said, **"Effective leadership is putting first things first"** (Habit 3). It means making a conscious decision to focus on activities that are critically important but that are often set aside in lieu of activities that become urgent.

To demonstrate the idea of "first things," Covey adopted a grid based on two axes: urgency and importance.[3] This two-by-two box produces four quadrants of activities:

1. Urgent/Important
2. Urgent/Not Important
3. Not Urgent/Important
4. Not Urgent/Not Important

A quick inspection illustrates that we tend to spend the majority of our time, especially at work, on the things that are urgent, not necessarily important: the crises, the distractions, the daily irritants.

	Urgent	Not Urgent
Important	Crying baby Kitchen fire Some calls **1**	Exercise Learning Planning **2**
Not Important	**3** Interruptions Distractions Other calls	**4** Trivia Busy work Time-wasters

Yet, it is the urgent and important things—the stuff that requires a fire extinguisher—that covet the attention of the leader. Worse, leaders can easily fall prey to the urgency of *unimportant* things. Answering emails is a good example. We've become trained to respond to the buzz or the ding of mobile phones. We develop a habit; a habit that says we must *immediately* address any email that hits the inbox—just like Pavlov's dog.

While the typical leadership day is loaded with both tactical and trivial interruptions, the truly important challenges often remain unaddressed. Leaders become victims of a "here-and-now" mentality, focused on making reactive decisions, solving tactical problems, and pointing people in the right direction. *Critical* leadership tasks suffer. And who is the #posterchild for this trap? The BOSS. However, as equal opportunity critics, our observation is the KIDS that have become leaders, typically stumble down the same path.

So, things we know should be done, when balanced against the many fires we encounter (or create) daily, get tossed aside. Worse, we concoct a quiver full of convenient excuses for ignoring or infinitely procrastinating those important things.

Way back in 1940, in a presentation to the National Association of Life Underwriters (NALU), a man named Albert E. N. Gray offered up a #knowledgebomb even the KIDS can respect:

> The common denominator of success—the secret of success of every man who has ever been successful—lies in the fact that he formed the habit of doing things that failures don't like to do.[4]

The secret to success? Practice the habits that those who fail aren't willing to do.

Like putting first things first.

The Big Lie

Not surprisingly, few leaders have developed that habit. Some do, but most don't. The question is: Why?

In that address to the NALU, almost fifty years before *7 Habits* hit bookstores, Gray offered this explanation:

> Why are successful men able to do things they don't like to do while failures are not? Because successful men have a purpose

strong enough to make them form the habit of doing things they don't like to do in order to accomplish the purpose they want to accomplish.[5]

We're not suggesting you're a failure. We *are* suggesting that, most likely, you're not doing a lot of really important things that will have a significant impact on your organization. Despite the obvious benefits, leaders often fail to do the first things—the "most important things"—and we wanted to know why.

So, we asked.

We asked leaders of companies, big and small, in dozens of industries. In fact, it is a consistent part of our conversations with leaders—whether we're discussing training, leadership, strategic planning, or any other critical leadership item. We want to know what keeps leaders from focusing on the really critical leadership tasks.

What we've found is that essentially all leaders have the same answer. Over and over, when we discover one or more critical organizational needs have fallen by the wayside, we've heard one specific phrase. Without fail, four words are used as the excuse-du-jour for failing to get the *most important things* done:

"I don't have time."

But, here's the thing: *The way you use your time is a choice.* However, you have convinced yourself that you have absolutely *no* choice, and you choose to suit up with the firefighting equipment and spend your days working on the urgent, both the important AND the unimportant.

Have you stopped to consider that there will always be crises and "urgent" needs unless, and until, something changes? Have you considered the idea that changing the way you invest your time, and using some of it to address those organizational issues, could actually be a solution to the short-term challenges you consistently face?

This is the truly big, scary lie of leadership: If you continue to work really hard, even though you are not doing the **most important things**, eventually something will change.

Sounds a bit silly when you say it like that, doesn't it?
#understatementoftheyear

Cause and Effect

We have never encountered four more dangerous words in the leadership vocabulary. Note how destructive this short phrase is to the organization:

- **I don't have time** to work on strategy, but I'm not sure why my employees aren't all rowing in the same direction. *The inefficiency is killing us.*

- **I don't have time** to manage communication and ensure that critical messages get pushed down through the organization, but my employees completely swing and miss on critical items. *Poor communication is killing us.*

- **I don't have time** to develop training and standardize key processes, but my employees seem stagnant and disinterested. *The lack of engagement is killing us.*

The simple question is this: If you don't address these things as the leader, *who will*? And if you don't address them, what will change? Scary answer: Lots of things—for the worse.

Again, it's not that you don't have time, it's that you have chosen to spend your time doing something else. You've prioritized some *other* task and made the decision that *it* is more important to you than being an effective leader.

Of course, you probably don't look at it that way. You may have never even thought about it in that sense. You're a BOSS; you just get stuff done. You're freaking great at it.

The reality is, when you "don't have time" for *real* leadership activities, you're simply choosing to invest your most valuable asset in short-term stock that repays little-to-nothing in the long-term.

What might happen if you change your habits? Consider the results for Bill Gates, Harvard dropout, founder of Microsoft, and, currently, the richest man in the world. Sure, he was smart and driven and focused, but he also made time for the most important things:

> While leading Microsoft, Gates would go on a secluded retreat twice a year; during that time, he would immerse himself in reading and thinking about technology trends affecting Microsoft's business. Because his "Think Week" reading material included reports written by Microsoft employees all over the world, this practice allowed Gates to glean strategic insights from developments employees were seeing in the marketplace.[6]

The essence of being a great leader is understanding the most important things and choosing to give them an elevated importance, compared to the tactical, technical, or trivial things that dominate your workday. Employees are not responsible for communication (quality or quantity). Employees don't create strategy. Employees don't develop your employees.

These are the responsibilities of leaders!

And now, the good news! We will show you how to solve this problem. REALLY solve it. The kind of rock-your-world, why-didn't-I-think-of-this-before solution that we have been told over and over is a game-changer.

Come to think of it, we get that "game-changer" comment a lot.

Now we're fairly certain you can see very clearly why leadership is so freaking hard. In addition to all the standard leadership challenges associated with building a high-performing team, you have to contend with complexity, change, distractions, AND generational issues. And the nice, big bonus is that there is never, ever enough time.

But we didn't write this book *just* to be snarky and sarcastic. We are prepared to show you how to go to war against these problems—and unlock the enormous potential in your four-generation workplace.

As the Pops loves to say on the *Counter Mentor* podcast, "Stay tuned. Coming right up, we'll break it all down for you . . ."

Key Points to Remember

1. Time is a leader's single most valuable asset.

2. Effective leaders understand the value of "first things first."

3. The four most dangerous words in a leader's vocabulary are "I don't have time!"

The **COUNTER Mentor**
Leadership Model™

HAVE WE MANAGED TO GET YOUR ATTENTION? Yes, it's a war out there, and you are over-matched.

Okay, not really. The KIDS just love drama, so we had to throw some in.

YOU. GOT. THIS.

You just need to acquire the knowledge, the skills, and the habits of a successful cross-generational, technology-savvy, hyper-connected leader. Which, of course, we are going to outline for you.

We are going to help you become a Counter Mentor Leader.

Chapter 13

The Problem with Leadership:
Practicing What You Can't Define

"Leadership is not an easy subject to explain."[1]

Max De Pree

AS OF THIS WRITING, there are more than 139,465 books available from Amazon on the topic of leadership. And we've read just about all of them.

Okay, that's not true. Pops has read a bunch of them. Robby has read tweets about a lot of them. #slacker

 I'm just more efficient than the Pops.

The point is, there is no shortage of books on leadership. Which would easily lead us to believe that leadership is a deep, dark cauldron of secrets that only a select few can access and master. How many books would you have to read to get a sense of what leadership is and learn how you can be good at it?

Our objective is to help you understand that, from one perspective, leadership is actually quite simple. Well, simple to understand, anyway—it's the execution of leadership responsibilities that creates all of the problems.

That probably sounds a bit arrogant. After all, the words *leadership* and *simple* probably don't belong in the same sentence. Who in their right mind would believe the idea that leadership is *simple* (especially after reviewing all the new obstacles in the chaotic, four-generation workplace)?

Let's start with the fact that there isn't even a standard definition for leadership. The truth is, there are dozens of different definitions, and enough variations to keep you completely confused. We make this point clearly with each client we work with by asking the company leadership team this simple question, "What is the definition of leadership?"

As you can imagine, the answers are all over the place. People usually start out with a list of character traits (which gets very long). Others mention military generals or American presidents as examples. Or movie characters (Russell Crowe's Maximus has been mentioned). And there is always reference to New England Patriots quarterback Tom Brady's astonishing comeback in the 2016 Super Bowl. #GOAT (Greatest of All Time)

See the pattern? Exactly. There isn't one.

KIDS, do what you do best—Google "What is leadership?" We did, and our search produced more than 123 *million* hits, and the second entry on the search page is an article entitled "What Is Leadership?" by *New York Times* bestselling author Kevin Kruse. His article, penned in 2013 (!), says this:

Such a simple question, and yet it continues to vex popular consultants and lay people alike. I've now written several books on leadership for employee engagement, and yet it occurred to me that I never actually paused to define leadership.[2]

Say what? No definition of leadership?

We suspect it dawned on Mr. Kruse that it might be a bit confusing to teach and coach on a topic in which the topic itself is not even defined, something we have found that is true about a lot of what is written about leadership. That's not to minimize those efforts; it's just to recognize that it's very difficult to get better at something you can't even clearly define!

In addition, the "experts" can't even decide on the differences between a leader and a manager. Is a manager a leader? Is a leader a manager? Do they overlap? Mr. Kruse provided his opinion:

Leaders have a unique ability to rally employees around a vision. Because their belief in the vision is so strong, employees will naturally want to follow them. Leaders also tend to be willing to take risks in pursuit of the vision.

Managers, on the other hand, are more adept at executing the vision in a very systemic way and directing employees on how to do so. They can see all of the intricate moving parts and understand how to make them harmonize. Managers are usually very risk-adverse.[3]

This also is quite common in leadership literature. People love to put the manager and leader in two separate boxes and draw a very thick line between the two. The picture of leadership is one of a swashbuckling risk-taker who inspires and motivates with grandiose dreams. The manager, on the other hand, is responsible for the soul-crushing drudgery of execution and the responsibility of *directing* employees (the BOSS loves that whole "directing" thing).

We're sure that's not Mr. Kruse's intent, but his definitions contribute to the idea. In an effort to distinguish between the role of manager and leader, he could easily lead someone to believe that managers are NOT leaders and really shouldn't be! Leaders rally the troops; managers direct them. But here's the problem: If managers have employees working for them and don't lead them, who does? Is this suggesting that one person manages you and another person leads you?

 "Nice. These are the same people that think the KIDS are screwed up."

The bottom line? Leadership is anything but simple, and it is badly in need of a common definition—which, as you can probably guess, we will provide you.

Defining Leadership

So, let's assemble a definition of leadership that makes sense, one we can work with as we progress. Do we offer it as the be-all, end-all definition of leadership? Well, actually . . . yes. At least for our purposes, as it relates to leadership in the workplace. If we can agree on a definition of leadership, we can all work toward a common objective!

NOTE: We're not suggesting that others are wrong in their research or in their definition of the term. We, to borrow a phrase, stand on the shoulders of giants. However, we want to be able to anchor back to a specific, simple, easy-to-understand, actionable definition that doesn't require a subscription to *Harvard Business Review* to comprehend!

Here is our definition of leadership:

Leadership is the art and science of getting things done through other people.

Immediately, you can see a problem. While people most commonly get promoted for *getting things done*, leadership is about getting things done *through other people*. No wonder there is a disconnect. Let's unpack our definition:

Leadership is the art . . . Learning how to be a transformational leader is a never-ending task because every person and every situation presents a unique challenge. The connection that is required to transform potential into performance is different with each and every individual under your care! They have different personalities, backgrounds, demographics, education, and experiences. Their nature and their nurture are all different, and it requires that you engage your emotional intelligence (EQ) to determine the right way to engage them. We would assert this is an *art*.

and science . . . There has been an incredible amount of research done on what it takes to be an effective leader. There have been studies on neuroscience, motivation, discipline, grit, mindset, communication, management, efficiency, and other topics we don't understand! The list literally goes on and on and on. We believe leaders should continually study and grow to gain an acute understanding of the methodologies and techniques needed to function effectively as a leader in the wide array of circumstances and environments that exist in the workplace.

of getting things done . . . We've never known a leader who did nothing. Undeniably, a leader must have the ability to drive progress, fuel growth, increase productivity, create synergies, and adapt to constant change. Leaders should always engage in producing results.

through other people. The trick is not to try and get things done ALL BY YOURSELF. Micromanaging your people, and mandating that everything must be done exactly the way you would do it, is NOT leadership. We would define that as Taylorian Management—not Counter Mentor Leadership. This short phrase ("through other people") is what makes our concept of leadership so effective today! It has very powerful implications:

1. **Leadership is relational.** We don't say that leadership is "forcing people to do exactly what you say when you say it." That would be a dictatorship.

2. **With that relationship comes trust and safety**, which manifests itself in your ability to *influence* others. The reason you can get things done through other people is because you've **invested in the relationship**, built trust, and *earned the right to influence* that person's behavior!

Reality check: Yes, we recognize this may be hard for those of you who enjoy being the BOSS. Most of you were promoted because you were the best at your old job. Your knowledge, skills, experience, and results were better than everyone else's, so you got promoted to management. At that point in your career, it was all about DOING, but when you become a leader, everything changes. It's no longer about you!

Once you commit to Counter Mentor Leadership, you don't get out of bed thinking about all the things *you* need to get done today. You get out of bed thinking about what you need to do to *enable your people* to get things done today. Your first thought is people (who produce results), not results (that you direct your people to produce).

We call it Counter Mentor Leadership because you are doing things differently—sometimes *completely* differently. You are mentoring, learning, growing, and engaging your people—all at the same time. Gone are those days of lacing up your Superman boots or putting on your Wonder Woman cape in the morning and working all day to fix every problem yourself.

You are now a people-developer. A coach. A motivator. A listener. A communicator.

You're a LEADER. Simple, right?

Key Points to Remember

1. You have to understand what leadership is before you can do it well.

2. Leadership is the art and science of getting things done through other people.

3. Leadership is relational (not generational) and fully dependent upon trust.

Chapter 14

You Can't Lead if
You Don't Know How

"Leadership cannot really be taught. It can only be learned."[1]

Harold S. Geneen

A S WE TOLD YOU PREVIOUSLY, leadership is primarily a set of skills that can be learned.

Don't take our word for it; take a run through all the research on the topic. Or, you could read the bestselling books from leadership gurus like Blanchard, Covey, Maxwell, De Pree, and Welch.

Of course, that doesn't mean that all leaders are created equal. Far from it. Not all leaders have the same motivation, the same desire, the same emotional intelligence, or any number of other characteristics important to leadership.

On the other side of the coin (that would be Bitcoin for you KIDS), just because individuals actually *learn* the skills of leadership doesn't mean they are (or will be) good leaders, because, like all skills, mastery requires practice and development. For example, we both know how to play chess. But neither of us is a Grandmaster chess player. We don't practice. We don't play often. We're not studying to get better. And we're not *that* offended if you watch a game and note that we're not very good.

 "Although Robby would love a nice trophy."

 "I'm just happy if the Pops stays awake during the game."

Raise your hand if you've actually had leadership training. Not just a leadership seminar, or a leadership book or two. That doesn't qualify as training; it just qualifies as "exposure," and we're relatively sure you don't want your doctor to just have some "exposure" to medicine. What we have in mind is ongoing, behavior-changing, habit-forming, leadership *learning*.

Our point here is pretty simple. When you promote the best player on the team to management, you lose your best player and you gain . . . what? An underperforming leader? A new micromanager? Someone who has no idea how to lead or coach or develop a team?

What we are describing is the death spiral that is micromanagement. The more you do FOR someone, the more dependent that person becomes. The more dependent that person becomes, the more resentful she or he is because there is no control, no autonomy, and no ownership. In fact, the *quickest* way to stifle learning and creativity on your team is to solve every problem, take control of every project, and make every decision. When those habits creep into your leadership, the first casualty is trust, and no team or company or leader survives very long without trust.

A Random Act of Leadership

The youngest in our family, Scott, was hired at a local fire department in Oklahoma. As early as any of us can remember, Scott talked about being a firefighter. We have vivid memories of him as an eight-year-old wearing a fire helmet everywhere he went. He was worried that if he took it off, he "might not be a fireman."

He started down that path, becoming certified as an Emergency Medical Technician (EMT) and later advancing to become a nationally registered Paramedic (NRP). Then, at twenty-five years of age, he joined the local fire department and achieved his boyhood dream.

His first day on the job made quite an impression on him. After the usual orientation that new hires go through—paperwork, tour, meet-and-greet—he was introduced with two other new hires to the platoon captain. After some initial conversation, the captain began to explain the responsibilities of new recruits and how their training would be conducted. He grabbed some cleaning supplies and led the three new recruits into the bathroom area, explaining that the new guys were expected to start with the basics, including a thorough weekly cleaning of the bathroom. #rookie

Did we say thorough?

We're sure you get the idea, but, just in case the recruits weren't clear, the captain proceeded to show them exactly what he meant. He got down on his knees and cleaned every toilet—front, back, top, bottom—with a scrub brush. Not just one toilet. *Every* toilet, as the recruits just watched. Once he finished that, he went to work on the rest of the bathroom, pointing out the particulars of how to do the job right and what the final result should look like.

If you want to know what leadership looks like, there might be no better example.

Is there any chance those recruits won't know what is expected of them in the future? Is there any likelihood that they won't know how to do the job? Most important, is there any chance they will ever complain about having to do the "dirty work"?

In this one amazing demonstration, the platoon captain provided incredible clarity for his new recruits: what the right result looks like, how the work is done, the attitude that is expected, and the type of culture they are joining. Oh, yes, there is a pecking order, but—as you can see—no one is above doing what needs to be done to make this team successful.

Of course, the captain could've just provided a job description, pointed to a "values" statement on the wall, and given the recruits some marching orders. (Sound familiar?) In other words, he could've done what the majority of managers do, but the mission of a firefighter requires a critical level of clarity, as you can see in the Firefighter's Creed:

By wearing the Maltese Cross I accept the responsibility of my chosen profession and it is a privilege that I must earn every day.

My loyalty to this community and my crew is beyond reproach. I humbly serve as a Guardian to my community always ready to respond to those who are unable to help themselves. I do not advertise the nature of my work or seek recognition for my actions. I voluntarily accept the inherent hazards of my profession placing the welfare and security of others before my own.

I serve with honor on and off duty. The ability to control my emotions and my actions regardless of circumstances sets me apart from other people. Uncompromising integrity is my standard. My character and honor are steadfast.

My word is my Bond.

We expect to lead and be lead [sic]. In the absence of orders, I will take charge, lead my crew, and accomplish the task at hand. I lead by example in all situations.

I will NEVER Quit![2]

For some reason, a large part of corporate America doesn't seem to understand this fundamental component of team building. They see Navy SEAL teams, or SWAT teams, or emergency medical teams, and they believe that their excellence is derived solely as a result of the *nature of their work*: that because they save lives, take grave risks, or work under enormous pressure, they are naturally focused and effective.

That couldn't be more wrong. The mission doesn't provide the clarity; the leader provides it.

Although the mission requires that critical level of clarity—due to the nature of the firefighter's work—it doesn't happen automatically.

It happens because leadership causes it to happen.

The Building Blocks of Leadership

One thing is absolutely certain. Scott trusts his platoon captain.

Implicitly. Completely. Unhesitatingly. After just one day on the job, he was all-in and ready to run through walls.

Why?

Because "Attitude reflects leadership, Captain." (One of Robby's favorite lines, from one of our favorite films, *Remember the Titans.*[3]) Translation: Leadership, first and foremost, is the ability to influence others, and when people trust the leader, almost anything is possible.

On the other hand, people will NOT follow anyone for any substantial amount of time whom they don't trust. Their attitudes will deteriorate, and they will move along. They MIGHT stick around a little while for some short-term incentive. They MIGHT stick around a bit to see if things will change. They MIGHT stick around for a short time because they lack options, but it won't be long. Especially with the KIDS, this transition will happen *quickly*.

Understand this: Trust is the cornerstone of leadership, and without it, the organization—your team, your department, your company—is on a collision course with high turnover, low productivity, shrinking margins, and unfulfilled potential. You don't merit trust just because you're a BOSS or the manager of the team. You earn that trust. *That trust is the interest on your investment in other people.*

That's why we say leadership is an "other people" exercise. Before your employees will invest themselves in you, you must first invest in them. To earn that trust requires you to become other-people focused, which involves making a conscious and consistent effort in four critical values:

- *Loyalty:* an investment in your commitment to the well-being of **other people**
- *Humility:* an investment in the interests of **other people**, considering them as important, if not more important, than yourself
- *Service:* an investment of your time and energy in developing **other people**
- *Gratitude:* an investment in your appreciation of the efforts of **other people**

These four areas are critical to leadership—and to trust—because they are *reciprocal* attitudes. In other words, the principle of reciprocity applies:

- When you serve others, *they typically respond in kind.*
- When you express gratitude to others, *they typically respond in kind.*
- When you listen to others and consider what may be important to them, *they typically respond in kind.*
- When you are loyal to others, *they typically respond in kind.*

When you consistently invest in your people—directly and individually, NOT through some lame "recognition program" or insignificant gesture like "Blue Jeans Friday"—incredible things happen. The reason is simple: People trust leaders who truly value them and the work they contribute.

However, when people don't feel valued, they don't trust. And when people don't trust you as a leader, several things are certain to happen:

- You will have to do everything yourself.

- You will have a revolving door of new employees coming in as the old ones bolt for something better.

- You will have to solve every problem as your team's creativity (and interest) dries up.

- You will be another victim of the self-fulfilling prophecy "You just can't find good people."

The alternative is to rely on your title, position, or authority to compel others to work. You can be a tyrant and force people to do it your way (right up until they leave). You can micromanage every employee because "no one can do it better" than you. Don't call that leadership. It's not. It's Taylorian Management.

Instead, just realize you haven't acquired the skills of a leader.

Key Points to Remember

1. Clarity is essential if you want your people to perform at the highest levels.
2. The mission doesn't provide the clarity; the leader provides it.
3. Effective leadership requires you to invest in your people.
4. When you invest in others, they will respond in kind.

Chapter 15

Counter Mentor Leadership: The Model

"Be daring, be different, be impractical, be anything that will assert integrity of purpose and imaginative vision against the play-it-safers, the creatures of the commonplace, the slaves of the ordinary."[1]

Cecil Beaton

ERIC DORNE WAS THE BOSS.[2] He was THE poster child. Boomer. Old-school. Supervisor, turned Executive. It was his way or the highway: "When I say 'Jump!' you say, 'How high?'"

Command-and-control to the max.

To be fair, his style of management had obviously worked; it got him to where he was—Senior Vice President and Chief Information Officer of a once-iconic American company.

Before landing at the helm of the technology team, Eric earned his stripes in the aisles of one of the largest supermarket companies in the United States. Starting his career in the 1970s as a grocery sacker,

Eric climbed the ladder until he ended up—thirty years later—in a corner office of the company's corporate headquarters.

He was living the American Dream.

However, at this point, Eric's story takes a rather dramatic turn. He opted not to take the path that ended with the *gold watch*. Instead, he opted for something new and different. Instead of shepherding his old organization through bankruptcy filings and downsizing, and sailing off into the sunset, Eric—with all the excitement and enthusiasm he could muster (rumor has it he almost cracked a smile)—accepted the CIO position in a rapidly growing Fortune 500 distribution company, a leader in the natural and organic food industry.

Robby had the opportunity to work with Eric for just over three years. He witnessed the ups and downs of Eric's transformation from BOSS to Counter Mentor Leader firsthand, so he will tell you the story.

Uncovering Counter Mentor Leadership

I was first introduced to the company as a consultant on an in-and-out, thirty-day contract. My job was simple: help the organization make sense of its data and create a plan to get the people—leaders and doers alike—bought into the notion of treating that data as an asset (yes, this was right in the middle of the BIG DATA craze).

Before I could start on the project, however, I had to interview with Eric, who was leading the IT organization. To say my first interaction was uncomfortable (and intimidating) would be an understatement.

My interview (what I referred to as "The Interrogation" later) evidently didn't go well from Eric's perspective.

"You were way outside the box, you talked too fast, and you were too young and enthusiastic!" Eric told me over lunch four years later.[3] "You're 'we can do that, we can do anything' attitude definitely made me uncomfortable. I was uncertain about you and what we were going to be able to accomplish."

However, Eric cautiously moved forward with bringing me on, going so far as to add a "no questions asked" clause in the contract to cut me loose if things didn't go well. The BOSS was in full-blown CYA mode.

As we reminisced on the past, Eric explained, "The organization was at a point that it was struggling to manage growth and struggling to attract IT talent. I knew we needed to do things differently."

Doing things differently, in this case, was challenging an immature organization to break out of the past and make quantum leaps in performance. As you can imagine, there was resistance.

Like almost every BOSS, Eric was a bit freaked out by the KIDS, but why? Eric's answer could not have been scripted any better:

Generally, Boomers—especially those managers and executives in corporate America—are insecure, rigid, and reluctant to adapt to the pace of change. There is a prevailing thought and attitude towards Millennials of, "What can they know? They need to pay their dues and earn their stripes before they can have an opinion or disagree!" Today, the pace is so much quicker. Millennials have gained so much knowledge and experience so much quicker than we did. It definitely frustrates us.

Although my first few interactions with Eric were very tactical—reviewing analysis, detailing plans, facilitating meetings—he quickly realized there was something I offered as a "young and enthusiastic" twenty-six-year-old that he didn't have: a different perspective.

I really needed the different perspective. You looked at problems, and saw opportunities, through a very different lens than I did. I think those differences in thinking revealed many opportunities I may have seen much later or may have missed altogether.

After agreeing to a long-term engagement, Eric offered me a very interesting opportunity: to create a new organization within the IT department, one that was focused on the people side of the technology transformation he was driving. At the same time, I would act as an advisor to his team and a challenger of the status quo. To say I was stoked would be a massive understatement!

> You had an energy and a fearlessness to go along with your intellect. Both in expressing your opinions or disagreeing with me and in terms of risk. My generation was all about mitigating risk—your generation isn't like that at all! Your generation isn't afraid of the chain of command and will do whatever it takes to get the job done or do what you think is the right thing—no matter what!

Eric later gave me insight into his reservations and the risks he saw associated with this opportunity.

> I knew the biggest obstacle I had to overcome was convincing the rest of the organization—specifically, the executive leadership team—to take you seriously. Clearly, we proved the value, but it took time. I'll admit it was not as long as I expected!

It was incredible to watch his attitude toward me, and the other KIDS on my team, transform. In less than a year, we went from being "too young and energetic" to becoming a group of trusted advisers. He asked us hard questions, and he listened thoughtfully.

We built a team of wicked smart, energetic twenty- and thirty-somethings who interacted regularly with the executive leadership team and worked on the highest-profile initiatives. As we were reminiscing on what we built in those three years, I asked Eric the most important question: What value did we bring?

You brought an intellectual, strategic, outside-the-box way of thinking—all from a very different perspective. You challenged me in a way I could understand, but from a perspective I didn't think about. In my past life, you would never challenge a superior the way you pushed me. It made me uncomfortable at first, but I learned to understand the unique value.

You always pushed me to think beyond the short-term . . . How many times did we argue about tactics? Your generation just doesn't show up, take notes, and take orders. You received a different education than I did, had different experiences than I did. You weren't afraid to ask hard questions, even if you already knew what my answer would be. You made me think.

What I love about the younger generation is they are generally well-educated and very comfortable providing real feedback. Not just "good soldiers," but real thinkers that push the whole organization. Especially their leaders.

The most incredible part of Eric's story is how *he* changed. After thirty years of Taylorian Management, Eric began to embrace what Pops and I later labeled Counter Mentor Leadership.

I took this as an opportunity to reinvent myself. We reinvented the IT organization and, at the same time, I changed my style and my beliefs about the younger generation and how they interact in the workplace. I realized I could really learn from them.

Let's be clear: it isn't easy! Even today, I find myself wanting to revert, to go back to my old-school ways of leading. I know I can't if I want to be successful in the new world. I must be different, be a different kind of leader. When I left my former company—after thirty years and growing into an executive role—I knew I needed to listen more.

I realized the world was changing and I needed to get smart people around me that thought differently and actually listen to them—not just surround myself with those that would simply implement my ideas, but provide me with new and different ideas. Even if it makes me uncomfortable.

Based on his experience, I asked Eric what he thought was the key to attracting and retaining young talent. The power of his answer is in its simplicity,

Face time with the boss is critical. You must give that high-potential Millennial access to the top and ensure they know they're important. They need to know that you're invested in them. In those conversations, you must give them meaty, incremental challenges. Challenges that they see as meaningful to the boss and to the organization. I don't think you necessarily need to give them constant promotions, but new, intellectual challenges keep them engaged.

#truth #countermentorleadership

What Counter Mentor Leadership Looks Like

As you can probably surmise from Eric's commentary, the transformation from Taylorian Manager to Counter Mentor Leader is not easy. It requires a significant shift in the way you think about leadership, and it demands that you sharpen skills that are not usually talked about, much less celebrated, in the typical leadership book on sale at the airport.

Here are the ideas that frame Counter Mentor Leadership:

- **Counter Mentor Leaders are intentional about their time.** One thing we have learned about leaders is that they never have enough time. This isn't shocking; actually, it's quite a cliché. But those individuals who learn how to overcome the *I-Don't-Have-Time* syndrome are the ones who become transformational leaders. Quite simply, *leadership is about changing how you invest your time.* As a Counter Mentor Leader, you understand that your time is your most valuable asset, mostly because it is finite—and perishable. Counter Mentor Leaders choose to focus their time in those areas that provide an incredibly high return, and we'll explain how they do it.

- **Counter Mentor Leaders are emotionally intelligent.** Leadership is relational, and in order to truly influence others, you must engage your brain, bury your generalizations and stereotypes, and build a relationship. Driving up your emotional intelligence is the path forward to becoming a Counter Mentor Leader. More than ever before, successful leadership is a result of investing in increasing your emotional intelligence. We'll show you the data to prove it.

- **Counter Mentor Leaders are next-level communicators.** This is not breaking news, but it's clearly something we need to remind you of: communication is the foundation of every relationship. Your people cannot succeed without complete clarity. It's impossible. They will grind toward an arbitrary goal they assume is correct. However, while communication is vital to effective leadership, most managers have very little idea of how to develop those skills. We'll show you how to become a crazy good communicator.

- **Counter Mentor Leaders are great coaches.** An incredible thing happens when you invest your time in developing people (instead of just doing it yourself). You begin to exponentially expand your effectiveness and increase your reach! By coaching and developing your people—teaching them how to think and execute like a leader—you extend your capacity and drive productivity. However, coaching takes time. It requires you to be focused and intentional. The upside is better performance, increased engagement, and—BIG BONUS—you actually start getting time back! We'll show you how to be an effective coach and make it a standard part of your leadership skills.

- **Counter Mentor Leaders are strategic thinkers.** Taylorian Managers are focused, almost exclusively, on the tactics. They were raised on the notion that their value is in doing. They were praised for getting stuff done. As a Counter Mentor Leader, you will develop and communicate your team's strategy and direction. You will define their purpose and make sure they know exactly where the finish line is. *This can only come from you!* No one else. If they are not clear on where they are going, they will become little more than functionaries. We can't make you better thinkers, but we will definitely show you how to spend more time doing it.

COUNTER to the Old-School Way

Now that you know what a Counter Mentor Leader looks like, we want to give you a brief overview of the COUNTER methodology that will be detailed in the remainder of this section.

As you know, we believe leadership is the *art and science of getting things done through other people*, and we believe that transformational leaders invest their time in three areas that have a high return on that investment: communicating, setting strategy and direction, and developing people. This is the foundation on which we built Counter Mentor Leadership. Everything we discuss will be in alignment with these principles. Our model is built to do things COUNTER to the Taylorian Management philosophies we all grew up seeing.

DISCLAIMER: Change can be hard. Some of you have been successful as a Taylorian Manager—at least in terms of creating results.

You probably have ulcers. You probably experience a lot of turnover. You may have a toxic workplace culture. But you have been successful with old-school practices.

Our suspicion is that it isn't all that rewarding—or tolerable—or you wouldn't be reading this book. The challenge for you is the difficulty of change, and the reality is that good results often prevent people from looking for GREAT results.

Dig in! We can assure you that, once you know how, you can definitely make the change to Counter Mentor Leadership. We've seen it happen over and over again. Our approach is captured in a seven-step model packed into the acronym COUNTER (to remind you to do things *differently*):

- **Communicate desired outcomes.** Everything begins with communication. You will only be as successful as you are an effective communicator. Communication begins during the talent identification and acquisition process and continues through onboarding, training, and coaching. Everything communicates, and communication is everything!

- **Own the relationship.** Talking about a relationship is one thing; creating and *owning* the responsibility for that *relationship* is quite another. That relationship is the difference between engagement and disengagement, which means it is the difference between success and mediocrity.

- **Understand the different perspectives.** You are absolutely correct—the KIDS and the BOSS have very different perspectives. They value different things and want different types of recognition and attention. They were raised differently, taught differently, and received a different type of degree. Once you understand them, you can take the steps to leverage those differences.

- **Negotiate the obstacles.** There are several new obstacles in the workplace today: generational differences, complexity, distractions, technology, and a ridiculously quick pace of change. Counter Mentor Leaders understand the impact each of these obstacles has on the workplace, and they consistently negotiate their way around them.

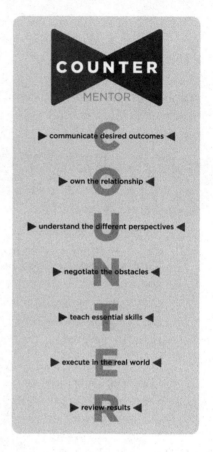

- **Teach essential skills.** It's never been more important to grow and develop your people. The KIDS entering the workplace crave this development, and the BOSS is finally starting to consider that he or she may actually need to start doing things differently. You have to identify the critical skills that each employee needs to be successful, and you need a plan to systematically develop those skills.

- **Execute in the real world.** As you change your behavior and start to act COUNTER to the old-school, Taylor-inspired management practices, your people are going to be cautiously optimistic. They will start to get excited and engage in ways as never before. None of this will matter if you revert to the old way of doing things the first time it gets hard. Life happens; mistakes will happen; failure will happen. How you react and coach your people will be the difference in success and failure for you as a leader.

- **<u>Review</u> results.** Finally, we are big believers in the importance of real-time performance review. We hate the annual performance review, but we can stomach the annual ritual if it is preceded by active coaching and a weekly one-on-one conversation. Transformational leaders understand that these things are the keys to accountability and true behavior change.

This is Counter Mentor Leadership. It will revolutionize your workplace!

Key Points to Remember

1. Leadership is relational. In order to truly influence others, you must engage your brain, bury your generalizations and stereotypes, and build a relationship.

2. Leadership is about changing how you invest your time.

3. Counter Mentor Leadership is built on doing things COUNTER to the commonly accepted ways of Taylorian Management.

Communication:
So, You're Saying There's a Problem?

"The great enemy of communication . . . is the illusion of it."[1]

William Hollingsworth Whyte

I T'S THE FIRST DAY of a two-day strategic planning meeting. The Pops is facilitating.

The client is in distribution, and their marketplace is changing dramatically because of—wait for it—technology. #shocker

Here's the story from Pop's perspective.

The Communication Problem

The entire leadership team was on hand: CEO, CFO, Director of HR, Director of Sales, Director of Operations, two product line managers, and three division sales managers. Early in the first day, to get the conversation started and people's blood pumping, I started off the meeting with a simple question that each person was asked to answer from her or his own personal perspective:

> "In your opinion, what is the single most important thing the company needs to do *today*?"

The discussion started with a couple of pressing operational issues, and then some concerns were voiced about sales, but after a while the conversation turned to the subject of communication. To put a fine point on it, the problem being described was the *lack* of communication in the company.

In short order, the entire group was deep into it. Voices were raised. Assumptions and accusations were made. A few faces began to turn colors.

At an opportune time, I stopped everyone and focused their attention on me. "If I'm hearing you right, you've got some serious communication issues."

People nod. The CEO didn't appear to be very happy.

"You got that right," someone said.

 "The Pops is a total pro at stating the obvious."

 "You lost me at 'total pro.'"

"So, when are you going to fix it?" I asked.

The room didn't respond; just a bunch of blank stares.

"I mean, you obviously have a serious problem with communication. The question is simple—when are you going to fix it?"

Clearly, it is far easier to *discuss* the problem than to consider how it might actually be *solved*.

The Communication Conundrum

This is a story we've seen repeated several times. People will complain for days about communication problems within the company, but they never stop to consider the role they play in creating and exacerbating the problem. They know there is a problem; they just don't realize *they* are the problem.

Communication is . . . well . . . difficult. Ridiculously difficult for something we do all day, every day. You would think all that practice would help, but not so much. The truth is, communication is difficult enough just between two people in a marriage. So, how difficult is it in a company of hundreds? Or thousands?

The challenge is that poor communication can destroy a company, just as it can destroy a marriage. Slowly, insidiously, lack of communication will create a dysfunctional organization, but companies consistently fail to identify and address the core issues. Frankly, many companies believe that communication issues are just something that will always exist—as in, "It is what it is." But if leaders don't improve communication, they must understand that the issue will never solve itself. And it's not a problem without serious consequences since poor communication is a primary cause, if not THE primary cause, of employee disengagement.

Which is why the first step in the COUNTER process is to **radically improve your communication**.

STOP!

Before you decide to skip this chapter because (a) you think you communicate just fine, thank you very much (isn't that cute?); or (b) you don't want to get into this "touchy-feely," hold-hands-and-sing-Kumbaya stuff (which is nonsense), ask yourself one question: Would your employees say your company (or department) has communication issues?

We're willing to bet our life savings that they would.

Actually, there is very little risk in that wager, since every single company we've ever worked with has had communication challenges. Not minor problems. BIG ones. Here is a laundry list of potential communication problems we consistently encounter:

- Unproductive meetings (so frequent, it's a running joke)
- Managers who don't listen well (or, usually, not at all)
- A lack of clarity in direction or plans
- Changes that no one can explain or account for (and then more, and more, and more)
- An ineffective "open door" policy (when, in fact, employee input is discouraged)
- Feedback that is nonexistent or not helpful
- An unclear definition of real success
- The use of email as the primary method of communication (doesn't everyone read email?!)
- A lack of recognition or encouragement for employees
- Annual performance reviews—enough said
- The company values are a mystery (unless someone bothers to look them up)

Believe it or not, that's just a start. There are plenty more. One of the first things we always hear in employee interviews is how poorly their company—and their leader—communicates. And poor communication is a monster reason why your team is not reaching its performance potential. And who bears the responsibility for communication?

Yes, that would be you. The leader.

So, if you don't communicate well . . . well, you're just kinda screwed, aren't you? And we don't care what generation you're from. This is an equal opportunity problem—Boomer, Gen X, Millennial, Digital Natives, whatever. Every generation thinks they do it better than the rest, but they're all mistaken. Poor communication is not a function of race, color, gender, ethnicity, age, or anything else. It's a function of self-awareness. It's a function of intent and effort.

ANYONE CAN IMPROVE COMMUNICATION SKILLS. Unfortunately, very few want to engage the required focus or put in the effort, and many lack the awareness to know they need to work harder at it.

Oh, by the way, if you really are a good communicator, congratulations! It's fairly rare, but it happens, and you will enjoy this chapter as much as anyone because you will recognize the truth in it.

The 1-on-1 Management® Leadership Cycle Explains the Real Value of Communication

In 2008, the Pops wrote a book called *1-on-1 Management: What Every Great Manager Knows That You Don't.*[2]

"The Pops LOVES to remind me he's already written a book."

"To be fair, Robby has written several letters to Santa and enough tweets to be considered a novelist."

In the book, the reader is introduced to a simple model called the 1-on-1 Management® Leadership Cycle. This model illustrates how effective leaders intentionally create employee engagement. As we laid it out in earlier chapters, employee engagement is a description (and a measurement) of how "connected" or "bought in" an employee is to the company.

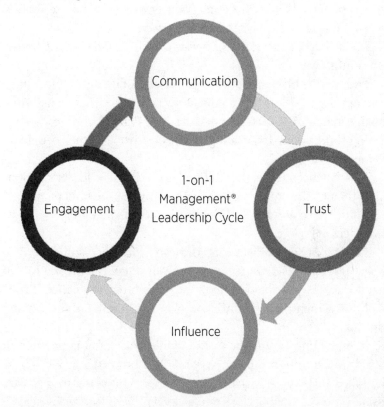

Empirically, we know that more engaged employees create better results: they are safer, they are more productive, they are better with customers, and they turn over far less often than their disengaged counterparts. That makes understanding *how* to create engagement a primary function of leadership.

So, if the objective is to create engagement, the question is: How do you get there?

First, it is practically impossible to engage someone you cannot *influence*. Although a leader might offer a short-term incentive (we would call it a "bribe") in order to influence an employee's performance, that is not engagement. That's renting a certain skill for a defined period of time. We don't want employees who are renters. We want engaged employees who are *owners*.

According to experts like Covey, Maxwell, and Blanchard, leadership *is* influence.

They define influence as "the power of producing an effect in an indirect way."[3] Doesn't that sound eerily similar to what transformational leaders do? It certainly matches our definition of leadership: "getting things done (producing an effect) through other people (in an indirect way)."

This is where leadership *actions* occur. It's the leader's actions that influence the employee and directly impact the level of engagement, but those actions will only influence if the employee *trusts* the leader.

Surely it is self-evident that you can't influence someone who doesn't trust you. Of course, you might influence someone to run away as fast as possible (we see that quite often; it's called Taylorian Management), but the influence we have in mind is positive and inspiring.

So how important is the need to build trust? You might as well ask about the importance of oxygen. Or money. It was Zig Ziglar who joked that "money isn't the most important thing in life," but, he said, "it is reasonably close to oxygen on the 'gotta have it' scale."[4]

That's about where trust falls on the leadership scale. With it, your company thrives. Without it, there is no leadership, and, in the end, no company. Which brings into play every single thing a leader does, since trust is based on the sum total of what people see, hear, and understand about a person.

Our friend Randy Conley is the Trust Practice Leader at Ken Blanchard Companies. His work is focused on the importance of trust in leadership, and he warns against overlooking the importance of trust:

> Trust isn't just a soft interpersonal skill that fills our relationships with warm fuzzies, unicorns, and rainbows. Trust drives bottom-line results in organizations. The *Great Place to Work Institute* has shown that high-trust organizations have 50% lower turnover than low-trust organizations, and employees who trust their leaders perform 20% better and are 87% less likely to leave the organization. Our own research [at Ken Blanchard Companies] has shown that people who trust their leaders tend to perform at higher levels, use their discretionary energy to benefit the organization, remain with the organization, endorse the organization as a good place to work, and be a good organizational citizen.[5]

So, here's the payoff pitch: How do you create trust?

The answer is complex and detailed. There are so many things that impact whether or not a person is considered trustworthy. However, in the final analysis you can attribute it all to one general thing—effective communication.

Here is your first and most important lesson in communication, one that you've been told a thousand times by your mom, grandma, elementary school teacher, and Twitter feed: EVERYTHING communicates.

Fine, they didn't all say it *just* like that. They said things like, "Don't take that tone with me, young man," or, "Don't you roll your eyes at me, missy," or something else, but you get the point: communication is not simply what people *say*—it's how they say it.

That's only the start. Communication also includes what you don't say, which often communicates just as powerfully as what you do say. It includes what you do, which everyone agrees will communicate far more loudly and lastingly than anything you ever say. Communication also includes what you choose *not* to do. For example, if you choose not to deal with an underperforming employee or follow through on an action that your employee longingly asked for help on, that inaction communicates volumes about you to the team.

In the final analysis, *everything* you do is communication, and your people soak it up like a sponge.

Good or bad.

Key Points to Remember

1. Communication is the foundation upon which all other leadership activities are built.

2. Communication is a function of intent and effort.

3. Trust, the backbone of leadership, is dependent upon thoughtful and effective communication.

4. Communication is not just about what you say, it's also about how you say it, and it includes the things you don't say and what you do or don't do. Everything communicates!

Four Critical
Areas of
Communication

"Science will never come up with a better office communication system than the coffee break."[1]

Earl Wilson

SIMPLY, effective leadership hinges on your ability to communicate. We can't say it any more directly that that. Unfortunately, we don't do as well as we should. Despite a dozen different ways to communicate, most companies just don't do it very well. That said, becoming a more effective communicator will make you a better leader, help you attract better talent, dramatically improve employee engagement, and make your life much easier.

It might even make it a little easier to deal with the KIDS—that alone is probably enough incentive to improve your communication skills! In the next chapter, we'll share the magic of the Counter Mentor 1-on-1 Meeting (CMM), the foundational cornerstone of our

COUNTER approach to leadership. That's because effective communication is best accomplished when two people are face-to-face, engaging in real, two-way dialogue (not CYA emails or LOL texts).

Need proof? Recent research reviewed in *Harvard Business Review* contrasted the use of email and face-to-face communication to make requests for donations. Forty-five participants in the study were each asked to make donation requests of ten different people (450 asks), one group using email and the other making the request face-to-face. Interestingly enough, participants in each group were confident that about five people would donate, meaning that, if true, neither method would be much more effective than the other. In reality, they misjudged just a bit:

> Participants who made requests over email felt essentially just as confident about the effectiveness of their requests as those who made their requests face-to-face, even though face-to-face requests were 34 times more effective than emailed ones.[2]

SERIOUSLY? *34 times?!*
Yes, Tonto, that would be correct.

"Raise your hands if you know who Tonto is. Outstanding, BOSS! Wait. KIDS, you do, too?"

"Yeah, we saw the Johnny Depp version. Awful. 31% on Rotten Tomatoes. BOSS, raise your hand if you know what Rotten Tomatoes is."

According to that research, you would have to ask two hundred people by email to equal the results of just SIX face-to-face requests.

Despite that, say the authors, most people tend to believe the email request will be *more* effective. #urbanlegend

Thus, our focus will always be on face-to-face interactions for driving communication.

First, let's make sure you understand the four critical areas of communication and why they are important to your success—which, as you've learned, means your people's success!

Develop Relationships

When the Pops was a young manager, managers were taught that you couldn't "be the boss and be a friend." The idea was that you couldn't have a difficult conversation, enforce a tight deadline, correct poor performance, or demand a "friend" stay late if you had a relationship beyond "I speak. You listen."

We would describe that point of view as stupid. Complete and utter rubbish. Really, it's just the stuff of amateurs. Bush league.

 "That's our G-rated opinion."

In the workplace, there are really only two alternatives—compel (coerce) people to do something, or create an environment in which they actually want to do it voluntarily. The second approach helps ensure that they believe in the task at hand and that it moves them and the team, closer to achieving the stated mission. It also makes them feel like valued, contributing teammates.

So, which approach is more effective?

Well—full transparency here—companies can be successful at some level with micromanaging, dictatorial, Taylorian Managers. But at what cost? High turnover. Poor engagement. Dismal morale. But why do it—especially when research shows that leaders who build relationships can be even more successful, without the costly side effects of micromanagement?

In 2011, Green Peak Partners published the results of a study conducted with Cornell University's School of Industrial and Labor Relations. The study involved executives in a variety of companies with revenues ranging from $50 million to $5 billion, and the results were conclusive:

> The study shows that harsh, hard-driving, "results-at-all-costs" executives actually diminish the bottom line, while self-aware leaders with strong interpersonal skills deliver better financial performance.[3]

That's bold! Managers with strong interpersonal skills are far preferable to "harsh, hard-driving executives," *especially over time.* Allow us to summarize (this would make a great tweet): The "hard" technical stuff of leadership doesn't move the needle like the "soft" transformational stuff does. #countermentorleadership

A 2014 article took that conclusion even further. In a *Harvard Business Review* article entitled "The Hard Data on Being a Nice Boss," author Emma Seppälä says that "tough" managers apply pressure to increase performance, but the side effect is an increase in stress that "can lead [employees] to look for a new job, decline a promotion, or leave a job." She concludes,

> Taken together, this body of research shows that creating a leadership model of trust and mutual cooperation may help create a culture that is happier, in which employees help each other, and (as a consequence) become more productive in the long run. No wonder their nice bosses get promoted.[4]

But don't get the wrong idea. This doesn't at all mean that leaders can't be demanding and have an expectation of high performance.

For some reason, there are those who consider those things to be mutually exclusive. #misguided

Take a look at great teachers, great coaches, great parents, and great corporate leaders. They are uncompromising when it comes to performance. What they don't do is lose sight of the value of, and the connection to, their people.

Align Expectations

We will discuss how to set expectations in greater detail later. Along the way, we will illustrate that you will never be able to manage employee performance effectively, or fairly, unless you establish crystal-clear expectations that are mutually aligned.

With clear, specific expectations, we are right back to creating a workplace that engages employees! Once again, the data is crystal clear. Research by Gallup indicates that clear expectations may be the most important element in employee engagement. Unfortunately for employees, most managers do a poor job of communicating those expectations:

> Gallup research suggests that setting clear expectations may be the most foundational element. Only about half of all workers strongly indicate that they know what is expected of them at work. Expectations—or a lack thereof—have the power to make or break worker engagement. Even if employees feel energized and motivated, those who lack clear expectations and spend too much time working on the wrong things can't advance key initiatives to create value for an organization.[5]

Engagement aside, imagine how much better things are for employees when they know exactly what's expected of them. If only managers knew how to set *clear* expectations. Yes, we know it seems fairly straightforward, but imagine for a moment this common "expectation": "You need to be prepared to work hard if you're going to get this done." Or this gem from the BOSS managing a sales team: "You need to make more calls."

Is there anything more nebulous? More open to interpretation? And exactly how helpful is this magnificent piece of advice? "Work harder? Geez, never thought of that, BOSS." "Make more calls? Holy cow, if only that would've crossed my mind."

Getting everybody on the same page will make your management role so much easier, and we'll show you how to do it right. #teaser

Reveal the Big Picture

The trend in corporate America is to hire a person to do a specific job. Nothing more, nothing less. The company has a position, that position has a job description, and that job exists in a vacuum. Head down, headphones in. Do your job. Don't ask questions.

With few exceptions, that's the way the BOSS likes it, but it's a complete train wreck. When people don't know what the "mission" is, or they're not sure what their own destination is ("What does success look like for me?"), they cannot, and will not, do their best work.

Jason Fried is a cofounder of Basecamp, a web-based project management and collaboration tool. In 2015, a small group of employees began brainstorming on some new ideas for the software, which soon led to a small team working on a new project that impacted the entire company, which led to problems. Why? They didn't know the big picture.

According to Fried, 80 percent of the company wasn't up to speed on the changes being made to the product or why those specific changes were being made. Although it wasn't true, many employees felt as though a whole lot of effort was going into a project that wasn't really making the product any better. As Fried shared in a 2015 issue of *Inc.* magazine entitled "The Danger of Keeping Your Team in the Dark," the fault for the misconception was entirely his:

> What I saw, and they couldn't see, was the bigger picture. We have a great vision, but it had been locked away in the heads of a few people who knew that what we'd built so far was just a foundation, and that now we would be able to move on to the real innovations. The team's blindness to that was my fault, of course. It's easy to forget, as a leader, that when employees don't get the wide view, not only does the point of their work escape them, but it can also lead to real frustration. It's hard to feel pride and ownership when you don't understand where things are going.[6]

Confusion. Blindness. Frustration. The results of ineffective communication.

The irony of this challenge wasn't lost on Fried. Basecamp is a collaboration tool designed to foster improved communication!

Fundamentally, great players want to play on great teams—they want to have a collective sense of purpose, working toward a common objective. At the same time, those players want to know how they can grow and learn and advance their careers. They want to have a clear line of sight to the next level, and the level after that.

Imagine a race where the runners have no idea where the finish line is, don't know the distance of the race, and have no idea what the reward will be if they finish well (or what "well" means!). In what universe does that make any sense? Yet, that is often the approach, as the BOSS assumes that a project and a paycheck is sufficient motivation for an employee.

When those same employees are working toward an objective they understand and believe in, the level of engagement is extraordinary.

Explain the "Why"

When we were young (for the Pops, this was somewhere between dinosaurs and cowboys), it didn't take long to figure out that you don't ask adults why they want you to do something. Anyone older than thirty probably has this response tattooed on their forehead: "Because I said so."

Oh, NOW I get it! And all this time I thought there might have been a really good reason for what you're asking me to do, but by all means, KEEP IT TO YOURSELF! I don't need to UNDERSTAND why you've asked me to do something. After all, following orders is so . . . motivating. #obviouslysarcastic

Actually, this whole concept is a hot-button issue for the BOSS. We'll talk about it more in a future chapter, but to the BOSS, asking "why" is a sign of disrespect. However, this is not an issue the KIDS created, it's a *people* issue. People want to know—in fact, need to know—WHY decisions are made, WHY changes are implemented.

You *must* get this! Whether it is a decision, the direction of the company, or the motivation behind an objective or task, understanding "why" allows people to get on the same page and make the work meaningful to them. Mindlessly following orders will never lead to best efforts or top performance.

As we will repeat over and over, leadership is a pay-me-now-or-pay-me-later proposition. So it takes you a couple of minutes to explain the rationale behind a decision or the motivation behind a new idea. Big deal. The alternative is WAY worse. One way or another you're going to pay, but the immediate investment in time is far less than the long-term time you'll lose in fixing the mistakes and eventually doing it yourself.

And that doesn't include the costs of dealing with plummeting employee disengagement.

Conclusion

Geez, BOSS, how to end this chapter? We have thrown down some serious evidence for improving your communication game. If you haven't gotten the point by now, it might be time to find some folks in the office who might use this book.

Actually, check that. Tell them to buy their own copy.

However, if you've caught on that this "touchy-feely" stuff is dope, then the next chapter will show you how to up your game.

 "Dope?"

 "Not a good word choice for the BOSS, I admit, but *dope* is modern slang for AMAZING!"

Key Points to Remember

1. The most effective communication, by far, is done face-to-face.

2. There are four critical areas of communication: developing relationships, setting expectations, clarifying the big picture, and explaining the "why."

3. Communication—like leadership—is a pay-me-now-or-pay-me-later proposition.

Chapter **18**

The Counter Mentor 1-on-1 Meeting (CMM)

"Human communication has its own set of very unusual and counterintuitive rules."[1]

Malcolm Gladwell

CLEARLY, all of the tools that have been added to the communication arsenal in the past three decades have done very little to improve the quality of communication in the workplace. We've done everything we can to make communication easier and faster, but we've swung and missed on *better* (in terms of effectiveness).

There's plenty of tools to choose from—email, text, Slack, Basecamp, Skype, FaceTime, and WhatsApp to name a few—and there are still the old-school favorites: the telephone and face-to-face. However, from our perspective, the most effective "tool" that you MUST dust off and utilize to improve communication is *time*.

No, BOSS, that's not an app. We're referring to actual time. Since effective communication is a function of dialogue, interaction, and understanding, time actually becomes the limiting factor in communication.

No time? No chance of communication. Period.

Coming to the realization that leadership is the art and science of getting things done *through other people* should help you understand the need to invest in those people—specifically, invest your *time* in them—if you are going to help them develop their potential. And when you develop them, you actually multiply your ability to GSD (get stuff done). That makes everyone happy.

 "GSD? I thought we weren't gonna do TLAs."

 "We gotta speak to the KIDS in a language they understand."

 "Oh. You mean we should quote *Friends* episodes?"

 "Or *Game of Thrones*, yes."

This is THE best-kept secret of transformational leadership. Most managers tend to look at a new investment in time as *additional* time needed. However, the reality is, if you invest your time in people proactively, we will show you how to actually recoup that time and then some.

Here's a tweetable summary for you:

> If you don't have time to spend communicating NOW, how
> in the world will you have *more* time later? #mindblown
> @countermentors

(Just kidding, BOSS; go ahead and use a highlighter on that sentence so you don't forget it!)

The principle is simple: You can invest time in your people *now*, or you can wind up spending a lot of extra time later fixing the many problems created by *your* poor communication!

Pay me now, or pay me later.

Let's figure out how to invest now and eliminate the wasted time down the road. The single most important thing that you can do to communicate effectively with your people is to invest your time in weekly, high-quality communication with your employees. Not surprisingly, extensive research at the Gallup organization has revealed that this practice is a significant driver of employee engagement.

> Gallup has found that consistent communication—whether
> it occurs in person, over the phone or electronically—is connected to higher engagement. For example, employees whose
> managers hold regular meetings with them are almost three
> times as likely to be engaged as employees whose managers
> do not hold regular meetings with them.[2]

Don't worry! We're not talking about adding another group meeting to your already overburdened schedule—meetings that most of the KIDS (and every other employee) despise because they are done so poorly. Instead, the meetings that we will add to your already overburdened schedule will be one-on-one meetings. Not to worry, however! As we said before, you will get that time back, so stay with us.

Face-to-face, one-on-one meetings are, without question, the very best way to facilitate effective communication! The good news is that video calls (Skype, for example) qualify as face-to-face calls. Even an old-fashioned telephone call (the way Pops did one-on-one meetings back in the day) is better than nothing.

The only problem is that we have found when we mention the concept of a "one-on-one meeting," people tend to jump to wild conclusions about them and make a variety of bad assumptions.

Like these:

- I already do one-on-one meetings. (Yes, but not the way we'll show you.)

- I don't know what I would do. (We'll show you that, too.)

- I don't have time for individual meetings. (Absolutely you do, and we'll show you how.)

- Employees won't talk. (Yes, they will.)

- Employees won't *quit* talking, and I don't have time to play counselor. (It can happen, but we'll show you how to avoid the problem.)

- I have my own work to do; I can't waste that much time. (We get that one a lot, but you will change your mind, we assure you.)

The bottom line is that if you don't want to invest in your employees, you will find an excuse.

You'll decide you "tried that once and it didn't work," or you'll spend thirty minutes telling us why you don't have time, or some other nonsense. But if you want to transform your team's results, the one-on-one meeting—done the *right* way with the template we prescribe—*is a game changer.*

We know because we've heard that said over and over.

The one-on-one meeting we prescribe is powerful and wildly effective. To distinguish it from other not-so-powerful-and-effective one-on-one meetings, we give it a specific name: the Counter Mentor 1-on-1 Meeting (CMM, for short).

What Is the Counter Mentor 1-on-1 Meeting (CMM)?

Pops has been teaching a specific one-on-one meeting approach for a dozen years, using the same basic format he utilized in his career as a manager and executive. He wrote about it in his book, *1-on-1 Management: What Every Great Manager Knows That You Don't*:

> Great managers realize that creating high performance is substantially contingent on developing a relationship of trust with each employee. 1-on-1 Meetings provide the means and opportunity to connect directly with each individual, to develop a coaching and mentoring relationship, to provide consistent feedback on performance, and to communicate more effectively.[3]

Our one-on-one meeting is quite different from your typical, run-of-the-mill, one-on-one meeting. For example, traditionally, when managers take some time to review a project with an employee, they call it a one-on-one meeting. If an employee pops into the office to ask a question, the manager says, "Oh, I have one-on-one meetings with my people." In fact, a manager can have a random conversation over a cup of coffee, and suddenly it's a "one-on-one" meeting.

In the words of sports broadcaster Lee Corso, "Not so fast, my friend!"

Here's the deal: Just because you're meeting one-on-one doesn't mean you're qualified as an expert in the Counter Mentor 1-on-1 Meeting. Not even close. The CMM has a very specific format, and the intent and results of this meeting make it unique and very powerful. It accomplishes a number of very important objectives for the leader, many of which are not currently being met at all.

Following the CMM format allows you to:

- Create a conversation and build a relationship
- Develop mutual understanding and alignment of expectations
- Provide individual, personalized attention to your direct reports
- Develop your understanding of the employee's perspective
- Provide for real-time performance management (including critical feedback AND encouragement and recognition)
- Encourage employee input and feedback

Just a single thirty- to forty-five-minute meeting each week does all that, and more.

At this point, BOSS, you may need a paper bag. You're probably hyperventilating, or you've fallen out of your chair and hit your head. *"Forty-five minutes? EACH WEEK?! For every one of my employees? Are you outta your mind?!"*

Here is our wild guess: you currently manage twelve (or fifteen, or twenty, or more) people, and you couldn't possibly spend even thirty minutes per week with each employee because that would be SIX HOURS (or more) every single week. Sound right?

Well, it's possible we've heard that one before.

First, if you have more than six to eight direct reports, you have too many. For all but a few select situations, trying to impact more than eight employees (we prefer six) is highly problematic. Mike Myatt, author of *Hacking Leadership* and one of the world's most recognized authorities on leadership, addressed span of control in an *Inc.* article entitled "Span of Control—5 Things Every Leader Should Know":

Every leader is different, and as a result, has different needs
with regard to numbers, skills, cultural dynamics, etc. If you
don't have the skills to lead or manage a broad span, yet
attempt to do so, it will be your undoing. If your focus is too
narrow, you'll find yourself with blind spots and operational
gaps. The average number of direct reports for Fortune 500
CEOs is 7.44 . . .

It's not the number that's important, but whether you're
getting what you need out of whatever number you have.[4]

With respect to Mr. Myatt, the number is important IF you're
responsible for developing employees. Span of control has been
researched and debated for decades. The military model, perfected
over two centuries, dictates six direct reports (sometimes even four).

In the workplace, over time, companies have experimented with
up to twenty-five direct reports, often going so far as to compen-
sate managers based on the number of people on their team. But,
leadership is not about the number of people you have, it's about the
number of people you can directly influence—the number of people
whom you can help transform individual potential into improved
performance. To be able to develop the potential of your people and
truly build a relationship, we believe you simply cannot have ten or
twenty or thirty direct reports.

Second, when you invest three or four hours of total time each
week in the CMM with your direct reports, you will quickly recapture
that time in the future. It may sound daunting at first, but when you
conduct these meetings you know exactly what is going on with each
of your people (their priorities and plans for the upcoming week), and
you will have accomplished all of the critical things we listed above
as well: recognition, relationship, coaching, etc.

We can tell you this with enormous confidence: not only will
you be far ahead of the game in terms of understanding your people,
but you will easily get that time back—and more—as you eliminate
the dozens of mini-meetings (drive-bys, phone calls, instant and text

messages) you engage in to catch up, get updates, fill in the blanks, understand issues, clarify misunderstandings, and type those long emails that would be completely unnecessary if you would just have a face-to-face conversation!

Now, let's get tactical: When should you schedule these meetings? In our experience, Monday mornings are ideal—you can look forward to the new week. Fridays are next best, since you can reflect back on the week and look forward to the next week. However, any day of the week can be used—we just prefer Monday or Friday. The key is to schedule them for a day when you *know* you can conduct the meeting the majority of the time.

The basic concept of the meeting is to make it the *employee's* meeting. It is time that you set aside to give them access to YOU, their leader—to ask questions, get clarification, and provide input. Which means that, as a general rule, the employee should be talking about 75 percent of the time and you should be listening intently.

BOSS, if the idea of *listening* is not completely familiar to you, it means that you are actively trying to hear AND understand what the employee is saying. Normally, for you, it's the other way around—you expect the employee to do all the listening—but not in this case. And, fair warning here, this is not a meeting where you jump into BOSS mode and solve every problem, or show employees how much smarter you are!

Yes, you will have the opportunity to offer direction and clarification and advice (we'll show you the best way to accomplish that), but it is critical to first understand this is not a production meeting or a project review meeting! Instead, it is a conversation with a very specific purpose: to create understanding, build a relationship, develop trust, and understand performance (good and bad) in real time. Translation: this is the opposite of what typically happens in the completely worthless corporate exercise known as the annual performance review. We call that a #wasteoftime.

The Counter Mentor 1-on-1 Meeting (CMM) will easily create the most effective performance management tool you have ever seen.

In the next chapter, we'll show you the simple, easy-to-use format that makes this meeting so effective.

Key Points to Remember

1. The single most important thing that you can do to be effective with your people is to invest your time in weekly, high-quality, face-to-face communication with your employees. We call it the Counter Mentor 1-on-1 Meeting (CMM).

2. Leadership is not about the number of people you have; it's about the number of people you can directly influence—the number of people whom you can help transform individual potential into improved performance.

3. Time invested in communication now will save you a TON of headaches in the future.

Chapter 19

The Counter Mentor
1-on-1 Meeting (CMM) Format

"I admire machinery as much as any man, and am as thankful to it as any man can be for what it does for us. But, it will never be a substitute for the face of a man, with his soul in it, encouraging another man to be brave and true."[1]

Charles Dickens

STILL WITH US, BOSS?
Don't worry, we're not suggesting that you won't be offering advice or direction at certain points in the CMM, but your primary objective is to create a dialogue that allows your employees to assess their own work performance, take responsibility for their work, contribute ideas, and feel like an integral part of the team.

This means you MUST resist the temptation to fix every issue and tell them exactly how to do everything. Instead, you should be *listening*.

This is where the magic happens. We've been doing this type of one-on-one meeting for more than twenty-five years. (Okay, Pops has been doing them for twenty-five years—he's old—but Robby has *only* been doing them for the last decade.) When done well, we find that after four or five meetings, we have a very good idea of the employees' capabilities, what motivates them, how they plan, how they execute, and how we can begin building on their strengths.

How? By following the template and listening carefully.

However, your biggest challenge will be to listen without jumping into let-me-tell-you-what-to-do mode. If you're the BOSS, that's probably your nature—you fix things, you make decisions, you tell people what to do. We've learned that approach doesn't place people in a position to take ownership of their own work, which, of course, is what you're always screaming for employees to do.

This meeting gives you the perfect opportunity to encourage—and teach—your people to think critically. Most of the time, your objective is to encourage your employees to create their own plans and think through their own solutions rather than relying on you to provide a solution for them. All that does is create dependency. So, instead of **telling**, we will focus on asking the right questions and **listening** (have we beat this concept to death enough?!).

Here is the CMM format:

- **Review**—Discuss key events of the previous week.
- **Preview**—Outline significant events for the upcoming week.
- **Plan and Prioritize**—Establish critical objectives to be advanced or completed, establish expectations, and discuss resources needed.

Pretty simple stuff. Review last week. Preview the upcoming week. Understand the plans and priorities the employee has set for the week. It sounds simple—and it is—but the insights you will gain very quickly are amazing!

Note: We have found the same questions tend to come up over and over again about the Counter Mentor 1-on-1 Meeting (CMM), and many people are uncomfortable with facilitating their first meeting. There are two key resources you should download from *https:// countermentors.com/resources*: "CMM Frequently Asked Questions," and "How to Do Your First CMM."

That first meeting is very important since, for many managers, this may be the first time you've ever scheduled a one-on-one meeting. Many employees assume there is a problem, "Have I done something wrong?" They may even fear getting fired or downsized. These resources will walk you through getting started and help you avoid several misconceptions or missteps.

Let's unpack the meeting format a bit further.

Review

If you're not adequately prepared for the CMM, you need to know that it will be tough to get these meetings started. So let's prepare. Ready? Here's what you say: "Tell me about last week. Give me the highlights."

See? Not so bad! Consider yourself adequately prepared to start.

Seriously, the objective here is to create a general review of the past week. What happened? How did things go? What's working, or not working? We strongly advocate that managers encourage positive self-talk with this simple question: "Tell me something great that happened last week." We've found that getting started with good news can set a productive tone for the balance of the meeting.

Let's be clear: This is not designed to be a session for employees to gripe about the company or criticize other employees. If, during the first few meetings, the employees move in that direction, simply tell them you would love to have that conversation (even schedule it so they understand your sincerity), but, for now, the goal of the meeting is to focus on *what* transpired last week: the high points, the challenges they encountered, their progress on key initiatives they are working on, etc.

Here is the Pops with an explanation from his book, *1-on-1 Management*:

> You may find that employees are prone to getting bogged down in too much detail, so encourage them to give you the highlights from the past week and reserve discussions regarding details until the end. This provides a summary or overview of the previous week in just a few minutes, leaving you with a good understanding of progress and direction.
>
> There are situations where you will want to pursue more details. For instance, if the employee describes a problem or challenge that occurred, dig into the details and prompt them to describe how they dealt with the situation. One of the objectives . . . is to encourage critical thinking, and this process will help you to understand how the employee thinks and solves problems, and will also provide the opportunity to coach them in key situations. . . .
>
> Another opportunity to dig into additional details might be if the employee describes a key project or assignment that has been completed, or a task that has furthered the company's key values or objectives. This may provide a perfect opportunity for you to recognize or praise the result, either in the 1-on-1 Meeting™ or at a later time when you can do it publicly.[2]

If you listen carefully in the CMM, you'll pick up on some critical points that may need your attention and require coaching or change.

You MUST resist the urge to start solving all of the problems! DON'T START FIXING THINGS. Instead, ask good questions and prompt your employees to think through, and verbalize, what they think may need to be done.

Once you've done a high-level review, it's time to move on to the next step in the meeting.

Preview

After you spend some time understanding last week, it's time to talk about their plans for the coming week. You want to have the employees outline their key activities and discuss any new projects or tasks that need to be added to the workload.

Here's the easy way to get started: "Tell me about this week. What are your plans and priorities?"

It is here that something interesting begins to take shape, and this is where the performance management aspect of the CMM starts. Each week, you review what the employees did the previous week, and, with the exception of your very first meeting, you have the ability to compare what they did to what they *said* they were going to do in the Preview section of last week's meeting.

This simple process allows you to determine the following:

1. How well employees think critically and set priorities
2. How well they plan their work
3. How well they execute those plans

Deficiencies in any of those three things become coaching priorities for you. If they don't assess their current situation well, you can help them learn how to prioritize their work. If they don't plan well, you can teach them how to plan. If they don't execute on their plans effectively, you can address that issue and coach them to improve.

Cool, huh?

We'll talk much more about accountability and how to get your employees to take ownership of their work later, but this is a huge step in that direction. Do NOT plan everything for your employees; instead, when a problem arises, ask them to present *their plans* on how they think they should proceed. Here is a quick example:

EMPLOYEE: I seem to keep missing a small detail in these projects.

LEADER: What do you think the problem is?

EMPLOYEE: I'm not sure. I just seem to overlook something I should catch.

LEADER: Okay, let's do this. There are different ways to approach this problem. I would like you to think it through and create a plan for solving the problem (*the result you want*). Let's get that done by our next meeting and you can show it to me then (*the time frame*). Solving this one problem will not only make your life easier, it will save you time down the road that you spend now dealing with the fallout (*the "why"*). Make sense?

EMPLOYEE: Absolutely. I'll get started right away.

LEADER: Outstanding. Is there anything you need from me?

The effective leader will establish an expectation for results rather than micromanaging the details. Even if you know exactly how to solve the problem, it's in your best interest to teach your employees how to think critically and solve problems.

Yes, that takes more time. And yes, that will make your employees far more productive, and you will get that time back over and over in the future.

Plan and Prioritize

As employees outline the upcoming week's activities and objectives, you want to prompt them to establish their own plans and set their own priorities. We understand this may happen within a broader context of priorities that have been established by you, but rather than telling people what to do next, you should encourage *them* to determine the critical "next steps" of each project or task.

Ask them to share their priorities and their timelines. If you are not in agreement with any of those items, ask questions that allow them to explain their reasoning.

The key here is to talk less and listen more.

At the end of the CMM, finish with these questions:

- "What do you need from me?"
- "How can I help you this week?"

Managing Performance with the Counter Mentor 1-on-1 Meeting (CMM)

There you go. Simple beyond description, yet incredibly profound and revealing if you can learn to listen and probe in the right areas.

Think of all that you learn during this simple weekly conversation. You gain insight into morale and attitude; you understand how they think and plan; and you determine if they execute and manage the critical details. During that time together, you are provided with the perfect opportunity to set clear expectations, to provide feedback and recognition, and to coach when it's needed. You clearly demonstrate that you are invested in their development.

Highlight (or tweet) this: In the final analysis, overcoming generational challenges is not about learning to "manage" the KIDS, it's about learning to be a more effective leader. #truth

All of your people need time and attention, not just the Millennials and Digital Natives. All of them need your encouragement, support, and coaching—even the Boomers. They might not admit it, but they do! And all of them need to have their performance assessed more frequently than once a year.

The Counter Mentor 1-on-1 Meeting (CMM) is stunning in its simplicity, and even more stunning in what it provides as a return on your invested time. By following the simple format (Review, Preview, Plan and Prioritize), you will become acutely aware of any performance issues in real time and have a consistent format and opportunity for addressing those challenges as they arise.

We have one final bonus to give you. Chances are pretty good that you do some kind of annual performance review at the end of the year. Or in January, or March, or whenever you finally get around to it.

You hate it. Your employees hate it. Unfortunately, the annual performance review is a dumpster fire—yet another old-school idea that stinks but just won't die. However, since you'll do somewhere around forty-five to fifty CMMs each year with your direct reports, the annual review is easy!

No surprises. No delays. No drama. In fact, you can start discussing the annual performance review a few weeks in advance and complete it in one of your last CMMs of the year.

Sweet.

Our Data Is Better than Your Excuses

In September 2016, Robby began working closely with a $900 million, privately held distribution company. They were a national company that primarily grew through the acquisition of regional businesses with less than $100 million in revenue. His initial work revealed that the bulk of the leadership team had never had any formalized leadership training whatsoever.

About six months into the engagement, he had trained approximately 70 percent of the leaders—from supervisor to CEO—on how to correctly execute the Counter Mentor 1-on-1 Meeting (CMM). He used this opportunity to quantify the effectiveness of the CMM with this client; specifically, we wanted to understand the correlation between the CMM and employees' level of engagement.

The results were startling.

Robby asked more than eight hundred employees to self-report how often they met with their respective manager in the CMM. The survey results indicated that employees who "Never" had one-on-one meetings with their respective managers—when compared with those who "Sometimes" had one-on-one meetings—had an engagement score **25 percent lower** than the "Sometimes" group.

If that's not strong enough, when the "Never" group of employees was compared to those who reported "Always" having the CMM with their manager, the engagement score was **35 percent lower**.

Mary Kay Gribbons, HR leader for the organization, was not surprised with the results:

> I've done one-on-one meetings for years. When I worked at American Airlines, I had a manager that did them and I carried it forward when I got promoted. However, I like the Counter Mentor 1-on-1 Meeting so much better. This works. It provides

an easy-to-use tool that enables me to both hold my people accountable and recognize their great work.

I've been leading people for a long time. This has been a game-changer.[3]

"Game-changer." We really love those words.

By now, you should clearly see the value here. Stop and think about all the time you have wasted because something isn't communicated, or because you don't quite understand an issue, or because you're trying to deal with a problem by email that grows exponentially as you argue your points (that will be taken out of context and used against you!).

Think about the performance drag that happens because expectations aren't aligned and employees aren't all rowing in the same direction. With the CMM, communication improves, performance issues are quickly identified and addressed, employees receive real-time feedback, and expectations are defined and agreed upon.

Bonus: While all of this is happening, you are building trust and creating a culture of engagement!

However, be warned. There is a way that you can flush all of those benefits down the toilet, and turn the CMM into a complete waste of time. All you have to do is allow our Counter Mentor 1-on-1 Meeting to become the *1-on-1 Beating*.

We've seen it, and it's not pretty.

This happens when you turn the CMM into a forty-five-minute performance review—in painstaking detail. You focus on each deficiency and prescribe detailed solutions because, after all, you know best. If you go that direction, you will make things even worse than they already are. That kind of attention is not at all helpful and will only escalate disengagement.

Don't turn the CMM into something it's not designed to be, and definitely don't start if you don't intend to make it a habit. We've been using and teaching the CMM for a very long time. If you do it right, it will make you a far better leader.

With every generation.

Key Points to Remember

1. The power of the CMM is in its simple format: Review, Preview, Plan and Prioritize.

2. In the Counter Mentor 1-on-1 Meeting (CMM), You MUST resist the temptation to fix every issue and tell your people exactly how to do everything. Instead, you should be listening.

3. By following the format (and not making up your own!), you will become acutely aware of any performance issues that exist—in real time—and have a consistent format for addressing those challenges as they arise.

Chapter 20

Own the
Relationship

"Leaders must own everything in his or her world. There is no one else to blame."[1]

Jocko Willink and Leif Babin

IN THE INTRODUCTION to his bestselling book *The Five Dysfunctions of a Team*, Patrick Lencioni shares the following observation:

> If you could get all the people in an organization rowing in the same direction, you could dominate any industry, in any market, against any competition, at any time.[2]

We enthusiastically agree with the wisdom in that statement, but anyone who has rowed crew will tell you there is much more to dominating on the water than simply rowing in the same direction. There is cadence, coordination, technique, strength, and race strategy, to name a few.

Still, the idea is powerful. Getting everyone rowing in the same direction implies a common objective that everyone understands. In the ideal situation, all team members are passionate about that objective and are giving their very best effort.

However, in the workplace, what qualifies as "rowing in the same direction" is usually a manager telling people what to do and stressing the importance of the task at hand. In crew, that would be a little bit like telling eight people to jump in a boat and "row *that* way, and don't forget how important winning this race is." Clearly, getting eight people in sync—actually unifying the team—is a bit more complex than that.

The next step in the COUNTER Leadership process is to take very specific steps to get your employees on the same page and rowing in the same direction. We refer to it as "owning" the relationship— **taking the necessary steps to provide clarity, set clear expectations, and create a culture that fully engages the employees**.

Instead of just hiring individuals for positions and telling them to row as hard as possible, we like to make sure they know *how* to row, *where* to row, and *why* we're rowing in the first place. We also want to make sure the boat is in great shape, they have the right oar, and the reward for winning is clearly defined.

And you? Continuing the rowing analogy, you are the coxswain (pronounced COX-en)—the boat leader, the person responsible for direction, cadence, coordination, and instruction. If you don't do your job well, the team will never reach its potential.

You're not surprised that communication is *still* the foundation, are you?

Mary Whipple was a coxswain for twenty-one years. She led the U.S. to an Olympic silver medal in 2004 and golds in 2008 and 2012. Add world championships in 2006, 2007, 2010, and 2011, as well as collegiate national championships in 2001 and 2002.[3] #winning

Translation: She is a world-class coxswain (literally, a boat servant[4]), the person on a rowing team (a crew) who sits in the stern— the back of the boat—and directs the boat during a race. She is the coach in the boat, responsible for cadence, synchronization, racing strategy, and motivation for the crew. What the coxswain doesn't do is row.

Prior to the 2012 Olympic finals, the *New York Times* published an article about her impact on the team:

> Like a symphony conductor, she made sure her rowers matched one another as they took each stroke. Under race conditions, she turned on her magic. Nearly every boat she coxed in practice races won, no matter the lineup.
>
> "She had the ability to get eight strong women all working together," said Anna Cummins, who rowed with Whipple in college and on the national team. "When you lock into that, the power is something you can't even quantify."
>
> Whipple also is a master at calling a race, telling her rowers where their boat is relative to the racecourse and to other boats. If they are behind, she finds the precise words that make them go faster. Not all coxswains can do that.[5]

Boat *servant. Coach.* Symphony *conductor.* As it turns out, this whole idea of getting people rowing in the same direction is the perfect analogy for leadership.

From our perspective, when a leader takes ownership of the *relationship* with an employee, it's not unlike the coxswain's role—a coach in the boat whose work directly impacts individual and team performance. It also means the leader clearly understands that a low-performing team is a reflection of ineffective leadership and that a high-performing team is not possible without an effective leader.

Jocko Willink and Leif Babin, both former Navy SEALs, make this point clear in their book *Extreme Ownership: How U.S. Navy SEALs Lead and Win*:

> For leaders, the humility to admit and own mistakes and develop a plan to overcome them is essential to success. The

best leaders are not driven by ego or personal agendas. They are simply focused on the mission and how best to accomplish it.[6]

We are continually amazed at corporate leaders who are quick to blame their people and outside circumstances when their teams underperform, yet they roundly criticize team members who make excuses for their own failures. The typical response? "Why can't they take ownership of their work?"

To which we answer: "Why don't you take responsibility for your team's work? Aren't you the leader?" Let's revisit three key questions from chapter 7:

1. Who hires the employee?
2. Who trains the employee?
3. Who is responsible to lead the employee?

See the problem? There is no possible way for you to push the blame for your team's lack of performance on to your people. You hire them, you train them, you lead them; so when they fall short at some point (and they will), your first step is to make sure you didn't contribute to the failure.

Willink and Babin were members of SEAL Team 3 in Ramadi, Iraq, the most imperfect and unforgiving "work" environment possible. Opportunities to find excuses and lay blame at the feet of others were piled up like the sand they often had to battle in doing their jobs. That, however, was never acceptable:

Leaders must accept total responsibility, own problems that inhibit performance, and develop solutions to those problems. A team could only deliver exceptional performance if a leader ensured the team worked together toward a focused goal and

enforced high standards of performance, working to continu-
ously improve.[7]

Certainly, there is no question you can do everything exactly
right and some of your employees may not perform at the minimum
standard. They might fail or make a mistake of some kind. However,
if you've done your job well, they know what is expected, they know
how to complete the task, they've been trained, and the task is within
their capabilities. Failure is an opportunity to teach and develop—
that's where real growth happens.

The reality of people development is that you shouldn't mind
if your people fail. You almost *want* them to fail. But—this is critical—you just want them to fail *small*. Which, again, comes back to
your responsibility as a leader. If you put people in a position to fail
large and they are not prepared and experienced in that role, you've
not done your job well.

So, in the sense of being responsible and accountable for employee
success, we advocate that every leader should take "ownership" of that
relationship. We believe that owning the relationship means two very
specific things—creating clarity and setting clear expectations.

Creating Clarity for Your Employees

Creating clarity for an employee is no different from creating clarity
for an athlete, a soldier, an actor, or a musician.

Can a highly trained, highly paid athlete play well without a
well-communicated game plan? Or without a clear understanding of
what the coach expects from each athlete in the game? Can a highly
trained soldier complete a mission if the details of the mission are
incomplete or if the soldier's responsibilities are not well defined?

Geno Auriemma is the women's head basketball coach at the University of Connecticut. Even the most casual sports fan typically recognizes Auriemma, but maybe you aren't aware of his stunning record.[8]

When Auriemma arrived at UConn in 1985, the Lady Huskies were in bad shape, with only ONE winning season in the previous twelve tries. Since joining the team as its head coach, he has led the team to just about every imaginable record in women's basketball.

As of this writing, UConn has been in the NCAA tournament for twenty-nine consecutive years. They have been crowned NCAA champions eleven times. Auriemma's teams have averaged thirty-one victories per year—for a mind-boggling thirty-two years! And, just for good measure, he has also coached the USA Basketball Women's National Team to the 2010 and 2014 World Championships, and led the USA national team to gold medals at the 2012 and 2016 Summer Olympics.

Clearly, the man can coach. He certainly understands how to create winning teams. In other words, he is a ridiculously effective leader. So, what's his secret to enduring success?

First, Auriemma is fanatical about game preparation and the importance of practice.

I've never met anyone that was a great game player who didn't have tremendous work ethic and practice habits. The challenge for everyone, at least those who come here, is learning how to practice with such consistency that you know you are going to perform consistently when you go into a game.[9]

Makes sense. Fairly straightforward stuff: work hard, practice consistently.

Second, Auriemma is absolutely clear about what it takes to be a Lady Husky. His expectations of his players are well communicated and completely aligned. He took some time to discuss his approach to team building at a news conference during the NCAA women's Final Four in 2016:

So, recruiting kids that are really upbeat, and loving life, and love the game, and have this tremendous appreciation for when their teammates do something well, that's hard. That's hard. It's really hard. So, on our team, we—me, my coaching staff—we put a huge premium on body language, and if your body language is bad, you will never get in the game. EVER. I don't care how good you are.

If somebody says, "Well," you know, "You just benched Stewie [senior Forward, Breanna Stewart] for 35 minutes in the Memphis game a couple years ago." Yeah, I did. "Oh, but that was to motivate her for the South Carolina game the following Monday." No, it wasn't. Stewie was acting like a 12-year-old, so I put her on the bench and said sit there.

So, when I look at my team—they know this—when I watch game film, I'm checking what's going on on the bench and if somebody's asleep over there, if somebody doesn't care, if somebody's not engaged in the game, they will never get in the game. Ever. And they know that. They know I'm not kidding.[10]

They *know* he's not kidding.

How do they know? Because Auriemma makes it crystal clear. No guesswork.

In case the point is completely lost on you, these are "those KIDS no one can lead" playing for Auriemma—an incredibly demanding leader. Yet, he wins, year after year. He understands the huge challenges of coaching, including the generational divide that exists today. However, generations change, but leadership principles do not.

What specifically do you need to address in order to create clarity for your own employees? It boils down to roles, responsibilities, and performance standards. You need to ensure the following:

- The employee understands the Big Picture, the company's mission, and its vision for the future. The employee's role is clearly defined—specifically, it is apparent how the employee contributes to the success of the team and/or company.

- The values, norms, or guiding principles of the workplace culture are defined and understood, and the employee knows how these items are factored into performance reviews.
- The employee knows exactly how performance is measured and evaluated.
- Internal and external stakeholders are clearly identified.

Think about your hiring and onboarding process. Are these things covered in detail?

Or do you hire people and run them through a quick HR process to sign papers and give the policy manual a cursory review before sending them to a desk to get started?

These four items are a necessary component of any consistently high-performing team or enduring company. We challenge you to find an exception.

Nothing spells mediocrity more consistently than a lack of clarity.

Once you have those items addressed, the next step in "owning the relationship" is to ensure that your expectations are simple, clear, and actionable, and that you're creating a workplace culture that allows your employees to develop and thrive.

Key Points to Remember

1. As a leader, you *must* proactively own the relationship with your direct reports. Do not wait for your employee to take the first step.

2. Owning the relationship means a leader takes responsibility for creating clarity and defining expectations.

3. When you set CLEAR expectations, performance management gets WAY easier.

▼
COUNTER
▲

Expectations:
How to Eliminate the Excuses

"A thin line separates success from failure, the great companies from the ordinary ones. Below that line lies excuse making,
blaming others, confusion, and an attitude of helplessness."[1]

Roger Connors, Tom Smith, and Craig Hickman

ONCE YOU'VE CREATED CLARITY for your people, there is
another critical step to take in order to "own the relationship"
with each employee—you *must* learn how to set detailed, clear
expectations.

"Learn how? I mean, how hard can it be?"

You would be amazed. The idea may sound fairly simple, but
most leaders don't get their people rowing in the same direction
simply because they don't clearly communicate their expectations.

The really scary part is they *think* they do, but they don't.

You probably noticed that UConn basketball coach Geno Auriemma sets unequivocal, unambiguous, crystal-clear expectations. He sets the expectation for preparation and practice. He sets the expectation for watching film. He sets the expectation for body language *on the bench*, for crying out loud. As a member of the team, if your attitude or behavior doesn't align with the stated expectations—if you're not living up to the standards set for the culture—you don't play. Period.

One thing is for sure, when three-time Naismith College Player of the Year and WNBA first-round draft pick Breanna Stewart gets to sit on the bench for not meeting expectations, you can be certain every player on the team understands the expectation and the *intent* of those expectations. Namely, it's about the TEAM.

The question is, how do the players react to those expectations? Does it create resentment or disengagement? Here is what Stewart had to say after the 2016 season concluded:

> If we [her and fellow seniors Morgan Tuck and Moriah Jefferson] were to come to any other school as a group, we wouldn't have done what we did here. And that's crediting a lot to Coach, to the other coaches, to the other players we're playing with. He pushed us to levels that we didn't know we could even reach or play at. And once we bought into that, it was a great journey to be on.[2]

In case you harbor some idea that creating clear expectations and specific boundaries will only box in your employees and stifle their creativity, you need to understand you have it exactly backwards. Having clear expectations is liberating. It allows people to function with freedom. It prescribes exactly what needs to be done—and why!—and allows people to develop their potential.

Working in the dark only opens the door for excuses.

People's Excuses for Failure

"A problem only exists if there is a difference between what is actually happening and what you desire to be happening," said authors Ken Blanchard and Spencer Johnson in their classic book, *The One Minute Manager*.[3] At first glance, that may not necessarily strike you as profound; maybe it seems more like common sense. However, there is something critically important that is implied in Blanchard's observation—that whatever you "desire" to happen has actually been communicated effectively.

Think about the number of times that you have desired, or expected, something to happen in the workplace, whether it was a task to be completed, a deadline to be met, or a follow-up to be provided, and it didn't happen. How did you react? How did you feel? Where you irritated?

BOSS, we know exactly how you reacted. You connected the failure to the generation—"Those bleepin' KIDS!" Maybe it was just a minor annoyance. Maybe it actually was a big freaking deal. What is was, at any level, was conflict. From one perspective, that's what a manager does—manages conflict in the workplace. Not just conflict between people, but the conflict that occurs when employees don't perform as needed, or when an attitude or behavior has to change.

In its simplest form, conflict is simply frustrated expectations. That is, you expect one thing, but you get something quite different. Thus, clarifying your expectations is a key ingredient to managing conflict effectively.

For us, the interesting part of our job is watching how different people "manage" that conflict. Some get angry and stew over it. Some use sarcasm to try to make a point to the employee. Some express their frustration directly and escalate the conflict. Others ignore it completely, only to bring it up in a total meltdown when they "just can't take it anymore!"

For example, you hit the drive-through at Starbucks and order a caramel macchiato, but at the pickup window they hand you a cinnamon dolce latte. Depending on your temperament, you might be slightly frustrated (Robby) to genuinely irritated (Pops). Either way, you ask them to fix it for you and it's all good. Minor annoyance. Very minor conflict.

"I drink black coffee. This example is totally ridiculous. Why the stereotype?"

"You wear bow ties and funky socks. I just assumed you liked fluffy coffee."

Now, let's go inside the workplace, where you, for example, expect that one of your employees will complete a project on a certain day—a project that includes a specific set of deliverables for you to review. It is part of a much larger project that you are expected to report on to the CEO later in the week, and you need time to look at the big picture and make any necessary revisions. To your surprise, despite constant reassurances, your employee fails to meet the deadline. Suddenly, you're in panic mode, and your blood pressure threatens to blow out a vein in your neck.

Major problem. Significant conflict. You expected a result you did not receive. It has to be dealt with, which means there is a direct cost associated with it. Resolving conflict, big or small, always takes time and energy (and, as a result, money), even when you clearly communicated your expectations.

There's only one problem worse than frustrated expectations: when you *think* you've clearly communicated your expectations, but you actually haven't done so at all (more on that later). Now, not only are *you* frustrated, but the *employee* is also frustrated because she didn't know what your expectations were. This means that as you argue about details and discuss what you meant and what the employee should've known, the conflict will be more difficult to resolve and require far more of your valuable time and energy, which costs you even more money.

We will be blunt: It is ALWAYS in your best interest to communicate your expectations very clearly, primarily because the conflict will be much easier to resolve when you have communicated effectively. In fact, if your expectations are clear, then the expectations will resolve the conflict, not you! This is one of the big secrets to effective performance management, and we'll show you how it works.

The other aspect of this issue—setting an *unclear* or ambiguous expectation—is much more common. Managers like to say things like "work harder" or "get it done as soon as possible," and they actually believe they have been quite clear. We call that being delusional.

When expectations are unclear or ambiguous, it opens the door for excuses, and those excuses are *actually* valid! One of our all-time favorite business quotes comes from the late Robert Townsend, former CEO of Avis and author of the enduring 1970 *New York Times* bestseller *Up the Organization.*

> One of the most important tasks of a manager is to eliminate his people's excuses for failure.[4]

This statement is profound on different levels, but let's focus on the obvious: this statement implies there are things that a leader can do to eliminate the opportunity to make excuses for failure.

We agree. Strongly.

In our experience, the three most common "excuses" for failure—in a landslide—are these:

- "I didn't know."
- "I didn't know how."

- "I didn't have time."

How many times have you heard those excuses?

Take a closer look. If an employee doesn't *know*, whose fault is that? In case you're struggling, the answer is you, the leader. Yes, of course, you told the employee what he needed to do, didn't you? Except that you most likely left out a few critical details and, worse, made some assumptions you shouldn't have. Those assumptions, after a failure, sound something like this:

- "He should have known what to do."
- "I would've known what to do if it was me."
- "Why couldn't she figure that out? I did. It's not that hard."

These are the things we hear from leaders who are completely frustrated with employees who fail, falter, or miss deadlines. Instead of making things clear, these managers just assume people should, and will, know what to do. They are the kinds of assumptions that waste hours of time on the back end, and they cause problems that could have easily been avoided if you had taken a little time on the front end, spelled out the details, and ensured everyone was on the same page.

What if employees don't know *how*? Isn't that a training issue? Well—didn't *you* train them?

How about employees who don't have *time*? Don't you set their priorities? Either they really don't have time and you need to address the problem, or they're not working up to performance standards, and you need to deal with that issue.

Instead of genuine clarity, what we consistently find is haze. For example, these are not well-defined expectations:

- "You need to bear down on that project."
- "You need to get to meetings on time."

- "You need to make more customer calls."
- "Your attitude needs to improve."

Those may sound like clear expectations to you, but they aren't, and we will explain why. At the same time, we'll teach you how to do it right, which will help you eliminate a ton of frustration and conflict on both sides of the equation.

How to Set Expectations

In each of the examples above, there is quite a bit of ambiguity presented to the employee. It is that uncertainty that will set your hair on fire.

 "Pops, you don't have any hair."

 "I was the master of uncertainty. . ."

You might be thinking this is nonsense; after all, clear-headed people understand what those things mean, and given the context, they know exactly what needs to be done. Let's allow the KIDS to respond to your "clear expectations."

- "What does 'bear down' on a project mean exactly? Skip lunch? Make loud noises when something is hard? Push harder on the computer keyboard?"
- "Since we almost never start meetings 'on time,' what does 'on time' mean?"

- "'More' customer calls? How many more? And, by the way, does the quality of the call matter or does leaving a voice message count? Can I just shoot them a text?"

- "'Improve' my attitude? What's wrong with my attitude exactly? How would I improve it? Should I start now, or can I work up to it? Actually—you're right—I should spend the afternoon on the golf course working on my attitude."

That's how the KIDS feel about your "clear" expectations! Are you freaking serious? Here's the deal: Without crystal-clear expectations, you open the door to excuses, AND THEY WILL BE MADE. And you *will* be frustrated.

 "And you'll wind up with no hair, just like the Pops!"

 "I expect that the hair jokes will end at some point."

 "No—probably not."

Let's save you the headache *and* the hair loss. Here is the powerful three-step process for setting expectations effectively:

1. The *results* you desire must be clear.
2. The *time frame* must be clear and agreed upon.
3. You must explain the *why*.

Notice we didn't say, "You must show them exactly how you would do it and DEMAND they do it your way!"

Nope. That's not what a Counter Mentor Leader does.

A simple illustration will make this process quite clear. If you have children and you've asked them to clean their rooms, you've probably experienced the frustrations and the conflict of poorly communicated expectations.

Your expectation probably sounded like this: "You need to clean your room!"

We'll let the Pops tell it from his perspective.

Clear Expectations and Clean Rooms—From the Pops' Perspective

Let's say I tell my ten-year-old son—let's call him Robby—that he needs to clean up his room: "Son, you need to clean your room." I throw in the appropriate parental look that suggests I'm serious.

A couple of hours pass, and I take a quick look to see if the room is done. If you have kids, you already know, of course, that it's still a disaster. So, I track Robby down and very pointedly ask him, "Why isn't your room clean?" Here is how that conversation might sound:

ROBBY: Dad you just told me to do it a little while ago.

POPS: It's been exactly two hours and forty-two minutes, son. What part of "clean your room" didn't you understand?

Now I'm a bit frustrated, and Robby is a bit frustrated, but Robby gets to work on his room and emerges triumphantly thirty minutes later to inform me that his room is now FINISHED! Here is how that conversation might sound:

ROBBY (PROUDLY):   Pops, I finished cleaning my room.

POPS: Let's go take a look.

[Robby opens the door enthusiastically. Pops looks around. Twice.]

Pops: Where did you clean?

In case you don't have kids, let me help you understand something. Parents typically have a far different idea of what the word *clean* means than our kids do. And that's exactly why you never want to make assumptions, and why you want to make sure you take the time to ensure the results you desire are clearly defined.

True story. The good news is, when Robby and his siblings were kids, Mom helped them clean their rooms a couple of times, and she showed them how. They learned the skills required to properly clean, and they learned exactly what the word *clean* meant in our house. The result? When the kids cleaned their rooms, they knew exactly what it had to look like to pass muster. No misunderstandings.

It doesn't matter what the situation might be. If you are setting an expectation for a project, a meeting, a change in behavior, completing a task—whatever—make sure the end result is clearly defined. Remember, we aren't saying you should tell them exactly *how* to do it (that's what training is for), but what the end result looks like.

And, no, I never gave Robby a trophy for cleaning his room. Or for just showing up.

What Exactly Does "Sometimes" Mean?

The second aspect of communicating expectations is to **agree on the time frame**.

One of the biggest sources of frustration for managers is to use general terms for time frames. *Soon, immediately, next week, quickly, ASAP*—you name it, people have a general term for it. The problem is, there doesn't seem to be a commonly understood definition for any of these terms.

Furthermore, each of us is actually very confident in our own definition. Yours is wrong. Obviously.

In one of our training workshops, we give people a list of words and ask them to define the words in terms of percentages. For example, "When something USUALLY occurs, it happens what percentage of the time?" We insert words like *rarely, always, sometimes,* and *occasionally* and ask people to determine what percentage of the time that means to them.

Not surprisingly, the numbers span a broad range of possibilities. We've actually had people assign a percentage of 80 percent to the word *always.* #confused

Now, on top of the definition problem, add competing priorities, self-interest, and a general lack of enthusiasm for any given task. What is the end result of this frightening combination? Conflict. You get frustrated. Which leads to irritated. Which turns into yelling and screaming.

All because you didn't get a commitment for a certain time frame. Stop with the general terms and the lack of specifics. Instead, be specific, effective immediately.

To clarify, immediately means right now.

The Final Ingredient

No one does their best work when they don't understand the *why* behind the ask (or in most cases, the *orders*). Working in the dark is not conducive to good work OR a good attitude.

A lack of understanding *always* breeds mistrust, which, as you recall, is a key driver of employee disengagement. When you set expectations, make sure you offer up the "why" behind the expectation. If you don't, you leave the employee to speculate, make all kinds of wild assumptions, and spread discontent all over the company.

Assuming you don't already know, that doesn't work out very well. And it can be avoided with a short explanation.

With all three ingredients in place—a clear result, a defined time frame, and an understanding of *why*—you have a crystal-clear expectation AND you've removed a lot of potential excuses you won't have to deal with if things go sideways.

Key Points to Remember

1. Clarifying your expectations reduces the level and frequency of conflict.

2. Conflict is simply frustrated expectations.

3. To set clear expectations, you must:

    a. Make sure the desired result is completely understood.

    b. Define and agree upon the time frame.

    c. Explain the *why*.

Understand the
Different Perspectives

"No matter by what various crafts we came here, we are all now in the same boat."[1]

President Calvin Coolidge

I F YOU'VE MADE IT THIS FAR, you don't need us to tell you that the BOSS and the KIDS have very, very different perspectives on pretty much everything. We beat this topic up in the first few chapters, so don't worry, we're not going to rehash it—that's not the point of this chapter.

Success in this chapter means coming to a very important conclusion—one that is paramount to understand if you hope to transform from a Taylorian Manager into a Counter Mentor Leader:

Regardless of the generations, you MUST understand each individual's perspective.

Without an understanding of the difference in perspectives, you will be stuck in an endless loop of making assumptions that are wrong or misguided, which will keep you constantly frustrated and in conflict.

Who has time for that!?

In the film *Dead Poets Society*, Professor John Keating was a different kind of leader with a very different perspective.[2] "Different" was not the trait of a gentleman at Welton Academy in 1959. Keating laughed at the wrong times, he made jokes about "sacred" traditions, and he was even known to stand on a desk or two while reciting poetry. Today, he would have had a HUGE following on social media.

As a new professor at the "best boy's preparatory school in the United States," Keating knew the importance of connecting with his class of high schoolers. Personally, his objective wasn't just to help students achieve satisfactory grades on exams; he wanted to truly push them to think for themselves, and, in so doing, help them change their lives.

In his first meeting with the new class, he did something incredible. In a brilliant move to connect with his boys and set the tone for the class (in business, we call this "culture"), he immediately told them all to leave the classroom and follow him, a radical departure from the droning lectures of the typical teacher.

He made jokes; he poked fun at his students; and he worked to connect his boys to those from the past, imploring them to understand what real lessons should be learned from the older generation. He wanted to take them beyond the typical, "Do it the way we've always done it," idea, but he wanted them to observe and learn from the previous generations.

"They believe they're destined for great things, just like many of you . . . Did they wait until it was too late to make from their lives even one iota of what they were capable? Because, you see, gentlemen, these boys are now fertilizing daffodils. . .you can hear them whisper their legacy to you . . . Carpe Diem. Seize the day. Make your lives extraordinary."[3]

Robin Williams' portrayal of Professor Keating in the film *Dead Poets Society* was—and will always be—extraordinary. In the film, there is a fascinating juxtaposition between Mr. Nolan, the old-school, paddle-carrying headmaster, and Mr. Keating. The primary difference: Keating listens intently to the boys while seeking to understand their struggles, hopes, and dreams, while Nolan embodies the I-say-jump-you-say-how-high dictator (the BOSS has been around a LONG time).

It is the metaphor for what we've been discussing, the difference between a Taylorian Manager and a Transformational Leader. In the movie, Keating and Nolan had very different ideas about leadership.

And very different ideas about respect.

Respect: The Key to Understanding

One of our favorite exercises to facilitate with clients who are struggling through the "BOSS vs. KIDS" conflict is to ask them to define the word *respect*. Typically, there is a snicker, an eye roll, and an annoyed, under-the-breath muttering of, "How do you *not* know what respect is?" somewhere in the room.

The results of this exercise are shocking and predictable and eye-opening to everyone. Even the BOSS quickly changes her tune from "This is a waste of time" to "Okay, you have my attention."

Frankly, the simplicity of the exercise is what packs the punch and makes it so powerful. We all know the definition of respect, don't we? You've been taught—either directly or indirectly—from the moment you figured out how to interact with other humans.

It's hysterical how the stereotypes hold all over the world. From the BOSS, you get exactly what you'd expect: some borderline offensive, inappropriate version of "Sit down, shut up and do what you're told!" From the KIDS, you get a borderline whiny, frustrated cousin of "Just let me have an opinion, for once!"

What we're saying is there are *extreme* differences in the two definitions of respect provided by the KIDS and the BOSS. Clearly, each was raised in a completely different world. This insight is the key to understanding the different generations. It is also the key to building the bridge between those generations.

We have found that understanding respect is the decoder ring to translating the eye rolls and bitmojis that the KIDS use to communicate. (BOSS, if you don't bitmoji, ask someone under thirty.) Learning how the BOSS views respect is the shortcut to showing him or her that you are capable of challenging the status quo while still acknowledging the value of her time in the trenches. Learning how the KIDS define respect is the key to keeping them engaged and on the team.

The thing is, both the BOSS and the KIDS consider respect to be non-negotiable, yet they define it quite differently. The KIDS think you (BOSS) have to earn it from them. The BOSS thinks she deserves it because of authority and position. One expects to get it automatically; the other won't give it until it's "earned."

Can you say *conflict*?

The key to resolving this conflict goes back to "owning" the relationship. For the leader, it means having a conversation about this very topic. It is nothing short of amazing what happens when people try to see the world through someone else's glasses. You rarely agree on everything, but you're able to put things into a context.

Respect is a great example. When we have a conversation with a group of disgruntled KIDS who are upset that the BOSS doesn't show them any respect, we typically start by learning how they see the problem and how they arrived at their conclusions. Then, we show them the BOSS's perspective—how the BOSS was raised, how the BOSS views respect, and so forth.

Then we point out something that should be obvious, but usually isn't: The KIDS expect the BOSS to earn their respect, but they don't place the same requirement on themselves! They typically aren't working to show respect but rather are sitting back waiting on the BOSS to earn it—which is what they accuse the BOSS of doing.

Yes, it's usually slightly awkward.

Actually, it's just a huge difference in the perception of respect and which comes first—giving respect or earning respect. Communicating your expectations during the hiring and onboarding process and discussing the role of respect in your workplace culture will help you find the employees who are right for your team, and it will eliminate a lot of the conflict that exists in the absence of that communication.

BOSS, if you're not willing to hear and discuss the KIDS' perspective, don't expect to make a lot of progress in your culture. You don't have to agree, but you have to discuss, understand, and align your expectations with theirs!

Tactics: The Counter Mentor 1-on-1 Meeting and Reverse Mentoring

If you want to show respect and understand what respect means to your people, you need to take the time to build the relationship. Since we have different definitions (and backgrounds and experiences), you can't be expected to know everything about your employees from the moment they sign the offer letter. This is something you work on every single day, from the first day until you stop working together.

It's all about communication. (Isn't everything?)

We've already given you details around how to set clear expectations, and one of those expectations should revolve around respect! Building the relationship, however, goes beyond a stated expectation. There are two key tactics to leverage in understanding your people's unique perspective. The first is the Counter Mentor 1-on-1 Meeting (CMM), and the second is a rarely used tool called *reverse mentoring*.

Counter Mentor 1-on-1 Meeting (CMM)

We have raved about the effectiveness of the CMM. We truly believe it is the most powerful tool in your leadership arsenal. It gives you the opportunity to show support, interest, insight, value, recognition, and real-time performance feedback to an employee.

A 2016 article entitled "How to Make Your One-on-Ones with Employees More Productive" drives home the point:

> "Nothing quite beats a face-to-face, one-on-one meeting," says Elizabeth Grace Saunders, the author of *How to Invest Your Time Like Money*, and the founder of Real Life E Time Coaching & Training. "One-on-ones are one of the most important productivity tools you have as a manager," she says. "They are where you can ask strategic questions such as, are we focused on the right things? And from a rapport point of view, they are how you show employees that you value them and care about them."[4]

This face-to-face meeting is how you begin to develop a strong relationship, and it's also the perfect place to create an understanding of each employee's perspectives on the workplace.

Reverse Mentoring

Reverse Mentoring is exactly what it sounds like—mentoring—only in reverse. The "junior" employee mentors the "senior" employee. In the four-generation workplace, it makes perfect sense because the

KIDS know and understand things the BOSS does not! However, few companies are utilizing the tool.

In a 600-company survey conducted by the Delphi Group, a little more than half (56 percent) leveraged traditional mentoring, but only 14 percent—roughly one in seven—employed any kind of reverse mentoring program.[5]

We don't get it.

Leveraging a more junior employee to teach you about how things are done in 2018—technology, social media, productivity apps, etc.—provides an extreme level of insight and growth. So, why don't we do it?

Answer: It's different. It's change. It makes us uncomfortable. And, for the BOSS, it can look like a loss of superiority, a tacit admission of vulnerability. So the BOSS fights it and criticizes it and claims it's all a waste of time. And employees flee in droves to join companies willing to leverage any talent, regardless of generation.

We go into much more detail on reverse mentoring—and how to implement it in your organization—in chapter 26. For now, please understand there are HUGE benefits associated with reverse mentoring:

- You proactively close the knowledge gap between the BOSS and the KIDS.
- You empower high-potential employees.
- You bridge the gap between generations—driving understanding and empathy (things you really, really want as a leader!).

Remember, when we say you must understand the different perspectives, we aren't giving you the green light to make a fool of yourself! This isn't about being something you're not.

BOSS, we aren't telling you to be "young and hip."

KIDS, we don't expect you to watch *M*A*S*H* re-runs or take up crossword puzzles.

"See my hat? Some of us are just naturally hip."

 "SHAKING. MY. HEAD."

The greatness comes from simply working to understand the perspective of those different from you. Whether you're a first-time manager, a tenured executive, or a 1950s prep school English teacher, we can agree there are significant differences between generations. What's more, there are also differences between genders, personalities, and experiences. The critical concept you *must* take away in this COUNTER step is that understanding is critical to developing a relationship, and relationship is the key to trust.

By the way, this is not an *efficiency* exercise. **You CANNOT be efficient with people!** You can't go through the motions of a CMM meeting, check off the boxes, and expect your people to be all-in. If you're not prepared to sincerely invest, don't waste your time.

Professor Keating might say it like this: "Invest the time to understand. Others will only care when they know *you* care. That will make your leadership extraordinary."

Key Points to Remember

1. Understanding perspectives will help you understand actions.

2. People—especially those from different generations—define respect differently.

3. The key tactics to understanding the different perspectives are the Counter Mentor 1-on-1 Meeting (CMM) and reverse mentoring (which is easily done in the CMM).

4. You cannot be efficient with people! Understanding takes time.

Check out this related *Counter Mentors* podcast episode: "When Did Respect Go Out of Style?!" Visit cmtr.co/ep6.

Negotiate the Obstacles

"There is surely nothing quite so useless as doing with great
efficiency what should not be done at all."[1]

Peter Drucker

A S MUCH AS BUSINESS IS ABOUT PEOPLE—and it is ALL
about people—it is also about overcoming obstacles. Of course,
sometimes those are exactly the same thing, aren't they? The KIDS
understand: if only the BOSS would stop clinging to "the way we've
always done it" and get out of the way!

The problem is, few managers really stop to think about the
obstacles. Not because they don't encounter obstacles. Clearly, they
do—usually every day. But do managers stop and think about potential obstacles before to those obstacles becoming a fire that needs
fighting?

Not a chance.

How about you? Do you think about the next obstacle over the
horizon, or do you come to work every day toting a fire hose and a
fire extinguisher?

If you're like most managers, you simply plow ahead, exercising sheer power of will to overcome the challenges you encounter in the workplace. In fact, there seems to be a certain level of pride, and romanticism, associated with that idea: to encounter Mount Everest and simply decide to conquer it with no strategy, plan, or training (insert powerful orchestra music here—and Robby's dramatic eye roll).

Unfortunately, Everest is not something you *overcome*, as though it is simply a matter of working harder. Everest is five and a half miles tall. 29,029 feet, to be exact. You don't exactly wake up on Saturday morning and decide to "go summit Everest."

How big a task is it? Typically, climbers work their way up the mountain through four different camps over a period of time, just to acclimate to the altitude. At a certain point, the mountain becomes extremely unforgiving. Everything above 8,000 meters (26,247 feet) is known as the "Death Zone." Once you reach that altitude, the risks are enormous. Frankly, many people never make it off the mountain.

While more than 4,400 people can lay claim to standing on the earth's highest point, 282 people have attempted the challenge and lost their lives.[2] The truth is, whether you succeed or fail in your quest to summit Everest, absolutely nothing about reaching the top is easy. It is very costly, very difficult, and extraordinarily risky.

Without trying to be too dramatic, the process of becoming an effective leader in today's chaotic, four-generation workplace often feels a whole lot like climbing Everest. Some of the critical workplace obstacles, the ones that prevent Taylorian Managers from transforming into effective leaders, are the workplace equivalent of the death zone. Make a mistake in one of these areas, and the impact on your team's performance—and your leadership—will be significant.

Of course, these obstacles can be negotiated, but it's definitely not just a matter of working harder, taking on more responsibility, or carrying a bigger fire extinguisher. The answer is to identify those obstacles, make preparations, and take them on proactively.

In today's workplace, there are three Everest-sized obstacles we believe you must plan for and safely negotiate your way around if you are to be a successful leader:

1. How you invest your time.
2. How you engage your emotional intelligence (also known as emotional quotient).
3. How you deal with—and lead your people through—change.

Negotiating these three obstacles is no small task, but the payoff is enormous.

Your Investment in Time

In the workplace, time is the one thing that managers never have enough of. As we discussed earlier, "I don't have time" are the four most dangerous words in your leadership vocabulary, and it is the most common reason managers offer for failing to do critical leadership activities.

It's not that managers don't understand that they need more time to do those things; they just never seem to have any extra time lying around. Ironically, although managers constantly complain they never have enough of time, it's amazing to see how poorly they invest what they do have.

Invest? Yes, leadership requires an *investment* of time.

George Shultz, the secretary of state for President Ronald Reagan, shared his views about carving out specific time for the most important things in a recent *New York Times* interview:

> When George Shultz was secretary of state in the 1980s, he liked to carve out one hour each week for quiet reflection. He sat down in his office with a pad of paper and pen, closed the

door and told his secretary to interrupt him only if one of two people called:

"My wife or the president," Shultz recalled.

Shultz, who's now 96, told me that his hour of solitude was the only way he could find time to think about the strategic aspects of his job. Otherwise, he would be constantly pulled into moment-to-moment tactical issues, never able to focus on larger questions of the national interest. And the only way to do great work, in any field, is to find time to consider the larger questions.[3]

The idea of setting time aside to think transcends generations. It is remarkably simple, yet ridiculously uncommon. It is the difference between *leading by doing* and *leading by developing,* and there are consequences for each course of action.

The consequences for *leading by doing*—getting things done yourself—is to create a dependency on you in every aspect of your team's work and ensure you never have enough time to the get the most important things done. Conversely, the consequences for *leading by developing*—getting things done through other people—is to create a team of people who are effective without you, freeing up time for you to invest in additional leadership functions: functions that provide a *much higher* return on your time investment.

 "I'm thinking this is a no-brainer."

 "So, why doesn't your generation get it?"

This is exactly how you jump off the Taylorian Manager hamster wheel. **You start by investing a little time in leadership thinking**

each week. Then, you watch the results multiply into huge savings of time down the road. That's exactly what we coach leaders to do: set aside time each week to think.

We call it the *Leadership Window*. It's radically simple, but incredibly powerful!

 "Radically simple?"

 "Yeah, it's more simple than just simple. It makes simple look difficult. It's simple to the simple."

 "Now I know how my parents must have felt."

Three quick steps and you can make it a part of your leadership habits:

1. Set aside one to two hours of time each week and SCHEDULE it on your calendar. (Many of you just freaked out: *"Who has two hours in their week!?"* Okay, start with just thirty minutes if you need to.) This needs to become a HABIT. Make it a recurring appointment. Every single week.

2. Eliminate ALL distractions for that time.

3. Using the Counter Mentor Leadership Window™ form as a guide,* use that time to THINK, and ponder, and consider the leadership activities of communication, strategy and planning, and people development.

---

*To download the Counter Mentor Leadership Window™ and all other Counter Mentor forms, see https://countermentors.com/resources.

4. DO NOT use this time to answer emails, or work on budgets, or any other administrative stuff. You'll absolutely lose all the power of this process. (Perhaps your first thinking exercise could be about when to schedule time to do that stuff.)

Yes, it works. Yes, it will easily increase your leadership effectiveness. Exponentially! The idea is to focus *exclusively* on *leadership* issues—to spend time thinking through those items for which you never seem to have time.

It is so important to make time to think. Why? Because if you don't do it, no one else will. No one else is thinking about communication or strategy or developing people. Your employees aren't intentionally creating a path, a direction, a detailed plan to reach specific strategic objectives. Why would they?

Instead, we all come to work, put in our time, fight fires all day, and go home.

Wash. Rinse. Repeat. And, almost without exception, the most important things don't get addressed. We know, because we've seen it hundreds of times.

Your Investment in Emotional Intelligence (EQ)

Business, first and foremost, is about people.

We admit it—repetition is a BOSS technique. When it comes to learning, it's a pretty good idea, but when the repetition is reminding the KIDS over and over about "back in the day," it becomes unbearable.

Business is not really about products, or projects, or strategy, or funding.

It's about people.

"Surely, we've gotten that point across."

 "Have you ever seen the BOSS try to operate a remote? We should say it a few more times!"

Those other things are important, of course. It's tough to do business without a product, or capital, or a viable plan. However, it is the people in the business equation who create all of the variables. Without customers, there is no business. As Henry Ford famously said, "It is not the employer who pays the wages. Employers only handle the money. It is the customer who pays the wages."[4]

Employees aren't any different. They can be difficult in a hundred different ways, but nothing can get done without them. Douglas Conant, former CEO of Campbell's, said, "I strongly believe that you can't win in the marketplace unless you win first in the workplace. If you don't have a winning culture inside, it's hard to compete in the very tough world outside."[5]

Howard Schultz, former CEO and now Executive Chairman of Starbucks, agreed: "You can't expect your employees to exceed the expectations of your customers if you don't exceed the employees' expectations of management."[6]

Yet, we hear something said way too many times by a frustrated BOSS:

"You know, managing a profitable business would be so much easier if it wasn't for having to deal with people."

Yes, he usually means it exactly as it sounds, even if only a little bit. This may surprise you, but we absolutely agree! People are imperfect and often inconsistent, and dealing with people can be incredibly unforgiving.

But this is a perfect time for your very first lesson in emotional intelligence: Never say something like that *in front of* your employees. We're pretty sure it's not a trust builder; it's more like a culture killer.

The challenge for you as a leader is to get the most out of your people. Doing that means taking ownership of your *people* skills— **what is now typically referred to as emotional intelligence (EQ)**. Why? Because people don't work for someone they don't trust, and your trustworthiness is a direct result of the way you deal with people. Zig Ziglar simplified the sales process by saying, "If people like you they'll listen to you, but if they trust you they'll do business with you."[7]

This simple yet profound insight is directly applicable to leadership! Just change one word:

> If people like you they'll listen to you, but if they trust you they'll *follow* you.

Furthermore, you definitely ask your employees to take ownership of their work, so you probably should take ownership of *your* work, right? And what is your work? Getting things done *through other people*. See? That *people* thing just won't go away.

Think of all the ways you can stumble as a leader: bad decisions, poor communication, ill-conceived plans, bad hires. The point is, there will be more than enough challenges for you to overcome as a leader, so you probably want to do everything you can to prevent yourself from adding "My people don't trust me" to the list. That's why emotional intelligence is so critical.

John D. Mayer, a professor at the University of New Hampshire, and Peter Salovey, a professor at Yale, are recognized as being among the first researchers to define the concept of emotional intelligence:

> From a scientific (rather than a popular) standpoint, emotional intelligence is the ability to accurately perceive your own and others' emotions; to understand the signals that emotions send

about relationships; and to manage your own and others' emotions. It doesn't necessarily include the qualities (like optimism, initiative, and self-confidence) that some popular definitions ascribe to it. [8]

Daniel Goleman took that idea and made it commonplace in the business world when he published the internationally bestselling book *Emotional Intelligence: Why It Can Matter More than IQ*.[9] Goleman was among the first to suggest that effective leaders are those who develop their "emotional" intelligence, saying, "For leaders, the first task in management has nothing to do with leading others; step one poses the challenge of knowing and managing oneself."[10]

Goleman defined emotional intelligence as encompassing five areas: self-awareness, self-regulation, motivation, empathy, and social skills. Travis Bradberry and Jean Greaves, cofounders of TalentSmart® and coauthors of *Emotional Intelligence 2.0*, define emotional intelligence as the "ability to recognize and understand emotions in yourself and others, and your ability to use this awareness to manage your behavior and relationships."[11] Unfortunately, the authors say, almost two out of every three people they tested were not skilled at identifying their emotions and using them to their own benefit.

Okay, that's interesting to know, we suppose, but why should you care? Is there a connection to something tangible? The answer is yes. Absolutely, definitely, yes. Bradberry and Greaves explain:

> EQ is so critical to success that it accounts for 58 percent of performance in all types of jobs. It's the single biggest predictor of performance in the workplace and the strongest driver of leadership and personal excellence.[12]

The single biggest predictor of performance? Wow!

As it turns out, your EQ is an uncanny predictor of whether or not you will be successful as a leader. How is that for motivation? How much impact would it have on your team's performance if you, the leader, helped your employees develop *their* emotional intelligence? #crazyidea

In chapter 6, we shared a piece written by Matthew Lieberman, Professor and Director of the UCLA Social Cognitive Neuroscience laboratory. In the article, he notes that "social skills are a great multiplier," meaning that leaders with high EQ are more effective in the workplace:

> A leader with strong social skills can leverage the analytical abilities of team members far more efficiently. Having the social intelligence to predict how team members will work together will promote better pairings. Often what initially appear to be task-related difficulties turn out to be interpersonal problems in disguise. One employee may feel devalued by another or think that she is doing all the work while her partner loafs—leading both partners putting in less effort to solve otherwise solvable problems. Socially skilled leaders are better at diagnosing and treating these common workplace dilemmas.[13]

Yes, your emotional intelligence is a critical factor in your leadership effectiveness. However, this is one of those "good news, bad news" situations: The good news is that a higher EQ can propel you to a different level as a leader. The bad news is, as we discussed previously, fewer than 1 percent of leaders are results-focused and have high social skills!

Despite that, you should not see this as some rare talent that less than one in a hundred leaders possess. Instead, you should recognize that we don't train our leaders correctly! If a company was convinced of the extraordinary impact of leaders who have both a results-focused approach AND strong interpersonal skills, they would spend far more time developing the social skills of leaders. The return on investment would be dramatic.

This book isn't meant to be a deep-dive into improving your personal EQ. You should digest *Emotional Intelligence 2.0* in its entirety specifically for that purpose. On the other hand, we can tell you with great confidence that making a focused effort in two key areas we've already discussed—understanding the perspectives of your employees and improving your communication skills and habits—will have a substantial impact on your emotional intelligence.

Your Investment in Adapting to Change

William Arthur Ward once said, "The pessimist complains about the wind; the optimist expects it to change; the realist adjusts the sails."[14] His observation speaks to the three options we are generally faced with when we encounter obstacles in life—complain, hope, or adapt.

The problem is, change is stressful. It is difficult under the best of circumstances. And for many successful companies, it is actually seen as unnecessary. When companies achieve success, their biggest enemy is often the very success they enjoy. The ever-present mantra "This is the way we've always done it" is much easier to defend. After all *that* way made us successful. Why would we change? Why would we listen to the KIDS—they're just some twenty-something wannabes who haven't done anything!

This sounds perfectly reasonable, right up until it doesn't anymore and your company gives way to a more aggressive, more committed competitor that isn't scared off by *the way we've always done it*. It's why Jim Collins opened his bestselling book *Good to Great* with this memorable line: "Good is the enemy of great."[15]

NFL coaches understand this idea better than most. They can't afford to rest on the past. Contentment breeds mediocrity, and mediocrity gets you fired in a hurry. Past success buys very little time or favor in The League, so coaches either adapt or they get replaced.

Bill Belichick, the head coach of the New England Patriots, is one of those coaches who understands the value of change. In fact, he has turned it into an art form.

With the dramatic, come-from-behind 34–28 win over the Atlanta Falcons in Super Bowl LI, Belichick has now led the Pats to seven of the last sixteen Super Bowls and hoisted the Lombardi trophy five times. During that time period, not only has the game changed significantly, but the players on the team have changed from year to year (with the notable exception of Quarterback Tom Brady), and he has seen his coaching staff change several times.

Still, Belichick wins. That's what makes him the GOAT. (Do we really have to explain that one again?)

It is his adaptability—his ability to change—that is the hallmark of his tenure as the head coach of the Patriots. Defensive lineman Vince Wilfork, a member of the Pats roster for eleven seasons, referred to Belichick's ability to change in an interview prior to the 2014 Super Bowl win over Seattle:

> I think when you get so used to having a certain quality of players, and it changes, it's hard for you to adapt to change. And I think Bill had to do a good job of that ever since I've been in the league because we've changed so much.[16]

In the past sixteen years, the Pats have finished first in the AFC East fourteen times (they settled for second the other two years). Sure, having the greatest QB of all time is a giant factor in their success, but the game and its components have changed so dramatically that staying on top that long is as much a reflection of Belichick's ability to adapt as it is a reflection of Tom Brady's quarterback play.

Here is a stark comparison: During Belichick's seventeen-year tenure at New England, the Cleveland Browns, the Buffalo Bills, and the Miami Dolphins have each had nine different head coaches. The Detroit Lions and Washington Redskins have each had seven. And how have those teams fared in the playoffs? All FIVE teams combined have played in twelve postseason games and won exactly once. COMBINED.

No Division Champs. No Super Bowl wins.

Change is not optional—unless you're good with mediocrity. What we can tell you is this: Change is simply a decision. You can stick to what you know and do now, or you can adapt.

It is strictly binary.

Yes or no. Change or stay the same.

Succeed or become irrelevant.

Key Points to Remember

1. To overcome the common excuse "I don't have time" you must intentionally create a *Leadership Window* to address critical leadership issues.

2. The consequence for leading by doing—getting things done yourself—is to create a dependency on you in every aspect of your team's work and ensure you never have enough time to get the most important things done.

3. Leading by developing—getting things done through other people—is to create a team of people who are effective without you, freeing up time for you to invest in additional leadership functions: functions that provide a *much higher* return on your time investment.

4. Emotional Intelligence (EQ) is a vital leadership skill. If people like you they'll listen to you, but if they trust you they'll follow with you.

5. This whole book is about change. If you cannot adapt, you will not be an effective leader.

Teach the
Essential Skills

"I don't divide the world into the weak and the strong, or the successes and the failures. I divide the world into the learners and non-learners."[1]

Benjamin Barber

THE OBJECTIVE OF LEADERSHIP, as we say over and over, is to get things done through other people.

That means one of two things—either you hire people with all of the necessary skills, or you hire people with great potential and help them acquire those skills. Regardless, you have to create the right workplace environment or those talented employees will leave for greener pastures.

And by greener pastures, we don't mean "more money."

Teaching the essential skills means that the BOSS is intentionally helping the KIDS acquire the skills necessary to excel in any given position. It also means, BOSS, that you can teach your people the essential *leadership* skills in this book. #shamelessplug

We could write a whole different book that focuses on how poorly most companies approach the training and development process—if they even have one. First, most training is expendable, meaning that it's the first line item in the budget to be cut. Second, few companies have specific training and development plans for individual employees. Instead, they train reactively and sporadically—if at all. Third, in most situations, accountability to the training process is nonexistent, which means that any money spent on training typically has a very low return on investment.

But that's for another time.

The fact is, everything we've discussed won't be as impactful if all of your employees don't get better at what they do. Without question, the right workplace culture and transformational leadership go a very long way, but you still need your people to grow and develop key skills.

That should be your primary leadership objective (and, frankly, part of your compensation, but we'll leave that for that hypothetical "other book" as well)—ahead of results or primary job activities. Results will always take care of themselves when you get the right people, create the right culture, and TRAIN your people well.

Our friend David Burkus, the bestselling author of *Under New Management: How Leading Organizations Are Upending Business as Usual*, joined us on the *Counter Mentor* podcast to discuss several things about the "traditional" workplace that people are beginning to challenge. In some cases, the changes are radical departures from the old-school ideas about the workplace.

 "Shocker."

One of the key challenges we discussed with David is the number of hours employees work. Again, we're back to the importance of time, but now we're extending the idea to the employee rather than the leader. Here's what David had to say.

We labor under this misconception—especially in the West, especially in the United States—[that] we should brag about how little sleep we're getting and how many hours we're working. . . . In terms of productivity, in knowledge work, in coming up with ideas and solving problems, we should probably inverse that. We should brag about how much sleep we're getting and how much our brain is recharging. . . .

Let's be totally honest, an eight-hour work day in a knowledge work organization—if you had uninterrupted focus time, and no meetings scheduled that day—you could probably get everything done by lunch . . . the irony being the fact that [when someone] is working at the office twelve hours a day, they're still getting probably eight hours, or even seven hours, worth of work done.

Just because you hung around until your boss left doesn't mean you're doing productive work.[2]

The real shame of this issue is that the BOSS often equates the number of hours "worked" with the level of commitment to the company, while the KIDS know they could do the work in half the time, but they have absolutely no reason to do so. They are actually *incented* to work slower! "If I'm required to have my butt in the chair from eight to five, I'll make sure I spread the work out to last that long . . ."

We know because we hear it all the time—endless meetings, mindless duties, and no clear purpose create a mind-numbing existence for many employees! But at least they are in their seats, (allegedly) working, right?

So, the KIDS make you happy by logging more hours to do the same amount of work. Productivity decreases, engagement suffers . . .

 "Geez, this is starting to sound like a broken record."

"Like when you talk about the KIDS?"

The solution to this problem fits right into the COUNTER methodology. When you purposefully train and develop your people, individually, according to their needs, it benefits you in several ways:

- Career development is a HUGE driver of employee engagement.
- Employee performance improves as skills develop.
- Distractions are far less an issue when employees are mentored and challenged to learn things *they* care about.
- Learning leadership skills prepares high-potential employees for the next level.

This is certainly consistent with the research data provided by the 2016 Deloitte Millennial Survey:

> Of great significance in the current survey results is the finding that 71% of those likely to leave in the next two years are unhappy with how their leadership skills are being developed—fully 17 points higher than among those intending to stay beyond 2020. The most loyal employees are more likely to agree that:
>
> - There is a lot of support/training available to those wishing to take on leadership roles
> - Younger employees are actively encouraged to aim for leadership roles.[3]

Let's be painfully clear: This isn't just about teaching employees how to do *their* job. We want to develop the entire person. So, teaching the *essential skills* means we intentionally teach the employee three very specific things:

- How to think—to develop the skills to consider the entire process and scope of the challenge and develop a solution that is best for the *business*, not just the employee.
- How to communicate—to teach employees how to communicate effectively; it's the foundation of everything else they do!
- How to execute—to build an effective plan to work efficiently and collaboratively.

We know KIDS want to grow and take on leadership roles, but at first glance, many employees today—certainly younger employees—don't *appear* to have an interest in growth and development. But that appearance is often grossly misleading, and that's the real problem with all of your generalizations, BOSS. The truth, according to research at Gallup, is that many of the KIDS place a huge premium on career development:

> Millennials are much more likely than both Gen Xers and baby boomers to say a job that accelerates their professional or career development is "very important" to them (45% of millennials versus 31% of Gen Xers and 18% of baby boomers).[4]

The problem is they are often (but not always!) waiting for the BOSS to kick-start the process, which may look like laziness or a lack of initiative. Once in a while that may be true, but most of the time it's the BOSS making a bad assumption. Seventy-four-year-old Martha Stewart is a good example:

> I think every business is trying to target millennials, but who are millennials? Now we are finding out that they are living with

their parents. They don't have the initiative to go out and find a little apartment and grow a tomato plant on the terrace.[5]

Like many Boomers, Stewart loves to paint with the broad brush, doesn't she? But that's a bit like suggesting all female Boomers must be crooks.

Clearly that's not true, is it?

Pay Attention to Your Onboarding Process

Kelly Gallagher is visually impaired.

To put a fine point on it, that's a very positive spin on her condition. According to Ms. Gallagher, she "can see only a blur of whiteness when she stands at the top of a mountain, and depends on a guide to be her eyes."[6] Not quite blind, but not really seeing much of anything.

If you're wondering why she would be at the top of a mountain seeing a blur of whiteness, it's because she is an accomplished skier. Well, that's a bit of an understatement. She is actually a gold-medal Olympian. She won gold at the 2014 Winter Paralympic Games in the visually impaired Women's Super-G competition.

However, since she cannot actually distinguish the course, she skis with a coach. Skiing together, at speeds that typically hit 60 mph, her coach communicates with her via a Bluetooth headset. Can you even imagine plummeting downhill, whipping around flagpoles left and right, finishing with a time only a few seconds slower than an Olympic competitor with *perfect* vision—when you can't see anything?

UNBELIEVABLE!

To perform at that level—sighted or not—requires hundreds, if not thousands, of hours of coaching and training. However, it's not just any kind of coaching or training; it's the kind of training that has Gallagher mirror her coach in every phase of skiing. It is the sports equivalent of "job shadowing" or "mentoring." But, quite clearly, that training is not a one-time event; instead, it's an ongoing process that is consistently measured and evaluated. The results are amazing.

Think for a moment about that type of training—mirroring the actions of someone else over and over, while constantly communicating—and compare it to your company's **employee onboarding process**. The objective of an effective onboarding process is to prepare an employee to hit the ground running. Done well, it also creates the expectation that training is a cultural norm and employees are evaluated, in part, on personal growth and development.

The problem with most onboarding attempts is that they are woefully inadequate, and despite any good intention, they typically only hit the highlights: a review of the position's job description, an introduction to corporate policy and procedure, a primer on paperwork and workflow, and (if you're really lucky) a visit from IT to install necessary software applications.

One time. All at once. Half a day—tops.

Unfortunately, this type of onboarding typically serves only to create a *functionary*, not a functional employee. A functionary, not the most complimentary of terms, usually refers to a person of lower rank; someone with little or no authority who is tasked to carry out someone else's orders.

This type of "training" doesn't even focus on the really important stuff. What about the company's vision? How about corporate values or cultural norms? BOSS, we're betting big money you can't even say what your corporate values are without looking at the plaque on the wall. What good are they if you don't use them?

In an effective onboarding process, those values create boundaries that make leadership much easier. You should teach those values and reinforce them consistently. Just as important, you will need to identify and pursue the following questions:

- What skills and processes must employees master?
- What is the time frame in which you expect them to be learned?
- What does the training schedule look like to create that mastery?
- How will you ensure they have mastered those critical skills and processes?

Let's face it: the real reason companies fail to train their people is that they don't have a plan for training. There is not a detailed onboarding plan with a schedule and required certification assessments. There is not a short-term or long-term plan for skills development. There is not a coaching or mentoring plan in place. How do you teach the essential skills without a plan?

Not to worry. Here is a seven-step guide to creating that plan:

- Identify the **skills** necessary to excel in the employee's position.
- Identify the **critical outcomes** the position must produce (with metrics).
- Identify the employee's **gaps** in those skills.
- **Schedule** consistent training in all relevant skills.
- **Test** those essential skills, to ensure mastery.
- Provide observation and **feedback** on progress during your CMM meetings.
- Create a **mentoring plan** for the development of the *essential skills*—thinking, communicating, and executing.

Teaching the essential skills is the only way to increase your effectiveness as a leader. When you teach your people how to communicate, how to think, and how to execute, you enable yourself to focus on leadership activities—not doing everything yourself!

Which is critical since leadership is about getting things done *through other people.*

Key Points to Remember

1. Results will always take care of themselves when you get the right people, create the right culture, and TRAIN your people well.

2. In addition to job skills, there are *essential skills* you *must* teach your people: how to think, how to communicate, and how to execute.

3. Onboarding sets the tone for people development and creates the culture of growth and accountability from Day One.

Getting the Work Done:
Execute and Review

"The best-laid schemes o mice an men
Gang aft agley, [often go awry]
An lea'e us nought but grief an pain,
For promis'd joy!"[1]

Robert Burns

AT SOME POINT, the work has to get done. All of this leadership stuff sounds great in the classroom, but the important question is, can you apply it in the real world? Can you lead a team and create good results? More importantly, can you execute *under stress*?

"Absolutely!" you say.

So, you dive in head-first, preparing for a productive week. You make your to-do list, you schedule critical meetings, you arrange for resources to be available, and you roll in to work on Monday ready to make things happen.

Then Monday *happens*. Your plan takes three torpedoes amidships and gets blown to pieces by one customer disaster and then another. A critical HR issue pops up on Tuesday, and the alarm bells threaten to make your head explode.

Welcome to the Big Leagues. Mike Tyson described this situation perfectly when he said, "Everyone has a plan until they get punched in the mouth."[2]

But you're resilient. You're a problem-solver. You stay late Tuesday night to get some things worked out. Oh, yeah, you can still salvage the week! But, first thing Wednesday morning, the BOSS drops a high-priority, must-be-done-immediately project in the middle of your lap that crushes your Wednesday. And your Thursday. AND your Friday.

The good news? In those three days, another eighteen items get added to your already unmanageable to-do list for next week.

Awesome.

This is the world you live in. This is why you "don't have time," and it's exactly why you have to build a high-performance team that leverages your team's talent. Otherwise, you're nothing more than a self-limiting team of ONE: a lone performer with some assistants. BOSS, if you have to make all the decisions and solve all the problems, you'll never get ahead of the curve. Your stress levels will crush your health, and your vacation time will pile up like a rush-hour nightmare on I-5.

If you've been there, you know we're not being dramatic.

This is precisely why we include "Execute" and "Review" in the COUNTER leadership process. All that hard work you are putting in to build trust and earn the right to influence your people—communicating effectively, owning the relationships, understanding employee perspectives, negotiating the obstacles, and teaching the essential skills—all of that is useless if, when things get *real*, you revert to your old-school, Taylorian Management ways.

Working under stress is where your leadership is *really* tested. It's where your most important leadership moments occur, and it's where you develop the confidence to use the COUNTER leadership skills in high-stakes environments. You absolutely *cannot* afford to fold your tent and revert to micromanaging when things get tough.

Your people will start updating their resumes almost immediately.

The Reason You Struggle to Execute

They say hope is not a strategy. The truth is, it's not even a decent idea, much less a strategy. Hoping things get better is a give-up shot that relegates your team to mediocrity.

No, if you want to execute effectively—and consistently—you have to be able to create a plan that leads you to the result you need. However, and this seems strange to say, most managers have not been trained to plan any more than they've been trained to lead. People just assume that planning is a second-nature activity: that everyone knows how to create a functional plan. But, we've known plenty of managers and executives alike who don't know how to plan at all.

As in, NO IDEA.

We've seen managers claim their plan is "to do $50 million this year." That's it! No details and no explanation. The challenge is—and we can double-check this—we're pretty sure a number is not a plan. A number is just a number, and you still have to figure out the HOW—as in, HOW are you going to do $50 million?

Oh, by the way, a to-do list is not a plan either. A goal is not a plan. And "working harder" is definitely not a plan. It's a good thought, but a plan? Not so much. It's like any other good idea—they may be good ideas, but an idea doesn't qualify as a plan. Each of these things may be a *part* of a plan, but they don't qualify as a plan by themselves.

This is a consistent theme that we've seen across clients at every revenue level: companies just assume that anyone with a title above "supervisor" knows how to create and execute a plan. Instead of a real plan, however, you get goals, objectives, and big ideas. Even spreadsheets—with even more numbers (we just love when people present a budget and call it a plan).

But no plan.

Let's shed some light on the subject. To put a fine point on it, a plan is a **step-by-step process that is designed to achieve a specific outcome**. That process might include some great ideas, and a set of goals or objectives, and some numbers to measure progress—probably even some fantastic to-do lists at the tactical level—but those are all *pieces* of the plan, not the plan itself.

Imagine you're "planning" a vacation, and someone asks you what your vacation "plan" is. You respond by holding up a map and pointing to a resort on the coast. "That's our plan!" you exclaim. You know where you want to go, but you haven't figured out how to get there, what you'll need for the trip, or any of dozens of other details.

That is what often poses as a plan in the workplace.

In fact, whether you're in a small department or smack in the middle of a chaotic workplace, you know how a "plan" typically evolves:

- You're given a project of some kind.
- You're provided with an overview and scant few details.
- You're told to "figure it out as quickly as possible!"
- So, being a good soldier, you dive right into the tactics.
- You set meetings, you work twelve-hour days, and you spin your entire team into a frenzy attempting to solve something you actually don't quite understand.

Welcome to your worst nightmare.

Stress is through the roof, and your team's patience is running thin.

This Is How We Do Execution

The thing about planning is that it is nothing more than a process. Most companies understand *process*, but they don't have one for creating effective plans.

That's what we're going to do here—teach you how to plan. You'll get better as you practice, and if you want the advanced-standing course with all the cool bells and whistles all you have to do is call. Actually, make that a tweet: @countermentors.

Here we go.

Step 1: Validate the Mission (Where Are We Going?)

Great planners always take care to create a crystal-clear "destination," or mission. In this step, you answer a very simple question: "Where are we going?"

Quite often, a high-level objective may be provided for you, but that initial ask from the BOSS may be generic or vague. Like this: "Figure out why margins are slipping in the Northeast Region and make some changes." What usually happens is everyone gathers in a conference room, and the ideas start flying. HUGE mistake. Instead, you STOP and go back to step 1 and clearly define the current situation. What you will usually find is the details of the mission fall out on the table for you to see.

In this case, however, the mission must be much more clear. For example, in our hypothetical situation, the mission might sound like this: "Increase gross margins in the Northeast Region from 29.5 percent to 33.0 percent by the end of this fiscal year."

If you don't get clarity in the destination, it will be considerably more difficult to solve the problem.

Step 2: Define the Current Situation (Where Are We Now?)

The single biggest mistake made in the planning process is to dive directly into tactics or brainstorming. People often spend a lot of time and effort creating all kinds of ideas without clearly understanding their current situation. This makes little sense if you don't first have a clearly defined mission and then an understanding of exactly where you are NOW.

Think about it this way: Let's assume our destination (where we are going) is San Diego. Someone might suggest that driving is the best way to get to our destination, but careful analysis indicates that time is an issue, and driving won't work under those constraints. So, why would you spend hours discussing the roads to take and how much budget you will need for fuel, if driving is a bad idea in this context?

ANY idea is a GOOD idea, and ANY idea is a BAD idea; it all depends on CONTEXT. (KIDS, create a meme and put this on Instagram.)

Get the point? Your great idea isn't worth considering until we understand the context in which it will be used. So the next step in creating a successful plan is gathering information about the current situation and taking the time to clearly answer the question, "**Where are we now?**"

Understanding your current situation is critical for another reason. If, again, we're traveling to San Diego, that trip will look a lot different if we start in San Francisco as compared to starting in New York City. Many, many things about the plan can and will be completely different, depending on your starting location.

Whether you are developing a plan to implement something significant like a major technology change or you're looking to drive quick value by tweaking a process, you must have a complete understanding of the what, how, and why of *today*. If this step is skipped, you will often come up with a solution that doesn't address the root cause or right problem.

When you jump right into *get stuff done* mode and don't clearly understand the current situation, you are in danger of wasting a lot of time and money: you focus on the wrong thing: and ultimately, you produce the wrong outcomes.

Do you really have the time to correct wrong outcomes?

Step 3: Build the Action Plan (How Do We Get There?)

With a clear understanding of the current situation, you can finally get down to the strategies and tactics that answer our final question, "How do we get there?"

Here, we can finally begin to consider different ideas, but now we have a context to put those ideas into. We start first with strategic initiatives, before moving to the day-to-day tactics. For example, in our hypothetical mission from above to increase the gross margins in the Northeast Region, the action plan might include the following strategic initiatives:

- Address all customers with average gross profit currently less than 30 percent.

- Adjust product mix of top 60 customers in the region.

- Create tiered pricing strategy.

- Identify opportunities to add value at no additional fee that justifies a price increase.

- Identify most effective salespeople and analyze their territories.

Now, it's quite simple to assign each of these five strategic initiatives to one or more working groups, and those groups can develop the tactics to complete each initiative. Each step in the plan should be specific, actionable, and measurable, including the person who is responsible for the action and when that action will be completed.

If these don't exist, your plan is near worthless since you cannot hold someone accountable to generic, vague instructions.

Building out a plan in this fashion creates focus and clarity for the people responsible for execution. It is helpful to think of a plan as a very specific set of expectations, and you know exactly how to create expectations: a clearly defined result, a specific time frame, and an understanding of the *why* behind the plan.

This is how the Counter Mentor Leader plans: looking at where we are today, identifying where we are going, and determining how we will get there.

Now, to ensure the plan is well executed, the Counter Mentor Leader reviews progress and performance in real time.

Real-Time Performance Review

Creating a plan to effectively execute is critical, but this step drastically *decreases* in value if you don't review progress against the plan. However, it's not just the performance that needs to be reviewed; it's the individual responsible for that performance. You probably keep an eye on the mission to make sure it's accomplished, but do you review the individual as well?

Perhaps you do. Once a year, in the annual performance review. *Please.* Stop.

To be incredibly blunt, let us state unequivocally that the annual performance review—as it is typically practiced—is completely ineffective. In fact, it's almost completely dead.

For example, Accenture—a company of over 300,000 employees—almost completely eliminated the annual performance review process. Here's why:

[Management research firm] CEB found that 95 percent of managers are dissatisfied with the way their companies conduct performance reviews, and nearly 90 percent of HR leaders say the process doesn't even yield accurate information.[3]

Ninety-five percent?! Actually, we're surprised the numbers aren't higher! We can't find a single company that loves the annual performance review process. We can't find anyone who even likes it a little bit. Managers hate it. Employees hate it. And your bottom line REALLY hates it, which is more of why Accenture dumped the process:

The average manager spends more than 200 hours a year on activities related to performance reviews—things like sitting in training sessions, filling out forms and delivering evaluations to employees. When you add up those hours, plus the cost of the performance-management technology itself, CEB estimates that a company of about 10,000 employees spends roughly $35 million a year to conduct reviews.[4]

We know the process is completely broken. It's outdated, expensive, time-consuming, and worthless, yet we keep doing it. It is the perfect case study for the inertia of "that's the way we've always done it."

To recap: Annual performance reviews are a complete waste of time. Stop doing them. Join Microsoft, Adobe, Accenture, Deloitte, and Gap and make this ridiculous, ineffective, time-wasting, morale-killing process a thing of the past.

Instead, use the Counter Mentor 1-on-1 Meeting (CMM) to manage performance *in real time*. As we discussed in chapter 18, the CMM is the perfect opportunity to consistently review performance with each of your direct reports. It provides an avenue for coaching, development, recognition, and accountability (items we will discuss in greater detail in the next section).

Plus, as you will soon discover, consistent performance reviews will help you create the *nirvana* you rarely even allow yourself to dream of—a culture of accountability. Accountability cannot and *will not* exist without consistent, timely review. And, of course, review is nearly impossible if expectations and standards have not been clearly communicated.

COUNTER Is the Way Forward

We have been conditioned, both implicitly and explicitly, with the "fact" that a manager works in the corner office, issue orders (especially to the new, junior associates), allows a select few into the inner circle for guidance and advice, and pushes decisions down from the top. This type of "leader" doesn't seek the opinion of the KIDS, doesn't set aside time to be connected to his or her people, and rarely, if ever, has a strategic plan for attracting, developing, and retaining world-class talent.

Now you know that can change.

The COUNTER methodology is not a means of "managing *those* Millennials." It is a dynamic leadership methodology that works in the real world and consistently creates high-performance teams—even in the chaotic, four-generation workplace with all of its challenges.

Take the next step in your leadership journey—the step that is COUNTER to what you've been taught as a leader. This revolutionary approach will drive you to levels of performance you never thought possible.

Key Points to Remember

1. Execution is about staying on course when things get *real*. Don't let stress send you running back to your old-school, Taylorian Management ways.

2. A plan is a step-by-step process that is designed to achieve a specific outcome. It is a process you can learn, teach, and replicate.

3. The annual performance review is a tired, ineffective way to manage your team's performance and is absolutely dreadful at helping your people grow.

 Check out this related *Counter Mentors* podcast episode: "Annual Performance Reviews Suck!" Visit cmtr.co/ep3.

The Counter Mentor
Leadership Solution

NOW THAT WE'VE OUTLINED THE CHALLENGES that today's leaders face and summarized the Counter Mentor Leadership model, let's jump into the detailed tactics of how to apply our model in the modern workplace.

Chapter 26

Implementing the Counter Mentor Leadership Model

"I've learned that people will forget what you said, people will forget what you did, but people will never forget how you made them feel."[1]

Carl Buehner

O UR FRIEND ANNA was born and raised in a suburban neighborhood between cornfields and Walmarts in middle America.[2] She's an engaging, thoughtful, bright, tenacious, and passionate entrepreneur. She's one of those KIDS whom we love to interact with.

She's also a great leader.

Anna worked hard in high school, earned a full scholarship to Eureka College, and, following graduation, thought she might pursue a career in politics. So she took a big step and threw a Hail Mary in the form of an application to Harvard Law School. Since she was from a "regular, middle-class family," she perceived her odds for acceptance to be very low.

To her surprise, she got in.

That was nine years ago. Since then, all she has done is kick down doors and crush glass ceilings. She started, scaled, and sold a technology company in Boston, and she recently started on her next big idea.

When Anna was at Harvard Law, she entered on the politics track but quickly jumped on the big-law-firm train when the "reality of politics" set in. However, after a summer interning with one of the very big, very prestigious legal firms, she came to the realization she didn't like practicing corporate law either.

"Not even a little," Anna told us one Thursday afternoon via FaceTime. (That's what the KIDS do these days; they *leverage* technology!) "Actually, I kind of hated it." Though she didn't realize it at the time, this minor freak-out propelled her career to the next level.

During exams in her final year of law school, Anna and one of her classmates, Christine, were both wrestling with extreme levels of anxiety, trying to find an answer to the question, "What will we do next?" Those conversations sparked an idea—they wanted to change the way people donated their used luxury clothes and accessories.

"We saw an opportunity to use fashion as a force for good, all while disrupting a tired, outdated industry," Anna told us. "It was the perfect combination of what I'm passionate about—philanthropy, technology, and fashion."

With no seed money and a ton of enthusiasm, Anna and Christine began to develop what later became known as Fashion Project. Their goal was to leverage technology to maximize the value of used clothing and tap into people's desire to make the world a better place—all serving their ultimate vision of maximizing their positive impact on the world. In less than four years, they grew the organization to more than sixty-five employees and donated almost $1 million to charity.

Anna sounds like a proud parent as she describes the early days of the company:

> We were a family. We loved coming to work. We all worked harder than we ever had in our lives but also had more fun than we ever thought possible because we knew our mission mattered. We had our weekly team meeting over "family lunch" every Wednesday afternoon, with as much laughing as strategizing. We were chasing game-changing partnerships with major retailers, but still took the time to innovate and appreciate each other.

They landed the partnerships. It was the game-changer they expected.

Following the announcement of the North American partnerships, Anna almost immediately raised an additional $2 million in capital. "We went from being a blip on the radar to being *the* name in the fashion donation game, almost overnight," she told us.

Anna quickly discovered that, to ramp up operations and fulfill the new, exponential increase in demand, she would need to scale the business very quickly. She successfully took the company through their Series A round of funding, and raised another $7.2 million.

> And then the real problems started . . . As part of our Series A process, we created a formal Board of Directors and took on a number of new investors. We had people telling us it was time to act like a *real* company and that we needed *real* executives. So, we listened. We got some tenured, high-level talent.

What happened? Anna hired a BOSS.

Even though the company was experiencing success and explosive growth, she started to feel the tides changing. She didn't look like a retail CEO. She was just a twenty-something in designer jeans and heels, not a fifty-something in a suit. Her interactions with the *real* executives quickly became condescending ("Sweetie"), with offhand comments about her age.

"My perspective and insights were being discounted," Anna said, frustrated. "I was being told I didn't understand things about the company I built, and the industry I spent the last three years intimately learning—an industry I was disrupting."

Anna summed up the "classic, old-school" approach in a conflict that changed the trajectory of the company:

> I wrote an email warning the Board of Directors of what was coming [in the industry] and that we needed to take action now. I knew that we needed to raise more money much earlier than we thought, or we needed to sell. The response from the most outspoken board member was a more colorful version of "You are being emotional. We just need to stay the course and continue to grow."
>
> Everything about my note was fact-based and an analysis on what was going on in the market. It was actually a pretty dull read. The irony is, his response was extremely emotional.
>
> Looking back, that was a turning point. We didn't make the changes necessary, and what I predicted happened. The industry changed, and we needed to do something. By the time we did—we were already too late.

Next up: One of the members of the Board of Directors tried to fire her.

Anna remembers: "While discussing the future of the company and our options moving forward, he basically told me, 'We need a more traditional CEO,' and he suggested I be fired."

Thankfully, the other board members quickly squashed the idea, but the massive distraction—fighting to keep the company she built—consumed Anna for weeks.

Ultimately, the market turned. Their primary competitor sold, and three smaller competitors went out of business. Anna stayed on to lead the company through its hardest challenge—a sale. They were backed into a corner and could not get the funding they needed to stay ahead of the curve.

Unfortunately, Fashion Project didn't reach the level of performance it was capable of achieving, mostly—it seems—due to the inability of a few key board members to leave behind an old-school mind-set and management style. Anna was underestimated and undermined by the BOSS, simply because she was one of the KIDS.

Here are three important lessons from her story that you need to consider as you implement Counter Mentor Leadership:

1. **Don't judge a book by its cover.** Finally, a metaphor that the BOSS will understand. (Don't ever accuse us of being preferential to the KIDS.) This is the #1 thing you have to work to overcome! You've been programmed for so long to be a certain kind of leader and to perceive your role in a specific way, and you often find yourself unwilling to listen to someone who doesn't fit in that box.

   It's time to throw that habit away completely. You should form opinions of individuals based on how they perform, not what they look like. Most of the KIDS will, even if they don't like it, respect you for basing your opinions on their performance instead of the mythology created by a bunch of talking heads.

2. **Ask questions and listen.** You have incredibly talented people working for you. Yes, some of them are junior to you, and some might even be—*gasp*—KIDS. They have so much more to offer than you think. They have a different point of view, different experiences, different knowledge, and different ways of problem solving. They don't have the same *sacred cows* and unwritten rules. When you ask them questions and *actually* listen—this has the potential to be revolutionary. You are likely to hear new and awesome ideas, and you will see the KIDS' commitment reach a level you never thought possible.

3. **Think differently.** As you begin embracing new ways of acting, you must employ new ways of thinking. As we've detailed, there are new challenges that necessitate new ideas and new methods. You cannot use old methods to solve *new* problems.

Stop relying on your past experiences to solve your future problems. Engage the KIDS, truly assess the problem, and leverage the *right* approach.

How to Access the Power of the KIDS

The Counter Mentor Leadership model is unique in many ways, but one of the key components is the intentional, rapid development of the younger employees—the KIDS. This includes the process of reverse mentoring—pairing a senior manager with a younger, high-potential employee and creating an environment where they learn from each other.

Reverse mentoring is a term that was first popularized by General Electric CEO Jack Welch. Way back in 1999 (before Millennials invaded the workplace), Welch required five hundred of his executives to pair up with the brightest and youngest in the organization in order to learn about the latest fad at the time—the Internet.[3]

More recently, Gerald Hassell, the CEO of BNY Mellon, a $44 billion Fortune 200 company, implemented a reverse mentoring program at the bank.[4] Hassell asked a then-twenty-eight-year-old junior employee, Darah Kirstein, to help him understand issues from the KIDS' perspective.

Though somewhat uncommon, the idea of "reverse" mentoring is picking up steam. The reason is simple: the KIDS are the largest group of employees in the workplace, the average BOSS doesn't do technology well at all, and "the way we've always done it" doesn't work anymore.

However, in the same way that mentoring rarely happens by accident, reverse mentoring needs to be planned and intentional in order to maximize the gains in the long term. That relationship between older leaders and younger, high-potential employees can be extraordinarily powerful if leveraged properly.

Reverse mentoring serves at least three distinct purposes:

1. **Promote learning for the leader.** The process helps older leaders develop an awareness and understanding of new technology, new ways of learning, and new ways of thinking. This learning keeps the BOSS connected to the younger generation—their attitudes, perspectives, and opinions. More importantly, it fosters a "we" mentality that is much different from the traditional "us vs. them" workplace.

2. **Improve engagement.** The willingness to learn and accept input from the KIDS is a significant factor in creating trust and engagement. As we've clearly shown, more-engaged employees do better work, reduce costly employee turnover, and increase productivity.

3. **Create a competitive advantage.** Technology doesn't typically create a competitive advantage, but the successful *application* of that technology certainly might. Whole industries have been very slow to adopt social selling, marketing automation, digital engagement tools, and a host of other technology applications that can improve everything from communication to customer service, while dramatically impacting workplace efficiency and performance. Learning more about these new, innovative ideas can be a result of a healthy, consistent reverse-mentoring relationship.

It's critical to remember that reverse mentoring is a complete shift for everyone; it is *counter* to the popular, traditional point of view! The BOSS is used to being, well, the boss! The BOSS knows everything. The BOSS gives advice, not the other way around. If, all of a sudden, the BOSS is asking one of the KIDS for insight or perspective or, dare we say, *wisdom*, won't that be seen as a weakness?

Of course it will . . . NOT.

How ridiculous! The fact is, when the BOSS is not up to speed, and is unwilling to admit *that*, then she looks weak.

Becoming a Counter Mentor Leader is an exercise in humility. As the leader, you have a unique opportunity to proactively learn and grow from the KIDS, while maintaining relevance in an ever-changing world. Reverse mentoring gives you that opportunity, *if* you can just get out of your own way! #emotionalintelligence

The idea of reverse mentoring will be *incredibly* uncomfortable at first—probably for both of you. However, if you expect this relationship to be a win, BOSS, you must lead by example! You've got to make the KIDS feel something they may not have felt in the workplace before: personal value, and the opportunity to be fulfilled by contributing to something that matters.

Key Points to Remember

1. If you want to transform into a Counter Mentor Leader, you must stop applying extreme generalizations to entire groups of people. Instead, ask questions and *really* listen, and change your thinking from "We've always done it this way" to "How can we be better in today's environment?"

2. As a Counter Mentor Leader, you have a unique opportunity to proactively grow and learn from the KIDS, and maintain relevance in an ever-changing world.

3. Reverse mentoring is a powerful tool to help *you* grow while simultaneously developing younger, high-potential employees.

 Check out this related *Counter Mentors* podcast episode: "Reverse Mentoring: How About I Mentor You, Boss?!" Visit cmtr.co/ep14.

Chapter 27

If You Want Employees to Act Like Owners,

Quit Treating Them Like Renters

"When it comes to performance standards, it's not what you preach, it's what you tolerate."[1]

Jocko Willink and Leif Babin

WOULDN'T YOU LOVE to have your employees take ownership of their work? To be accountable?

If you want to get a lively conversation started, this one will do it. It is one of the most common topics we discuss in our work: employees and accountability.

The questions sound like this:

- "How do I get people to stop leaving at 4:58 P.M. and stay until the job is actually done?"
- "Why in the world can't people do things the right way?"
- "I told him what he did wrong, and he turned around and did almost the same thing again. How many times do I have to tell people?!"

Call it *ownership* or call it *accountability*—it generally means the same thing. It's when a person is *willing* to do whatever needs to be done—without being told every last detail—and is doing the job completely, all the way down to that very last detail.

Nathan Regier is the author of *Conflict without Casualties: A Field Guide for Leading with Compassionate Accountability* and a former guest on the *Counter Mentor* podcast. We asked him to join us on the show to discuss (among other things) the conflict created when accountability doesn't happen in the workplace. The question was, "How do we teach the KIDS to accept accountability and truly *own* their work?" Here is part of his reply.

> One of the big questions is, "Are we going to get out of the way of Millennials' consequences so they can actually experience responsibility, or are we going to keep trying to fix things for them, and micromanage them?"
>
> It's a really difficult, fine line. If we're going to let Millennials experience life and have consequences and learn to be responsible, they also need to be taught good skills on how to do that.[2]

Okay, we're not going to use the big paintbrush here, but the challenge Nathan describes is so common that leaders have to be aware of it. They don't own the patent on the problem, but there are plenty of KIDS who've never really been held accountable! On the other hand, there are some people in the workplace who simply *choose* not to be accountable (they shouldn't stay on your team long), but the problem with accountability goes a bit deeper than motivation—sometimes people simply don't have any experience "owning" their work. Whether it was helicopter parents (nice job, BOSS) who micromanaged their failures, or a succession of teachers who didn't correct mistakes for fear of doing injury to Johnny's or Jane's self-esteem, some people have not been introduced to the idea of being accountable for results.

We only bring this to your attention so you'll see another perspective of the problem. But that's not the real problem. The *real* problem is twofold:

1. The BOSS doesn't know how to create a culture of accountability; instead, he just expects everyone to "be accountable." It's a cute idea, but it lies somewhere between Neverland and Narnia.

2. When employees have performance issues, the BOSS doesn't truly address the issue. (More on that in the next few chapters.)

In both cases, the real problem is not the KIDS; it's the leader. Once you learn how to create a culture of accountability and you learn how to effectively deal with performance issues, you'll completely forget that some people come into the workplace without any experience with job "ownership."

What Is Accountability?

In some ways, the concept of accountability is one of the most misunderstood and poorly executed concepts in leadership. We know because we ask.

Ask managers what accountability means, and most will tell you it's doing your work the right way, the first time, the way they would do it, without being constantly reminded it's your job.

However, ask employees what accountability means, and the standard answer has something to do with who gets blamed when things don't go well. In fact, to most employees, being "accountable" means getting grilled, criticized, and/or publicly flogged, which is sort of the opposite of getting a trophy, so the KIDS are not big fans.

You'll never transform your culture into one of ownership until you understand that accountability is NOT the process of finding out who to blame for a mistake. Yes, it implies that employees should be willing to answer for their performance, but it does not automatically imply someone should get "blamed" or be publicly humiliated for a mistake.

That's called *workplace bullying*. Google it. It's a HUGE freaking problem in the workplace, created in large part by micromanaging tyrants who don't have a clue about leadership. According to the *Workplace Bullying Institute*, the BOSS is still the doing the majority of the bullying, and yet "72% of employers deny, discount, encourage, rationalize, or defend it."[3] #rant

That's just *bad* leadership. There's absolutely no excuse for that behavior in the workplace. Ever.

What accountability actually means is that an individual *willingly* accepts the responsibility to produce a certain result, is *willing* to own the responsibility for doing it the right way, AND is correcting any missteps along the way. The key is personal motivation. A person who is personally *motivated* to produce the right results will take ownership of the work and will be more than willing to answer for those results.

By now, you see the value of the Counter Mentor Leadership process in creating a culture of ownership. Every step in the process is designed to discover that personal motivation and to help an employee transform that motivation into killer performance. It helps you create owners! Because the first step in creating accountability— if you really want employees who enthusiastically take *ownership* of their work—is to start treating them like owners, not *renters*.

The difference between an owner and a renter is that owners have skin in the game.

They "own" part of the overall result, not just the blame for any mistakes that happen. With only a few exceptions, owners typically take better care of a home than renters would simply because they stand to lose personally if they don't, and they stand to gain personally if they take care of the home. And, icing on the cake, there is the pride of ownership. We've noticed that people tend to take better care of things they have paid for on their own.

Renters? Renters simply blame someone else, call someone to fix the problem, or cover up the problem with the quickest and easiest possible solution, even if that "fix" results in more work or more problems down the line. Because, frankly, who cares?

In the workplace, when your people "own" a project, they believe they have a stake in the outcome, so they inject their blood, sweat, and tears into the process. They take pride in what they produce. They take more care, pay more attention to detail, and work harder to get the right result—because they own it.

We define *accountability* as the process of "taking a personal interest in—owning—the results," as opposed to making excuses for mistakes and looking for something or someone to blame. The key is that **accountability is an attitude**, one that is modeled, cultivated, and instilled in others by a good leader.

Please! For crying out loud! Highlight this sentence: Accountability is NOT something you announce in a meeting. Like this: "I'm tired of this nonsense. As of today, you are going to start being accountable!"

Good luck with that.

Go ahead and tell HR to start processing new job applications.

How to Build Ownership into Your Culture

Building accountability into your culture is a process. It's not luck, and it's not some kind of magic potion. It's a process that is implemented by leadership. It requires the BOSS to put forth some effort instead of complaining all the time about employees not taking ownership.

There are four basic steps in the accountability process. Let's take a quick look at each step.

Step 1: Develop a "Freedom Box" for Each Employee

We've been teaching this for quite a while, but we never had a cool name for it until we met Jim Keenan (actually, it's just Keenan—nobody calls him Jim). He dropped this term on us in one of our interviews, and we loved it. So, we got his permission to . . . umm . . . steal it.

Keenan is the author of an insightful book entitled *Not Taught: What It Takes to Be Successful in the 21st Century that Nobody's Teaching You*.[4] He's a smart guy. Although he's from the forgotten generation (Gen X), he channels his inner Millennial—a lot. The KIDS would call him an OG.

 "You know Pops had to ask what OG means."

 "I swear you make this up as you go."

Here is Keenan's take on what the *Freedom Box* can accomplish:

In the sales world where I work, you can't win if everyone is doing the exact same thing. People are different. Everyone has their strengths and weaknesses, and companies need to capitalize on the unique strengths and skills of their teams. The *Freedom Box* is designed to do this. It's all about giving people the freedom to execute their way—the way that works best for them—while at the same time protecting the integrity of the organization.

Too many organizations try to be successful by making everyone the same, getting everyone to work exactly the same way. In sales, it's making the same amount of calls, using the same tools, setting the same amount of appointments, etc. The problem with this is, it doesn't capitalize on the unique strengths of each member of the team. The basics are the same, but people excel at different things and in different ways. In sales, you want—no you need—each member of your sales team leveraging their skills the best way possible.

For a leader, the *Freedom Box* is designed to do just that. It lets people OWN their job and their success. It allows them to feel as if they are making a difference and not just a cog in some machine. That's exactly what we need more of—people owning their jobs and taking pride in their results.[5]

Freedom with *ownership*? Isn't that EXACTLY what you want? Creating the *Freedom Box* is about setting a perimeter within which any employee can freely roam. Setting those boundaries makes it clear what is expected and what is acceptable in terms of getting things done. The "size" of the box is proportional to the employee's individual capability AND their willingness to take ownership of results.

Remember, one of the key drivers of motivation is a sense of autonomy. The KIDS crave it! And the best way to drive a sense of autonomy is to define a *Freedom Box* for each employee. Creating that box for each employee will force you to think critically about your team and the level of autonomy you want to give to each individual. By definition, the box will be a bit different for everyone. Some of your people are crazy-capable and deserve a lot of room to run; others are new or less experienced, so their box will be a bit smaller.

With everyone, however, the objective is to make that box as big as possible!

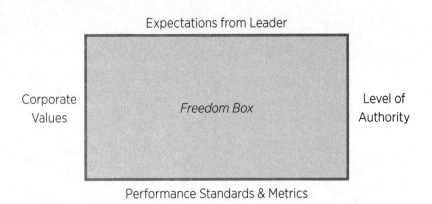

Here are the four primary boundaries of the *Freedom Box*:

- **Company values and/or guiding principles.** The values that define your organization are critically important. Don't have company values? Don't use the ones you *do* have? Then you clearly don't have a boundary on the box, and it's going to be much more difficult to manage performance issues.

- **Expectations.** As we discussed previously, the importance of setting clear expectations cannot go understated. Great leaders begin setting expectations during the interview process, continue through the onboarding process, and anchor back to these expectations in each of their Counter Mentor 1-on-1 Meetings (CMM).

  We are strong advocates of putting pen to paper and writing these down. It not only provides an increased level of clarity for your employees, it also allows you to understand, and think through, exactly what your expectations are. If your people don't understand exactly what is expected of them, it's going to create a real challenge when you need to address performance issues.

- **Level of authority.** Different employees typically have different levels of authority. Someone who has been with you for a decade and consistently exceeds expectations is going to have a higher level of authority than someone who just joined the team. This isn't due to favoritism or bias; it's simply due to performance history and the level of trust that is present.

  To keep this simple we like to teach four levels of authority:

  Level 1: Check with me before you do anything. This is for rookies, new employees, or someone without any experience in a particular project. You want to begin training this person to jump to the next level as quickly as possible.

  Level 2: Make the decision, but check with me prior to implementation. The idea here is to create a backstop for employees and let them practice what they learn. After they call it right a couple of times, you can probably elevate them to the next level.

  Level 3: Make and implement the decision, but keep me in the loop. The employees have the autonomy to make their own decisions within their domain, within the organization. Whether employees are working vertically or horizontally, they are free to engage as long as they stay within the four walls of the company. The second that they step outside the company, discussing terms with customers or opportunities with vendors, they must engage with you, the leader.

  Level 4: The buck stops with you. This is like being the CEO! These employees have complete autonomy. This is a rare level of trust because it implies that the employees have complete control to make any decision necessary within their domain—inside or outside the organization. Frankly, if you have an employee at this level, your work life is amazing! It also means you've probably got someone who is well-prepared to get a promotion.

Of course, you can define levels in different ways that make sense for your specific situation, but the point is to ensure that all employees understand the individual level to which they can make their own decisions.

- **Performance standards and metrics.** It's interesting how often employees don't know, specifically, how their work is measured. We like to ask employees this question: "How do you know that you are doing a good job?" They should be able to answer this question by telling us what is measured AND how they access that information.

  Beyond the key metrics, however, we want each employee to clearly understand what success looks like. So, measurement is not just a set of numbers; it is also a compelling narrative that helps your employees understand what's possible *when* they achieve those numbers!

Step 2: Clearly Define the Desired Result

Once the boundaries of the *Freedom Box* are in place, employees only need to know what the desired performance result looks like. Your expectations are clear and the employee knows what metrics are used to measure success; now it's time to define the finish line.

For example, a salesperson may be measured on revenue and gross profit, but what are the specific objectives? (An example might be $2 million in sales revenue at an average gross profit of 38 percent.) In addition, you might include specifics for new customers added, or sales in specific product categories, or penetration of specific markets. This critical step in the accountability process allows you to "zoom out" with your employees—connecting the individual's performance to the big picture while driving home a compelling sense of purpose.

The same process works for specific projects or new assignments; you need to specifically define what the results should be.

Step 3: Review Consistently

If you don't know how you could possibly review performance consistently, we would direct you back to chapters 18 and 19. It's called the Counter Mentor 1-on-1 Meeting (CMM).

 "The BOSS can be forgetful."

 "The KIDS have that effect on us."

Step 4: Address Performance Issues in Real Time

If you've done the first three steps properly, this step—the lynchpin in creating a culture of ownership—isn't scary or emotional or keep-you-awake-at-night stressful. This step is simply about having a conversation with an employee when you observe the *pattern of behavior* that is not in alignment with your expectations. Said differently, this happens when an employee isn't performing as expected or has (often unintentionally) stepped outside of the *Freedom Box*.

We'll outline how to do this in great detail in chapter 30, but you should know from the outset that addressing performance issues is not about emotion. You don't yell, scream, curse, or otherwise bully or intimidate your people. There is no passive-aggressive behavior or use of manipulation to get what you want. Instead, you will assume positive intent with your people and treat them like adults. If they choose not to act like adults or they cannot meet your expectations for performance, you will find it MUCH easier to act if you have done the first three steps well.

You Can Treat the KIDS Like Owners—Even in Politics

In a world of obnoxious twenty-four-hour news, 140-character hot-takes, political drama, and uncomfortably funny political satire, many people now form their opinions based on #fakenews, SNL skits, and *House of Cards* scenes.

No one *really* believes there is leadership in politics. This is exactly what makes Lizzy Guyton's experience so newsworthy:[6]

"I had zero interest in politics growing up. Frankly, I didn't have a political bone in my body," she told us on a sunny spring day in Boston. "Even in college, I was enjoying campus life and studying abroad—not participating in student government or debate club."

Graduating from a small liberal arts school in upstate New York, Lizzy was unsure what to do with her degree in English. She explained,

> When I graduated, I knew I didn't want to teach and didn't want to grind through another degree. I was kind of freaked out. After a lot of networking, someone struck a chord with me by suggesting I get into the communication side of politics. He hooked me with descriptors like "fast-paced," "lots of respon-sibilities," and "exposure." I was trying to find my passion and knew the worst outcome was I wouldn't like it.

She liked it. And she crushed it.

Her career started as a volunteer staffer in a senate campaign in 2010. She did "pretty much everything" and quickly found herself drawn to the communications side of the campaign. Her candidate won, and Lizzy joined the staff in D.C. as an assistant. In the next eighteen months, she was given more and more responsibility, and her career began to blossom.

After her stint as a staff assistant, she jumped at the opportunity to be the communications director on a congressional campaign in Indiana. Leaving the streets of the nation's capital, Lizzy moved to Mishawaka, Indiana, to support a strong female candidate. After a dogfight of a campaign, her candidate won and offered Lizzy the opportunity to return to D.C. as her communications director—at the ripe old age of twenty-six.

> When you join a campaign, it's a huge risk. You sacrifice every-thing, leave what you know and are comfortable with, to eat, breathe, and sleep the job. [The candidate] understood this and was incredibly gracious. She trusted our insights, and lis-tened. Looking back, it was an amazing thing to be a part of.

After acting as the communications director during Scott Brown's hard-fought yet unsuccessful senate run in New Hampshire, Lizzy jumped at the opportunity to join the staff of newly elected Massachusetts Governor Charlie Baker as his press secretary.

> I never thought I would be able to work at home [in Boston], for a Republican, in the press. I felt like the stars aligned. I underestimated making the jump from federal to state [gov-ernment], but, once again, it is trial by fire, and you're forced to learn the ropes.

Just over a year into her role serving the Commonwealth, Lizzy was promoted to Communications Director, responsible for lead-ing the Governor's communications team at just twenty-eight years young. #swag

We were really curious to ask Lizzy about the leaders she worked for. Politics is seemingly cutthroat and has a polarizing culture filled with tyrannical and ego-driven leaders. What were the things that made her leaders so effective and so gratifying to work for? Here is what she told us:

- **They were great listeners.** "Listening was paramount. Especially as a junior member of the staff, it was energizing to have a candidate or elected official who would take advice from someone half their age. But by simply listening—even if they didn't do what I suggested or they disagreed with what I thought—it made me feel valued."

- **They were intentional about building a relationship.** "Working in communications, I've learned it must be personal in order to be effective. To that end, my leaders had to give me the opportunity to get to know them in order to be prepared for me to write from their point of view, in their voice. This lends itself to building a relationship. The stronger the relationship, the better job I can do. Clearly, the better job I can do, the more successful my leader is."

- **They were serious about accountability.** "Campaigns are demanding. Holding office is all-consuming, and representing the interests of people bears an immense burden of responsibility. I was very impressed at how each one of my leaders held everyone accountable. There was one standard that everyone was held accountable to. This makes a difference. It's motivating to know that everyone has a shot to prove themselves and excel. There were no limits to how quickly you could succeed as an individual and as a team."

- **They trusted her, with their words and their actions.** "I don't think people, especially Baby Boomers, understand how motivating it is to be extended trust. When they put their trust in me—to be their voice, their eyes and ears, to give advice—it motivated me to want to be the best I could for them. That trust was critical, and I never would've been successful without my leaders trusting me."

BOSS, if you want to create a culture of accountability, there is your roadmap. Lizzy knew the boundaries of her *Freedom Box*, she knew exactly what the desired result looked like, and her performance was consistently reviewed.

But what about the KIDS? What can they learn from Lizzy's experiences? Clearly, she did a number of things to put herself in a position to excel, to be trusted in elevated roles at a young age. So we asked what advice she would give to others who want to progress quickly.

- **Be as invested as the boss.** "Trust is a two-way street. My leaders would never have trusted me if I didn't show them every moment of every day that I was as invested in the campaign, or the office, as they were—that I would work as hard and run as fast as they would. It wasn't lip service. I proved it; I didn't just say it."

- **Be prepared for what your boss needs.** "This is one of the biggest pieces of advice I give to interns or young people. Understand your business and your role completely. Think one step ahead so that you can be prepared for what your boss is going to ask and what information they're going to need before he or she even knows they need it. It not only shows your investment in them and the job, it shows that you're beginning to think like a leader. This is what will propel you to the next level."

- **Be confident, but be humble.** "[The Governor] once came down to a communications intern lunch, and I asked him to give them one piece of advice. His advice was simple: Don't lie. Yes, it's simple, but it is profound in this business. Saying, 'I don't know,' is a much better answer than setting yourself up for failure by making something up. The combination of humility and preparation are the answer. Be prepared and confident in your preparation. However, if you don't know, you don't know. Don't make it worse by making it up. We all have room to improve and, especially with a sleepless news cycle, there is always something new to learn."

Lizzy's experience can be the same experience for your people. Yes, she was a great hire. (BOSS, you're wondering where to get people like Lizzy. They're probably sitting in your office right now, bored.) However, it's unlikely she would've succeeded as she did if she had been working for one old-school BOSS after another—leaders who couldn't care less about the welfare of their employees. As Lizzy notes, it was strong leadership that allowed her to succeed:

> I've never felt the deck was stacked against me, either because I am young or female. I believe that I've had opportunities to excel because I have been inspired by strong leaders who have pushed me to be smarter, faster, and more motivated with each passing day.
>
> You have to perform at 100 percent in politics; that is a given. But some of the best motivation comes from the incredible determination and work ethic you are surrounded by in your leaders and your colleagues. It's an explosive environment that can often lead to strong results and progress. I was shown how to be fearless.
>
> That's my biggest piece of advice I give to anyone starting their career: find something that drives you and work as hard as you can. Stay humble, but don't be afraid to take a risk and speak up. That's how you are going to get where you want to go. It's not given; it's earned. I've been fortunate enough to have leaders that gave me the opportunity to own it.

Do you want your people to take ownership?
Treat them like owners.

Key Points to Remember

1. Accountability is not the process of assigning blame; it is the process of taking a personal interest in owning the results.

2. Accountability is an attitude, one that is modeled, cultivated, and instilled in others by a great leader.

3. Creating a culture of accountability is a process—one that cannot be done overnight. The key steps are:

   • Build the *Freedom Box*.

   • Clearly define the desired result.

   • Review performance consistently.

   • Address performance issues in real time.

 Check out this related *Counter Mentors* video podcast episode: "How Do You Conflict?!" Visit cmtr.co/ep23.

Chapter 28

The Problem with Problem Employees

"Don't fight the problem, decide it."[1]

George C. Marshall

W E'VE TALKED AROUND IT, but now it's time to speak to it directly—how do you deal with performance issues?

This leadership responsibility is easily the single most destructive leadership failure in the workplace: the unwillingness of managers, at every level, to deal with performance issues—poor performance, nonperformance, missed commitments, or attitude problems.

This is a HUGE problem, because problem employees typically remain problems. Sometimes for long periods of time. When we ask about performance issues—and we ask quite often—managers always admit they currently have underperforming employees (sometimes several), but that's not the real issue because *every* company has underperforming employees.

The challenge is that managers routinely admit they are doing little or nothing to address the issue!

Dave Brock is CEO at Partners in Excellence, and he is recognized as one of the best business coaches in the world. He is often forced to address this particular issue with his own clients, and the problem, he says, is that managers often just ignore poor performance:

> Somehow, we tend to ignore the poor performers—and that's a bigger problem than the poor performers themselves. We don't like dealing with them—they drain us; the discussion focuses on problems, not opportunities. There is conflict, potential for confrontation, which too many tend to avoid.
>
> When we do choose to address poor performance, it gets really complicated. If we intend to fire them, then we have to get HR involved, we have to go through all the stuff they make us go through—90-day plans, measured miles, and so forth.
>
> Too often, we just ignore them. Perhaps we wait for the next layoffs, taking care of problem performers by laying them off rather than all the hassle of terminating them.
>
> Or we just ignore them—out of sight, out of mind.[2]

Great business strategy, right? Ignore it—maybe it will go away.

The reasons managers give for their inaction are consistent and predictable:

- "I don't have time."
- "We're way too busy right now."
- "No, he's not great, but at least I know what I'm getting. Who knows how the next person will be?"
- "I don't know that I've done everything I can do to help her be successful."
- "If I lose him, I'll have to do his job AND my job until we get a replacement."

Let us translate into English we can all understand:

- "My priorities are out of whack."
- "I'm not a fan of conflict."
- "I don't like change."
- "I am currently overwhelmed and can't deal with it."
- "I really don't know how to handle this!"

The challenge is, when employees underperform and are allowed to remain on the job, it becomes an accepted part of your workplace culture. It permeates into the fabric of the company like cigarette smoke in a cheap hotel room.

And the worst part is, it puts a serious damper on employee engagement.

Do you know what that means? It means you lose TWICE. Once due to the performance loss from the underperforming employee and a second time when other employees' performance declines due to disengagement.

Two-for-one mistake, with double the penalty. Congratulations!

Let's be brutally clear: Employees will, over time, always settle on the lowest common denominator of performance. The level is set exclusively by you, the leader.

"I Am the Problem?"

Not long ago, Pops worked with a CEO who consistently had serious issues with one of his vice presidents. We'll let the Pops share the story from his perspective.

Is the Leader the Problem?

This client actually had more than one problem employee, but there was one particular director who was a really serious issue. The client told me he had asked the director to implement a new procedure inside his department, but the director never made it happen.

Oh, there was always an excuse. "We're working on it" was a consistent stall tactic. Another common answer was "We don't have time." My favorite was (seriously) "The employees don't like this new policy."

At first, like most managers, the CEO gave the director a pass after getting assurances that it would be done right away. However, after a couple of confrontations, the CEO had enough. He got angry. Then, he graduated to abusive language, often in front of other employees. Which means his failure to address the problem properly created a whole rash of other problems—inevitable collateral damage that is created when performance issues are not addressed.

At the time the client told me the story, this director was an ongoing problem, and the problem was getting worse.

After the client finished his story, he asked me what could be done to solve the problem. So, I walked him through a process of dealing with a "problem employee," a process that concluded with a frank discussion about the need to have consequences for nonperformance.

In response, he asked me an important question: "What happens if he doesn't do what I ask him to do?"

Good question.

Simple answer: "You let him go."

"I can't do that!" he blurted out. He just about came out of his chair. "You don't understand. This guy has very specialized knowledge. Guys like him don't just grow on trees! I can't run out and just find another person with his experience!"

After a short but dramatic pause, I responded, "So, he's holding you hostage."

He stopped and looked at me. I'm sure he thought I was criticizing his ability, suggesting that he had lost control, or something equally negative.

"Absolutely not," he replied. "He is NOT holding me hostage. It's just a big problem to find someone to replace him."

"You can't have it both ways," I told him. "Either there are consequences to his actions, or he is holding you hostage. If there are NO consequences to nonperformance, why would anyone do what you ask? Besides, if you don't follow through and create a culture where people do what their jobs require, then the employees are no longer the problem—YOU are the problem. Your corporate culture is determined by the actions and behaviors that are commonly accepted in the workplace, so your acceptance of nonperformance becomes a part of your corporate culture."

Now, for sure I had insulted him.

"Me?" he asked. "I am the problem? You must be kidding. He doesn't do his job, and I AM THE PROBLEM!?"

Now he was catching on. At least that's the way I chose to take it.

Although this "problem employee" continued to create significant challenges for the CEO, he was never sufficiently motivated to address it properly. And, not surprisingly, the issue dragged on for quite a while.

Finally, he had enough. He lost it one day, and finally bid the employee bon voyage.

And that's when things got interesting.

Most of the time, when a performance issue is finally addressed—when the boss finally gets enough and decides to do something about it—people flock to the manager's office to ask one simple question: "What took you so long?"

I'm betting you've experienced it. The relief when that guy finally—FINALLY—gets his walking papers is amazing.

Which is no surprise, because everyone in the building knows when people aren't doing their job well. And guess who they blame? Yes, absolutely, they blame the employees, but they also wonder why the BOSS isn't doing her job either, and the BOSS gets equal billing on the blame billboard.

That's right: They know you're not doing your job.

They know you have a responsibility to the entire team, and you're allowing that one person to compromise the team. They know their work is more difficult because you're doing nothing. They know you're making excuses for your inaction *while* you complain about the employee who is making excuses.

Isn't it clear what the real problem was?

Clearly the CEO was the root cause of his own frustration. His inaction, and then his misguided responses, created enormous stress inside the company. His anger often spilled out in front of other employees, making people massively uncomfortable.

The company culture was toxic, and his employees rapidly disengaged. Not shockingly, many of the employees were actively looking for new opportunities.

But, finally, after he dismissed the director, the extent of the damage done to the company became evident. Not only had the issue created significant morale problems; the most damaging of those problems was that the underperforming director had allegedly misappropriated confidential materials.

And then, the litigation started.

Was it the fault of the problem employee? Of course. Right up until the time the CEO became aware of it. After that, by failing to deal with it immediately, the fault transferred back to the CEO.

Yes—The Leader Is the Problem

We'll make it simple: If you have an underperforming team, or if you have individual team members with unaddressed performance issues, it is a *leadership* problem. Before you get sideways and disagree, let's review once again:

- Who hired the employee?
- Who onboarded the employee?

- Who trained the employee?
- Who manages the employee's performance?
- Who leads the employee?

If, in fact, that person is you, then how is nonperformance NOT your problem? You hire them. You train them. You lead them. In addition, you have the ability to deal with the performance issues that exist. How is it NOT your fault?

Granted, there are some managers without the authority to hire or to address performance issues, and, on rare occasions, the manager is not directly responsible for initial training. That lets the manager off the hook in many respects, but not the company.

You only have "problem employees" because you allow it. #realtalk

And when you allow it, it not only has a negative impact on the team and the company's culture, it also compromises you and your leadership credibility.

So, the real problem with chronic underperforming employees is, frankly, you. And the longer you wait, the worse the problem gets.

You have that employee, don't you? You must deal with this employee immediately or you will quickly see everything you worked so hard to build erode—slowly, but surely.

Key Points to Remember

1. When employees underperform and are allowed to remain on the job, it becomes an accepted part of your workplace culture

2. Employees will, over time, settle on the lowest common denominator of performance. The level is set exclusively by you, based on what you accept.

3. When you fail to deal with problem employees, it's no longer their fault; it's your fault.

Chapter 29

Good Coaching and BAD Coaching

> "We try to approach coaching with the idea that I'm going to present myself totally openly and honestly and communicate with everybody."[1]
>
> Steve Kerr

WAY BACK IN HIGH SCHOOL, the Pops was a football player. All five feet nine inches of him.

Yes, that included his afro.

 "Don't ask."

We'll let him tell you the story.

Experience With Good and Bad Coaches

The first two years, sadly, weren't a whole lot of fun. Losing can be that way. I played very little my sophomore year, and we finished the season with only two wins. I became a starter my junior year, which evidently didn't help a whole lot since we improved only slightly to 4–6, despite winning three of the first four games.

 "How about those leather helmets, Pops?"

Those first two seasons, we had the same head coach, a man who had been successful in the past but seemed to have lost interest or simply failed to adapt. Regardless of the reason, the fans thought he needed to move on, so he did, and the search committee found his replacement in a small Oklahoma town called Fairfax. His name was Larry Coker (the same Larry Coker who would later win an NCAA National Championship as head coach of the Miami Hurricanes).

Coker was a different kind of coach.

The previous head coach wasn't someone who connected with the players at all, but that part of the job was exactly what made Coker effective. In the first game of the season, we learned exactly how much difference an effective coach can make.

Unfortunately, we lost the game, starting the season 0–1. There were a few bright spots, but we didn't play particularly well overall, including a couple of costly mistakes by the kid with the afro.

In the two previous years, losing typically meant a lot of yelling, plenty of criticism, and an extra dose of running. Coker, however, approached it a bit differently. Monday—the first day back on the practice field following the Friday night loss—Coker and his staff met with the team in the locker room. It's been a *few* years since that meeting, but here is what I remember him saying.

"Guys, we just didn't play very well. We have a lot to work on, and we need to improve in several areas. But, I can tell you this: we're a good football team, and we are going to win a lot of football games."

And we did. With virtually the same players as the previous year, we peeled off eleven consecutive victories before finally bowing out of the state playoffs in the semifinals.

Taking over a losing team almost always requires a new coach to change the mindset of the players. Losing, as most athletes will tell you, can easily become a habit. The great Vince Lombardi once said, "The difference between a successful person and others is not a lack of strength, not a lack of knowledge, but rather a lack of will."[2] It is how a coach reacts to mistakes, failure, and losing that plays a huge role in the future success of a team.

It is a pivotal moment for most players—and for most employees—when they learn that failure is not a disaster! It's a game-changer when a player learns that failure can be an incredibly valuable tool in helping players (and employees) improve performance.

Make no mistake, Coker and his staff were plenty tough on us. They made us into better players, and they created an intense loyalty that my teammates and I still talk about almost forty years later. They forged a winning team by creating an atmosphere where mistakes became tools to learn and improve, not opportunities to criticize and verbally abuse.

We watched film. We saw the mistakes. We got better.

And along the way, our entire mindset changed completely. This was only possible because Coach Coker understood that coaching and leadership are cut from the same cloth—and it's always about the people.

Learning from Sports: Coaches Matter

It is the world of sports—a world most of us have some sort of connection to—that provides some of the best and most vivid illustrations of what a good leader (or a bad leader) can mean to a team. It also provides a very clear understanding of the role of coaching in leadership. In sports, coaches are not only responsible for leading the team, they are also responsible for improving the skills of individual players and teaching them how to function more effectively as a team.

Sports have played a huge role in both of our lives—both in high school and college. We've been both award-winning players *and* coaches. We have both experienced good coaches and bad coaches and recognize the powerful impact of each on an individual player and the overall performance of a team.

This experience leads us to see the connection to the workplace—to understand that a major aspect of effective workplace leadership is coaching and developing your employees. In fact, we would go a step further: If people work for you and they don't improve as a result of doing so, you are an ineffective leader. #boom

In addition to our own personal experiences in sports, we have studied dozens of great coaches, looking for patterns that predict their success. What we've observed is that successful coaches consistently develop a strong connection with their players. That connection builds trust and creates a window of opportunity to influence the player, which is the very definition of leadership.

In a 2015 *Sports Illustrated* article describing the relationship between Bruce Fraser, a coach on the Golden State Warriors staff, and megastar and NBA phenom Stephen Curry, writer Rob Mahoney describes the importance of the relationship between coach and player:

One of the core misconceptions regarding coaching in the NBA is the all-too-prevalent belief that trust between a player and his coaches comes implicitly. Respect can be demanded. Trust, though, can only be cultivated organically. When they were first matched to work together by Kerr, Curry was already one of the best players in the league and Fraser a newcomer to the organization. That liaison was functional enough to allow for basic drilling. But even for a player as coachable as Curry, willingness to receive instruction is directly linked to confidence and rapport.

"I don't think there's a manual for that," Fraser said. "It's just a feel. It's an intuitive sense that you have in establishing a relationship. You have to be a real person. I think that by things that you say and how you carry yourself—[the players are] watching everything."[3]

Providing real-time feedback to your players is a hallmark of coaching. That feedback helps players see the gap between current performance and what is needed to achieve greatness. Players then practice (and practice and practice) until they can execute those skills effectively, even under extreme pressure.

Yes, we'll admit it: both good and bad coaches do these things, but there is often a significant difference in the perception between the two. The *good* coach is perceived as genuine, helpful, and interested in the player's development, while the *bad* coach is typically perceived to be nothing more than critical. The first is generally referred to as *coaching*, and the second is referred to as *criticism*. Especially in the workplace.

Do you know what the difference is between coaching and criticism?

What we experience is that most managers see praise and criticism as techniques they use to subtly manipulate employees—a trademark of the Taylorian Manager. We can't tell you how many times managers have admitted they *need to do better* in providing praise, but when we ask them why, they claim they know they do too much "criticizing" and *probably* need to balance the scales a bit.

That's a problem.

What they really need to do is to develop a sincere empathy for their employees and help them develop their potential. That genuine concern for an employee translates into a real bond of trust between the leader and the employee. Without that trust—without the relationship—any type of feedback is much more likely to be perceived as critical.

Coaching vs. Criticism

Originally, the word *coach* was used to describe a large, horse-drawn carriage (think *Cinderella* or something that gets robbed in a John Wayne movie). It wasn't until the 1830s that the word developed into its more modern form. It was actually a slang term that is said to have been coined at Oxford University, used to describe a tutor who "carried" a student through an exam.[4]

Get the idea? A coach was an individual who helped a student succeed. The role was one of tutoring; teaching the student enough that a strenuous exam could be passed. Perhaps this is why so many managers are ineffective as "coaches." They don't have the patience or the capacity to teach and develop employees.

Instead, they resort to criticism.

The difference between coaching and criticism is the relationship created and cultivated by leaders when they engage their emotional intelligence. Managers who create a relationship with an employee are rarely perceived to be "critical" even when delivering tough, direct feedback.

Think about this for a moment. As a manager, you can say the exact same thing to two employees and get two completely different responses. You can call it constructive criticism, or feedback, or whatever you want, but you could have the same discussion regarding workplace performance with two different people, and it could be perceived two completely different ways:

- "Oh, she's fantastic. She really helps me see what I can do to improve!"
- "All she does is criticize me. She looks for something wrong in everything I do."

The feedback to each employee was exactly the same, yet there were two completely different perceptions of the conversation. What's the difference? Universally, we find the difference is the relationship: one has a strong relationship with the employee; the other does not. One is trusted and perceived to be genuinely interested in the employee; the other is not perceived to be anything more than in charge.

When we ask people to pick out specific words to describe coaching and criticism, these are the words that are most often used:

Coaching	Criticism
Helpful	Harsh
Understanding	Judgmental
Patient	Impatient
Teaching	Tearing Down
Caring	Insensitive

We could also produce these words if we asked people to describe a good relationship and a bad one. BOSS, this may be a shocker for you, but this isn't something the KIDS made up to get attention. This is an attitude commonly shared by employees of every generation.

Although both individuals, the coach and the critic, are trying to change or improve workplace performance, employee perceptions are remarkably different of the two. This leads many managers to believe that they have to choose one or the other. If you "criticize" the employees' work performance, they will think you are harsh and insensitive, but if you "coach," then all you're doing is being soft and allowing subpar performance.

That's #fakenews.

Effective leaders understand that **you can be demanding and empathetic at the same time**. Those two ideas are NOT mutually exclusive! However, many managers labor under the idea that being "soft"—their definition of empathy or having a people focus—is a barrier to getting the very best from people.

It's just not true. Even the "harshest" of coaches can build great relationships with players. Think about legendary Green Bay Packers coach Vince Lombardi—namesake of the NFL's championship trophy—who was famously described by Green Bay Packer player Henry Jordan as treating all of his players exactly the same: "like dogs."[5] He was tough. He was strict. But he was beloved by his players. Longtime NFL referee Jim Tunney said exactly that to Pat Williams, who shared the story in his book *Vince Lombardi on Leadership*:

> Vince Lombardi was intense and focused because he wanted perfection on the field . . . He was tough on his players. But he had a heart of gold, and he was sensitive to all of them. He loved his players, and in spite of Lombardi's gruff demeanor and shouting, they felt it. They knew he cared about them. Lombardi had a father-son relationship with each of his players.[6]

For all the KIDS who think anything good started sometime after 1980, let's talk about Gregg Popovich, coach of the NBA San Antonio Spurs and the current coach of the USA Men's Basketball team. To make it more relevant to you, Johnny Snapchat, one of Popovich's players is Tony Parker. He was married to Eva Longoria at one point—you probably follow her on social media.

Popovich (we would call him what his players call him, "Pop," but that would be confusing) has led the Spurs to twenty consecutive winning seasons at the time of this writing, which is a pretty good record considering only one other coach in NBA history has ever done that. He is also one of only nine coaches to win one thousand games, plus he has five championships as a head coach, an achievement matched by only four other coaches in NBA history.

So he is an excellent coach, but many of you (especially the KIDS) would probably call him mean. His antics during interviews are legendary in sports media (for your entertainment, visit *www.bit.ly/ SpursCoach*). He is direct. He doesn't pull his punches. He is not shy about correcting mistakes. He once told reporters after a game against the Dallas Mavericks that it was "a pathetic performance on the part of the Spurs."[7] The Spurs won the game.

Turns out, although Popovich may look like a tough coach, his focus is on creating strong connections with his players:

> So if you're just brutally honest with guys, when they do well, love them and touch them and praise them, and if they do poorly, get on their [butt] and let them know it and let them know that you care. And if a player knows that you really care and believes that you can make it better, you got the guy for life.[8]

Love them? Touch them? Praise them!? All of this "touchy-feely" stuff is a bit ridiculous, right? You can't be friends with your people if you hope to manage them!

Stop it.

Spurs General Manager R. C. Buford told NBC Sports columnist Joe Posnanski about Popovich: "The key is relationships. He's the best I've ever seen at building those relationships."[9]

We don't want excuses, BOSS. This is a late-sixties Boomer who makes a living coaching those KIDS you can't convince to come to work on time. KIDS with whom he has basically nothing in common other than a love of basketball.

Effective coaching doesn't get derailed by generational or demographic differences. Effective coaches—great leaders—understand that focusing on the value the individual brings to the team is what builds a powerful relationship.

And it's that relationship that allows a "demanding" leader to be seen as a coach, not a critic.

Key Points to Remember

1. If people work for you and they don't improve as a result of doing so, you are an ineffective leader.

2. The *good* coach is perceived as genuine, helpful, and interested in the player's development, while the *bad* coach is typically perceived to be nothing more than critical.

3. The difference between coaching and criticism is the relationship the leader has cultivated with his or her employee.

4. Effective leaders understand that you can be demanding and empathetic at the same time.

Chapter 30

How to Coach
Your Employees

"We spend a lot of time teaching leaders what to do. We don't spend enough time teaching leaders what to stop. Half the leaders I have met don't need to learn what to do. They need to learn what to stop."[1]

Peter Drucker

A FEW YEARS AGO, the Pops had the opportunity to coach a director of operations in the commercial construction space.

The client's primary motivation—something he mentioned early and often—was "constant improvement." To this end, he would regularly show up at a job and walk the site with the construction manager, moving from one area to the next, pointing out all the things that were wrong. He would pick the job apart one piece at a time, often confronting workers three levels below him to address an issue that needed to be corrected.

The fallout was predictable—team morale was a mess, and the end-of-year 360-degree evaluations for the director were not good.

However, he couldn't understand *why*. Since construction was all about results, how was pointing out mistakes not a good thing? How is focusing on constant improvement a bad thing?

Don't know?

"Thanks for playing, sir, and here's a lovely parting gift for being on the show."

 "Parting gift? Sounds dangerously like a participation trophy."

No one questioned the man's technical ability or his problem-solving skills, but his coaching skills would make Attila the Hun look gentle. Like many managers we encounter, he thought everyone in the company should have exactly the same motivation and behavioral style he does, and he struggled to connect with those who didn't.

The "constant improvement" idea is not a bad idea in and of itself; the problem arises in the way it's implemented. This gentleman thought he was "coaching," but nobody else on the team would call it that. For them, it was a constant barrage of criticism, which is a brutal demotivator for any employee—regardless of age, gender, or background. Especially for the KIDS. They want feedback. They *crave* feedback. But criticism? Not a chance.

The KIDS grew up in an environment where they routinely received feedback, much of which was the feel-good-about-yourself kind. Then, they got into the workplace and the feedback stopped and the criticism began. Research from Gallup indicates that only 19 percent of Millennials claim to receive routine feedback in the workplace, which presents a problem:

> All employees want some type of feedback from their manager. But millennials might require an even greater amount of it than do other generations in the workplace—perhaps because of their upbringing.

Millennials have grown up in an era of remarkable connectedness. They're used to receiving instantaneous feedback from parents, teachers and coaches. They've grown accustomed to having the immediate ability to ask questions, share opinions and provide commentary.

Simply put, millennials have engaged in a constant feedback loop from an early age. Given their perspective, it's understandable that this generation has an ingrained expectation for ongoing communication.[2]

The "constant feedback loop" can be your enemy if you ignore it; however, it can also be your friend. According to additional research at Gallup, "Millennials who meet with their manager on a regular basis are more than twice as likely as their generational peers to be engaged at work."[3]

BINGO! There is the connection you need to make: feedback is critical if you want to drive engagement with the KIDS! How you provide that feedback—in a way that will actually lead to behavior change and performance improvement—is the challenge.

For starters, feedback must be delivered in an effective way. As Steven Stosny, author of the blog "Anger in the Age of Entitlement," points out, "Criticism is an utter failure at getting positive behavior change. Any short-term gain you might get from it builds resentment down the line."[4]

The problem manifests itself when a hypercritical manager claims to be providing *constructive* feedback—that's classic BOSS speak for *criticism*. Unfortunately, that's a bit delusional. Stosny offers these stark comparisons between criticism and feedback:

Criticism focuses on what's wrong: *Why can't you pay attention to the bills?*
Feedback focuses on how to improve: *Let's go over the bills together.*

Criticism devalues: *I guess you're just not smart enough to do this.*

Feedback encourages: *I know you have a lot on your plate, but I'm pretty sure we can do this together.*

Criticism attempts to control: *I know what's best. I'm smarter and better educated.*

Feedback respects autonomy: *I respect your right to make that choice, even though I don't agree with it.*[5]

Here's some #breakingnews for you, BOSS: While changing things that aren't done right is certainly necessary to improving performance, consistently focusing on what's wrong is freaking irritating. If that's the way you approach "coaching," you will create enormous resentment. And turnover.

 "And mean tweets."

 "Yeah, like the BOSS would ever be reading those tweets."

Choosing to Create a Coaching Environment

To move out of the performance-crushing realm of constant criticism and into the performance-improving realm of coaching, your first step is to develop a relationship with your employee—one that builds trust. Fortunately, you now have the perfect tool for that very thing: the weekly Counter Mentor 1-on-1 Meeting (CMM).

Your second step is to provide consistent feedback in a way that focuses on employee growth and development—which results in performance improvement and does not devalue the employee. It should *never* be a session of finding fault, assessing blame, and fixing everything for the employee. Coaching is something "we" do together, not something "I" do to you.

With these two pieces in place, let's see if we can turn you into a high-performance coach. Here is the outline for creating an environment of coaching on your team:

1. You MUST set clear expectations.
2. You MUST address performance issues when they arise.
3. You MUST agree on needed changes and gain commitment to those changes.
4. You MUST focus on decisions and their consequences.

A few years ago, we worked with a client (let's call him Jack) who shared a personal story that perfectly illustrated these four principles. Jack, at the time of this story, was fresh out of college and recently married, but he had yet to secure a job in his chosen profession. So, one morning, he ventured out to find something temporary to bridge the gap.

Jack had worked in construction when he was in high school, so he grabbed his tools, tossed them into his truck, and went out looking for homes under construction. In his experience, home builders sometimes hired on temporary help to finish a job, so he thought his chances were pretty good.

Sure enough, after a couple of tries, he found someone who could use some help. "Have any construction experience?" the foreman asked. Jack assured the prospective employer that he had worked in construction, so the boss asked him if he had tools.

"In my truck," Jack replied.

"When can you start?" the boss wanted to know.

"Right now!"

The foreman seemed elated, hired him on the spot, and sent him over to work with a second employee, a teenage boy. Jack jumped right in, and together they began nailing exterior sheathing to the house.

After a short time, the boss came over and stopped the two.

"Listen, I'm going to need you to work a bit faster," he said, looking directly at Jack. "I can only afford to pay out a certain amount in additional labor on this house, so speed is important. Like this," he said, and he positioned a sheet of plywood on the house and rapidly nailed it in place.

Jack was a bit puzzled. After all, there were two of them working side by side, and the boss was clearly talking only to him. He looked at the teenager and then looked back at the boss.

"Yeah, I know what you're thinking," the boss said. "Here's the deal. This boy is my sister's son. I can't fire him."

Then the boss chuckled and said, "But I can fire you. Listen, I just need you to pick up the pace. If you can't work that fast, I certainly understand, but then I just can't use you."

Almost apologetically: *So sorry. I need you to be a little faster—or I just can't use you.*

"Does that work for you?" the boss asked.

"Absolutely," Jack replied.

From there, the job worked out fine, and Jack spent most of the summer working construction until he finally landed a permanent position in his field of study.

That is what effective coaching looks like, although the boss actually made a small, yet fairly common, mistake right out of the gate. He failed to set clear expectations with his new hire in the beginning, relying on the assumption that an experienced construction guy would automatically work as he expected. Instead—as typically happens—Jack adapted to the pace of an employee already on the job.

How the foreman handled it from there was perfect: he addressed the issue immediately, he demonstrated what the correct result looked like, he gained commitment to the necessary changes, and he focused on decisions and consequences.

Addressing Performance Issues

How do most leaders handle performance issues?

Frankly, really poorly. Actually #epicfail might be more appropriate.

Most managers will complain for months about poor performance to just about anyone who will listen, but then they will wait for the freaking annual performance review to *really* address the performance issue. (And by "address the issue" we mean they will include a bullet in the "Score Detail" section of the review.) #pathetic

Seriously? How is this, in any way, a good plan? Not only do you have to continue to deal with the performance problem until the review occurs—and the dip in performance that goes along with it—but also you can expect extreme resentment from other employees, an erosion of your workplace culture, and an additional wasting of time when you have to replace the positions when the other employees inevitably quit.

REE-DICK-YOU-LUS. (rə'dikyələs/adjective: deserving or inviting derision or mockery)

Imagine a football coach who has players on his team who need to improve or make changes but says, "Hey, we'll talk about this at the end of the season." #losingseason #jobsearch

Performance issues come in all sizes and shapes:

• Poor or consistently below-standard work quality
• Bad attitude
• Inability to work with other team members

- Failure to meet deadlines
- Anything Dwight Schrute would do

The good news is, if you're doing effective Counter Mentor 1-on-1 Meetings (CMM), you will pick up on any of these problems right away. Whether it's a one-time failure, a pattern of behavior, or a consistent performance issue, the Counter Mentor Leadership approach to coaching is very simple.

First, describe what you have observed. This is the actual performance or behavior. Nothing more! No general statements, no ridiculous uses of "always" or "never"—just a simple summation of what *actually* happened.

"Jim, I've noticed that you have come into the past three staff meetings ten to fifteen minutes late."

"Lauren, you missed the deadline by three days."

"Pat, I asked you to work closely with Kris on this assignment. There appears to be a conflict of some kind since I paired you together, and I was told that you were very upset with Kris yesterday."

The facts, and nothing but the facts. No embellishment. No finger pointing. No anger. Not something outrageous like, "*Everybody* knows." Everybody doesn't know—and even if they do, it isn't pertinent to addressing an issue *one-on-one*.

Your task is not to prosecute a case! You are trying to determine the cause and motivation without creating a more significant personal conflict, and move to productive behavior change that will help the employees develop their potential.

We've all done it. It's very common to accuse the person, add on irrelevant information (while making it seem relevant), or use emotion to make someone feel guilt or shame. It's the reason most conflict doesn't get resolved effectively.

Remember this (and tweet it): Conflict that doesn't get resolved almost always reappears in a scarier, more emotional form in the future. #leadership #conflict @countermentors

Here are the bad versions of the previous scenarios:

"Jim, what is your problem? I've said a thousand times that we need to be on time to meetings, and it's like you decide to be late *every single time* just to tick me off. I'm about tired of it."

"Lauren, you really blew it on this last project. Three days late? Seriously? You know, if you spent less time on Facebook and more time on the project, this wouldn't have happened. Do you realize that my boss wants me to fire you? He said the customer was really upset. I've never missed a deadline by three minutes—much less three DAYS."

"Pat, this nonsense with Kris had better get fixed in a hurry. I'm really tired of you two acting like a couple of spoiled kids. That little stunt in the break room yesterday was the last straw."

Lots of accusations. Plenty of manipulation. And, by the way, who is the manager *really* concerned about? These emotional, childish *accusations* are completely unacceptable.

After you describe what you have observed, you can add that you don't want to make any assumptions about what you've seen or heard. Then, prompt the employee to jump into the conversation by ending with a *genuine* question: "What's going on?"

Use a neutral delivery. Don't use that question to make an accusation. Your objective is to get the employee to fill in the blanks without feeling attacked or defensive. There is always a reason why something has transpired. Rather than making assumptions or accusing the employee of malicious intent, you simply want the employee to tell you what's going on and answer the question "Why did this happen?"

From there, it's simply a process of getting to the root cause, what we call the *core issue*. People will often answer with something vague or unhelpful (e.g., "Oh, nothing, really"). That won't do because you can't ask for change without understanding the real problem and the root cause that created it. If that happens, follow up with something like this:

> "Help me understand the problem. We've discussed the expectations for our team—that's not the result we're looking for—so let's figure out what we need to do differently. I'm not willing to make assumptions; I truly want to understand your perspective."

Again, to be clear, your objective is to prompt the employee to *begin talking!*

All kinds of things become apparent when people start expressing their thoughts and opinions. They might blame the dog for eating their homework, they might tell you that YOU are the problem, or—most of the time—they will tell you what happened and it's a straightforward conversation. You know, because you hire professionals who are adults and typically want to do a great job.

The most important thing you can do in this conversation is to continue to drill down. Remember, you want to address the root cause, not this symptom you've just observed. Don't stop with the surface answer. Instead use this simple phrase to go deeper into the conversation:

> "Tell me more . . ."

When prompted in this way, people naturally expound on the subject, which is exactly what you're looking for—more information that you can use to understand the challenge. Those three little words are magic! Remember, the more intimately you understand the challenge your employees are facing, the more effectively you can coach them.

Excuses and Blame

If someone starts blaming others or making excuses, that's a clue you can work with, but don't jump into accusation mode.

For example, if the response is, "Well, I can't get the project in on time if marketing doesn't get me the proposal materials," DO NOT run into that burning building without some additional information. Your response should be probing:

"Tell me more about that . . ."

Once everything is out into the open, the intent of your conversation is to determine what the employee needs to change, not figure out who to blame. Quite often, you will need to point out that other people or circumstances will impact results, but your objective is to help the employee see ways to navigate through those issues and solve problems rather than becoming a victim of other people's issues or mistakes.

"Lauren, clearly there are some things outside of your control, but let's talk about what you can control. What might you have done differently?"

Effective employees learn to maneuver around issues and challenges, solve problems, and still get their work done in the manner they agreed to—*it's your job to teach them how*!

As you collaboratively determine what needs to change, it is up to you to reset the expectation and gain commitment to that expectation. Remember—an effective expectation clearly defines the result, includes a time frame for completion, and explains the "why" behind that expectation.

> "Jim, I understand that you're frustrated with the staff meetings. Some of your objections definitely need to be addressed. That said, I want you to know that you always have the right to come in and tell me about something that's bothering you or to discuss something you think needs to be addressed. What you don't have the right to do is to be late to meetings as a form of protest.
>
> We will continue our conversation about changing some of the things in our meetings, but I need your commitment to come to meetings on time. It's important because it shows respect for everyone else in the meeting, it makes our meetings more efficient, and it maintains the values and expectations we care about. Can I get your commitment to start attending our staff meetings on time—starting with our meeting later today?"

The issue in the example above is a ***behavioral issue***. The new expectation asks for a change in behavior, and it is not necessarily related to performance. In other words, the employee might be doing great work, but the meeting issue is still a problem. When the problem is one of ***work performance***, your coaching conversation may lead to a commitment to engage in additional training to improve a specific skill.

In either case, you want to ask for a commitment to a new course of action and agreement from the employees that they will communicate early if the commitment will not be met.

This is extraordinarily powerful! This simple, yet incredibly valuable, advice is mentioned by the authors of *Crucial Confrontations: Tools for Resolving Broken Promises, Violated Expectations, and Bad Behavior*:

At the heart of every workable accountability system there is one simple sentence: "If something comes up, let me know as soon as you can."[6]

When you set expectations for your people, they will let you know about problems *before* they occur, and you will have far fewer *disasters* in your future!

Decisions and Consequences

Many managers find themselves dealing with the same attitude or behavioral problem over and over again. There is an incredible amount of frustration when repeatedly dealing with the same issue. Instead, you must get a commitment—a decision—to do something differently in the future. Once the employee makes that decision and commitment is given, you need not revisit the original problem. Instead, if you encounter the same problems in the future, your discussion should revolve around their decision *to not keep their commitments*.

This one step will keep you out of the endless cycle of behavioral problems. When people are asked to make a commitment to something, they have a decision to make. They decide whether to commit to a new action or behavior, or they decide not to. That decision has consequences. As one of our good friends likes to say, *"You get to choose your decisions, you don't get to choose your consequences."* Here is an example of how you gain commitment to the new (or different) way of doing things:

MANAGER: Jim, a few months ago we had a conversation about meetings and being on time. I've noticed that in the past three weeks, you've been ten to fifteen minutes late every week. What's going on?

Jim: Yeah, I know. I've had some things going on. It won't happen again.

Manager: Jim, I appreciate that, but I have a couple of concerns that we need to discuss.

Jim: Listen, I'm really sorry. I've just been tied up working on those projects you gave me.

Manager: Understood, but let's revisit a couple of things. We agreed that if you had any kind of challenge getting to a meeting, the first order of business was to let me know in advance. Remember?

Jim: Oh, yeah. I'm sorry about that.

Manager: Jim, the bigger problem is, if you make a commitment to someone and don't keep it, that breaks down trust. You made a firm commitment not only to be on time to meetings, but to let me know if you had to be late for some reason. You haven't done either of those things. Being on time is not really the issue here. The issue is keeping commitments and the trust problem it creates when you don't. Why don't you tell me what's going on?

See the difference? It's important not to be deflected by the quick apology. You need to get to the root of the problem, and allowing someone to continually skate on the same problem creates a cultural norm. Remember—culture is the commonly *accepted* behaviors and attitudes. If you continue to discuss the same behavioral issues over and over, you never get to the *core issue* (and other members of the team will begin to reconsider their employment arrangement).

Manager: Jim, I need you to understand. My expectations are clear—I expect you to keep the commitments you make. If you can't—or won't—I just can't use you.

Jim: WHAT? Are you firing me??

Manager: Not at all. I'm asking you to make a decision. I will support you either way, but if you choose not to keep the commitments you make, I just can't use you. It's your choice.

Behavior is always about choices and consequences. When someone acts a certain way, there *will* always be *natural* consequences—consequences that naturally follow.

For example, if you, the leader, consistently arrive late to work, people will naturally assume that you approve of that practice. If you consistently fail to address substandard performance, people will naturally question your leadership and lose confidence in you (and start performing at the substandard level!). Those are natural consequences.

However, when people choose one course of action over another, there may be imposed consequences. In our original example, if Jack, the construction employee, chose not to work at the pace required by the boss, that decision meant the boss just couldn't use him in that role.

There are times when you must bring people to that decision point, and sometimes they just won't want to choose the path you require. If you have presented the two choices and allowed them to make the decision, letting them go is simply their choice, not yours. At that point, letting those people go is the very best thing you can do—for you AND for them.

Our friend David Brock is the CEO of Partners in EXCELLENCE, a global consulting practice. Dave describes himself as a "ruthless pragmatist," and that would definitely apply to his thoughts about addressing poor performance in the workplace:

> Terminating a poor performer—after you have given them a fair opportunity and coaching to improve their performance—is the most compassionate thing you can do for the poor performer.

While it may not look that way, to them, initially, it forces them to find a role where they can contribute, where they have the potential for being an A player.

We are obligated to give them that opportunity—not withhold it, treating them as charity cases. We are obligated in our last conversations, as they leave, to coach them on the types of opportunities they might look for where they can perform and contribute.[7]

We hope you caught that. Keeping a marginal performer is NOT compassionate. It is not good for that person, it is not good for your team, and it is DEFINITELY not good for how people perceive you as a leader.

Coaching is about improving performance! It is also about helping people find the place where they can reach their potential. It's the final step in the process of creating a culture of ownership.

And it is the hallmark of the Counter Mentor Leader.

Note: We want to direct you to the outstanding book *Crucial Confrontations: Tools for Resolving Broken Promises, Violated Expectations, and Bad Behavior*, written by Kerry Patterson, Joseph Grenny, Ron McMillan, and Al Switzler.[8] The coaching approach we have used for years is based, in part, on the principles it teaches.

Key Points to Remember

1. The first step in coaching is to develop a relationship with your employee.

2. The second step in coaching is to provide consistent feedback in a way that focuses on employee growth and development—not just pointing out everything that's "wrong."

3. Here is the outline for creating an environment of coaching on your team:

   a. Set clear expectations.

    b. Address performance issues when they arise.

    c. Agree on needed changes and gain commitment to those changes.

    d. Focus on decisions and their consequences.

4. Behavior and performance come down to choices and consequences. When you ask someone to make a decision that includes consequences, it doesn't make you mean or insensitive; it creates accountability and makes you a good leader.

Chapter 31

The Spark that
Lights Performance

"But effort and courage are not enough without purpose and direction."[1]

President John F. Kennedy

WE'VE MENTIONED MOTIVATION several times. It's the spark that creates exceptional performance.

The problem is:

1. We're not all motivated by the same thing.
2. We're not all motivated to the same degree.

Understanding these two very simple ideas will help you unlock the vast potential that exists in these KIDS today.

The fact is, KIDS today are drawn to *meaningful* work—work that "means something" to *them*.

As it turns out, that's true of all your employees, as reported in the *Harvard Business Review* article entitled "What Millennials Want from a New Job":

> Even the most widely accepted stereotypes about Millennials appear to be suspect. Last year, IBM's Institute for Business Value released a report titled "Myths, Exaggerations and Uncomfortable Truths: The Real Story Behind Millennials in the Workplace." Based on a multigenerational study of 1,784 employees from companies across 12 countries and six industries, it found that about the same percentage of Millennials (25%) want to make a positive impact on their organization as Gen Xers (21%) and Baby Boomers (23%). Differences are uniformly minimal across nine other variables as well.[2]

This is the truth (and it's going to fire up *both* the BOSS and the KIDS): we are all humans and we are actually very similar. It's not to say that we are the *same*—we've proven that isn't true over and over—the point is to understand that you shouldn't accept every stereotype you hear! Our methods might be a bit different, but overall, employees want basically the same things and are *generally* motivated by the same things. So, the notion that you have to lead Boomers one way and Digital Natives another is just not true.

Counter Mentor Leaders understand that leadership—done the right way—overcomes the generational challenges because it's about the relationship. It is the great equalizer.

Performance will always suffer—for ALL employees—if they remain unmotivated, working in meaningless jobs without any sense of purpose. However, it will be *much* worse if that purpose is commonly understood to be nothing more than, "Keep your head down, do what you're told, don't make waves, and keep your opinions to yourself!"

That motivates NO ONE!

Companies often try to create a sense of purpose by adopting a set of core values. Done right, core values can be a huge asset (especially in the *Freedom Box*), but they're completely worthless when they're done wrong.

For example, we worked with an organization that had created a set of corporate values that included "people" as a value. Now, we understand that you can *value* people, but we struggle to understand how *people* is a core value. How you *treat* people? Sure. But "people"—by itself—as a core value? We have no idea.

The same company also decided that "profit" would be one of their core values (you really can't make this stuff up). We're relatively certain that profit is an objective of doing business, but we're completely lost as to how it is a core value. We don't think you need a Harvard Business School pedigree to see the potential conflict here, but just in case it wasn't obvious, Pops asked the question: "So, do these two values ever come into conflict?"

In unison, everyone in the room said, "Yes."

"And which one wins when they come into conflict?"

Insert uncomfortable, nervous laughter.

That wasn't predictable, was it?

Your people want to do something meaningful. KIDS, in particular, want to work where they can make a difference. It's not that getting paid isn't important; it's that meaning and purpose are critical. In fact, it's been said by many that today, "meaning is the new money."

The critical question is, how do you create that meaning and purpose?

A Take on Purpose from *Fight Club*

His face was beaten to a pulp. His pasty white skin had the look of an apple ready to be picked—shiny, ripe, and almost red. His ribs were cracked, his knuckles fractured.

He was in an intense pain.

The concrete floor was cold; it rumbled under the shouting of men—too many to count, but too few to get lost. Someone helped him up; he slipped on a cocktail of blood and sweat only to be caught by someone else. He looked across the room and grinned, "Again next week?" The crowd roared its approval.

He was *happy*.

He belonged. He was part of something. For the first time in his life, he knew he could do whatever he wanted—be whatever he wanted. He felt a sense of meaning and purpose—it drove him to levels he had only imagined in his boring, plain, pathetic excuse of a life.

He couldn't wait for what was next.

As he put his shirt back on, he made a half-hearted attempt to make the blood stop but was interrupted when it happened, his favorite part. The Leader stepped into the middle of the room.

The raucous gathering was reduced to a church-like silence, leaning in, urging the thick, humid air to loosen its grip on the moment.

The Leader was fiercely passionate. As he circled the room, his eyes darted from one person to the next, drawing each one of them in even further, making every person feel as if he was the only one in the room. At long last the Leader, with the command of a general and the swagger of an outlaw, spoke:

> "The first rule of Fight Club is . . . you do not talk about Fight Club!"[3]

For its participants, Fight Club defined motivation. It was the meaning they searched for in life.

Have you ever felt that at work? True purpose? The thrill of boundless motivation? Feeling like you could do anything, no matter the task, and never tire of it?

We're talking about the kind of motivation that drives you to believe you could run through a brick wall, if necessary. That incredible mixture of purpose, autonomy, ownership, and empowerment to use your passion and skills within a community working toward something meaningful!

Many of you are a bit confused. You may not understand how Tyler Durden (the Leader) was able to motivate a large group of men from disparate backgrounds without paying them a dime.

But then, you think, *"Oh, that's right; this is fiction!"*

So you're relieved: *"It's a movie! That's not reality. Durden wouldn't understand what it's like to manage people in the real world."*

Really?

We actually think he nailed it. When people find purpose, they believe they can do almost anything! The trick is to find that motivation.

Not convinced?

Let's add in a point of view you won't ignore, one that draws on four decades of research (the KIDS call that #science). It's found in Daniel Pink's 2009 bestselling book, *Drive: The Surprising Truth About What Motivates Us*, a book that reveals the real dominant motivators of human behavior.[4]

Here is Pink's own Twitter summary of his book (it's found on page 203 in *Drive*, which you should immediately purchase and read). **SPOILER ALERT**: Turns out, Tyler Durden was right—we're not motivated primarily by a paycheck.

> Carrots & sticks are so last century. *Drive* says for 21st century work, we need to upgrade to autonomy, mastery, and purpose.[5]

Really? Purpose is actually a primary motivator?!

Absolutely, and purpose—along with autonomy and mastery—serve as the three fundamental ingredients of human motivation. Let's take a quick look at all three.

Purpose

Purpose is *the yearning to do what we do in the service of something larger than ourselves.* "People don't buy what you do, they buy *why* you do it!" says Simon Sinek in a gentle croon. That's from his TED talk "How Great Leaders Inspire Action," an eighteen-minute presentation filmed in 2009.[6] It's been viewed more than 32 million times. Then there is the book *The Purpose Driven Life*, written by Rick Warren and released in 2002.[7] It seems to have touched a nerve—it's sold more than 30 million copies.[8]

People are *constantly* searching for how to find purpose! As a leader, you are capable of providing it.

What is that purpose, you ask? For some, it's impacting the community. For others, it's achieving a level of excellence in a class by itself. It might be making a difference or leaving a legacy or creating something entirely new. We don't know what your company's purpose should be. But we're pretty sure you could discover it in a thoughtful conversation with your people.

Purpose is the very essence of motivation. It can move an individual or a team to remarkable achievement *if* that purpose is relevant to the individual or team. Just so we're clear, casually suggesting in a staff meeting that something is "good for the company" is not going to qualify as providing purpose.

Autonomy

Autonomy is *the desire to direct our own lives.* People want to feel they have control over their lives. They want to have the opportunity to make decisions for themselves, and they're not terribly fond of taking orders, working in the dark, and doing whatever they're told to do (because you said so).

As a leader, when you tell people what do, when to do it, how to do it, when to start, and when to leave, you create functionaries. Resentful, unfulfilled, looking-for-another-job functionaries. They not only are demotivated, they also aren't thinking, or innovating, or taking ownership, or asking hard questions.

The Swedish company Spotify—with 30 million customers and $3 billion in annual revenue—works to maximize autonomy for their employees without sacrificing accountability. (BOSS, surely you have Spotify on your flip phone, don't you?)

> The watchword at Spotify is "be autonomous, but don't sub-optimize—be a good citizen in the Spotify ecosystem." A common analogy at the company is a jazz band: Each squad plays its instrument, but each also listens to the others and focuses on the overall piece to make great music.[9]

The jazz band analogy is a very good one. Musicians know how their performance contributes to the whole, but their individual contributions are unique and self-directed.

Mastery

Mastery is *the urge to continually get better at something that matters.* People are incredibly motivated by improvement. In *The 7 Hidden Reasons Employees Leave,* author Leigh Branham mentions four human needs—needs that he calls *fundamental* to human life. One of those needs is "to feel competent: expecting that you will be matched to a job that makes good use of your talents . . . [and] receive the necessary training to perform the job capably."[10] In other words, to achieve mastery in your specific role.

There is something eminently satisfying about mastering something—about knowing you've learned or accomplished something difficult or challenging that only someone highly skilled can do.

It's a reward in and of itself: a validation that you have achieved something special.

We're certain that autonomy and mastery will be much more meaningful—and will have considerably more impact in your organization—when your people are all working toward a common purpose. Purpose becomes that elusive "secret" ingredient.

However, with all due respect to Mr. Pink, we would add one additional component to his list. In our experience, there is one additional motivator, one that is a driver of behavior of individuals, sports teams, and even teens on the streets. We believe that fourth driver is community.

Community

Community is *belonging to a group of people that loves us more than we love ourselves.* We understand this idea is linked with purpose, but we think the differences are beyond nuance and should be discussed.

Humans, with few exceptions, crave community. It's the way we are wired. (Google "the psychology of community.") People want to be part of a team, a group, a gang, or a gaggle that accepts them, values their contribution, and truly believes they matter.

Throughout history, we've formed groups for survival, for healing, for growth, and to entertain the masses, from the Beatles to Manchester United. When you make your people feel less like a collection of disparate people and more like a community, you'll see a definitive improvement in your company culture AND your team's performance.

The Short Course to Creating Your Team's Purpose

Finally. You're convinced, right?

You've been going about the whole "motivation" thing completely wrong.

 "The BOSS is probably feeling pretty beat up at this point."

 "Imagine how the KIDS feel . . ."

We don't want to quit without getting you started down the path to creating your team's purpose.

The first thing you need to do is build a BIG bonfire and burn the idea that your team, or some of your people, aren't motivated. They are definitely motivated—by something. Your job is to find it, develop it, and get them to buy in.

The main problem? The culture you've created is probably less than motivating (to put it gently). So, first things first: stop blaming your people and start looking at yourself. Flip your whole thought process and think of your people as being capable of great things, even extraordinary things, if they work together.

Getting them to work together begins with a common purpose. Let's get very tactical for a moment about creating your team's purpose:

1. **Start with *your* thoughts.** Shut the door, close your email, turn off your phone, and focus. Write down in detail why your team or organization exists. (KIDS, copy the BOSS on this one; paper

and pen is actually a great idea here—there are too many distractions on your iPad or PC.) What is your company's goal or mission? Why is it important to you? What happens if you don't achieve it? Who is counting on you to reach the goal, achieve the mission, or do the job?

As you start this line of thinking, your mind will go in multiple directions, so make sure to capture all of your thoughts. This is the good stuff.

2. **Get input from your people.** Get your team together and share your thoughts. Open up the floor to input and ideas—the key is to get a real discussion going. This will turn up all kinds of thoughts, insights, and good ideas—and you don't have to change your intent, although you may wind up changing the words.

A point of caution. If people are turning up their noses to your thoughts on purpose, you have two choices: reject it because it doesn't resonate, or find people who are committed to the same passion you have. But take the time to consider that you might have created a purpose that people don't believe in. For example, if your purpose statement is "to build the company to $100 million in sales so I can sell it and retire," you might not get a lot of buy-in.

3. **Finalize your purpose statement.** After all of the discussions, analyze your findings and create your final version of the purpose statement. It doesn't need to be flowery or complicated—it just needs to be clear and compelling.

You want this to be a driver of motivation and a guide to people's behavior! If they can't retain it (or understand it), then you don't get either outcome.

4. **Communicate the purpose statement to your team.** Once you have the purpose statement in hand, you should review it once again with each of your direct reports and solicit additional feedback. Is it clear? Is it compelling? Will it serve to motivate our team to greater levels of success?

The last step is to begin the process of communicating the statement to everyone in the company. Almost without exception, at this point you're getting final sign-off and creating excitement.

In chapter 14, we shared the story about Scott and his platoon captain. We showed you a statement that outlined the Firefighter's Creed—their "purpose statement." It says:

> I humbly serve as a Guardian to my community always ready to respond to those who are unable to help themselves.[11]

It's clear. It's compelling. It creates a set of standards and expectations all its own.

It's *motivating.*

But it has no power and no value if it's not communicated. After all, a lot of companies go through the motions of creating a purpose statement (or mission statement), but no one in the building really knows what it says. Here's a list of our suggestions:

- If your purpose is too long to easily memorize, start over.
- If your purpose isn't communicated in every staff meeting in the company, don't bother.
- If your purpose isn't listed on your company's job descriptions and discussed during interviews and again during onboarding, don't waste your time.
- If you don't share your purpose with your customers, what's the point?

Tyler Durden gave those who followed him a true sense of purpose. You can too.

You don't have to be Tyler to create a purpose-driven team—you just need to shed your Taylorian past and practice Counter Mentor Leadership.

Key Points to Remember

1. A sense of purpose is an extremely powerful motivator for all generations in the workplace.

2. People are motivated by autonomy, a sense of purpose, mastery of their craft, and belonging to a community.

3. Hiring and retaining talent will be much easier when you define a clear and compelling purpose for your team.

Chapter 32

Reading is Easy,
Change is Hard

"The brain is a wonderful organ; it starts working the moment you get up in the morning and does not stop until you get into the office."[1]

Anonymous

HERE'S THE THING: Managers don't transform into leaders by accident.

The leadership model and supporting tactics we've described are simple to explain and easy to understand. They're straightforward and logical. However, in many ways, **they are counter to almost everything you've observed, learned, and experienced in your career**. This means that in order to truly implement the principles in this book—to become a Counter Mentor Leader—you're going to have to change.

And if there's anything we've learned over the years, it's that change is freaking hard.

Maybe harder than leadership.

There have been many great books written on driving successful change—personally and organizationally. John Kotter, Chip and Dan Heath, Charles Duhigg, and Stephen Covey are all on our must-read list![2] We are also huge fans of Hilary Scarlett. For us, her work was vital in understanding how the brain works and how we often set ourselves up for failure in the workplace.

That said, this final chapter isn't meant to be a general, exhaustive list on how to drive change. We simply want to give you insight into why the transformation of your leadership style is going to be difficult.

 "Although Robby's wife is actually a doctor, he definitely is not. Neither am I. But I can assure you that all of our neuroscience facts are based on *real* research by *real* doctors."

 "We *are* organizational therapists. Does that count?"

The problem we want you to recognize is that your brain is wired to reject change! You probably already have a sense of how much the average person dislikes change, but you may not know *why*. In fact, even if you like change, you typically don't like it at all when someone tries to change *you*.

There are two other key things you must understand:

1. Your brain's primary job is to keep you alive.
2. In an attempt to conserve energy, the brain takes shortcuts.

 "Shortcuts? "Sounds like one of the KIDS to me."

Keeping You Alive

Your brain is fascinating, and it's really good at a bunch of things that, frankly, don't really matter much—like remembering the last time your NFL team won the championship (as Patriots fans, our brain doesn't have to work very hard there), or the square root of 36, or how to ride a bicycle. However, what it's best at is keeping you alive.

Your amygdala, the part of the brain responsible for your *fight or flight* response, is diligently on high alert. If it perceives a *threat*—from a cheetah chasing you on the Serengeti to a competitor stealing your client in Scottsdale—it kicks into gear, preparing your entire system to deal with that threat.

The most important thing to understand when thinking about change is that, during *fight or flight*, blood actually flows AWAY from the prefrontal cortex—the part of your brain that does critical thinking and analysis. Which means, of course, that when your brain perceives a threat—like a big change or a bunch of small, seemingly unconnected changes—you are literally unable to think clearly.

 "That certainly explains a few things."

Key parts of your anatomy are shut down. Your digestion slows to a crawl (causing that uncomfortable feeling in your stomach), and your immune system is basically turned off. The resulting energy savings are all invested elsewhere. The brain instructs the heart to beat faster and harder, sending blood as quickly as possible to critical life-saving muscles: legs, arms, core. (Nope, not your brain!) At the same time, the brain directs the stress hormone (cortisol) to flood your system, causing you to be hyper-alert.

We're lucky. The brain is a lifesaver. It detects threats and works slavishly to keep you alive. But that response has some drawbacks in the workplace: in particular, more aggressive, irrational behavior when you need to be thinking analytically about how the change will impact you and your team. #scary

The Brain Takes Shortcuts

The brain, which represents only 2 percent of your body mass, uses up to 20 percent of your body's total energy production.

In an effort to conserve energy, our proverbial diesel engine takes shortcuts. For example, think about your commute to work every day. How many times have you gotten up in the morning, showered and dressed, made coffee, driven to work, sat down at your desk, and thought to yourself, "How did I get here?"

Here's another example. We have this idea that we see and perceive everything, but we really don't. Instead, the brain focuses on the thing it considers most important and conserves energy in other systems. That's why people will often miss a gorilla that runs across a stage in the middle of a bunch of people passing a basketball around. (To view this fascinating experiment, visit bit.ly/findthegorilla.)

Psychologists Christopher Chabris and Daniel Simons describe this experiment, and what happens in our brains, in their book *The Invisible Gorilla: And Other Ways Our Intuitions Deceive Us*:

> It's true that we vividly experience some aspects of our world, particularly those that are the focus of our attention. But this rich experience inevitably leads to the erroneous belief that we process all of the detailed information around us. In essence, we know how vividly we see some aspects of our world, but we are completely unaware of those aspects of our world that fall outside of that current focus of attention. Our vivid visual experience masks a striking mental blindness—we assume that

visually distinctive or unusual objects will draw our attention, but in reality they often go completely unnoticed.[3]

So, your brain is so focused on conserving energy, it relies on experience and prediction to keep you from running out of energy before noon!

Habits Make Change Even Harder

You're probably beginning to see why you're wired to reject change:

1. When a significant change is proposed, the brain perceives it as a "threat."

2. Sensing that threat, the brain activates its fight-or-flight programming (the amygdala does its thing).

3. You experience anxiety and a productivity-crippling fear about the future.

4. You (literally) can't think clearly, and you're subject to making poor decisions that can cause your worst fears to become reality.

Inside an already chaotic workplace, the prospect of change is now adding frustration, conflict, and a dip in workplace performance to the mix.

In her book *Neuroscience for Organizational Change*, author Hilary Scarlett explains the challenges created by change:

One big change might be manageable for a person, but lots of constant, unpredictable, seemingly small changes are what cause the real strain. Constant pressure mixed with uncertainty is very stressful. The combination of the two means that the

prefrontal cortex, which is responsible for our "executive function," is overloaded. Our brains are "limited capacity machines"
and as we overload them the limbic system interprets this as a
threat: the machine is under strain and can't function properly.[4]

One final challenge you'll face when transforming your leadership behavior: your habits. Your habits are a problem as well. Understanding them, and how they work against change, is also a critical
aspect of navigating your personal transformation. Charles Duhigg
is the author of the *New York Times* bestseller *The Power of Habit.* In
an interview with Terry Gross of NPR's *Fresh Air,* he explained how
habits work:

> "Every habit starts with a psychological pattern called a 'habit
> loop.' First, there's a cue, or trigger, that tells your brain to go
> into automatic mode and let a behavior unfold."
>
> "Then there's the routine, which is the behavior itself,"
> Duhigg tells NPR's Terry Gross. "That's what we think about
> when we think about habits."
>
> The third step, he says, is the reward: something that your
> brain likes that helps it remember the 'habit loop' in the future.[5]

Our habit-making behaviors, Duhigg says, have been traced to
a part of the brain called the *basal ganglia.* Further, research indicates that people revert to the basal ganglia's processing—those "habit
loops"—because, frankly, it feels good. When we implement the neu-
ral patterns of the basal ganglia, the pattern is reinforced again and
again. Said differently, the behavior is *entrenched.* This "hardwiring"
in the basal ganglia cements the behavior even further and every
time we execute that habit, we get a nice little hit of dopamine, the
chemical our brain drops that makes us feel good.

Here's the bottom line: Your brain is wired to reject change, and
your current hardwired habits make you feel good.

Yes, changing your leadership habits will be freaking tough.

How to Change Your Behavior (and Become a Counter Mentor Leader)

Without going into a complex, neuroscience-soaked roadmap to changing your behavior, we'll summarize it this way: to change a behavior, you will need to replace the old habits that are hard-wired in your brain.

Here is what that looks like in the real world, without all the big words:

1. **Identify an accountability partner.** If you hope to make and sustain real, lasting change, you must employ someone to help you identify your blind spots and hold you accountable. We always recommend someone you interact with on a regular basis—a trusted colleague or a high-potential direct report. If you select a direct report for this role, you have an opportunity to create a reverse-mentoring situation, but, beware, that may be a big step for you (and for your employee!).

   In the beginning, set up monthly off-site meetings to facilitate the conversation. Know that the first few meetings will be uncomfortable. If you stay the course and approach the conversations with humility and openness, your accountability partner will begin to give you outstanding insights that propel you to the next level of leadership.

2. **Include your team.** This transition is going to result in behavior changes that your team will immediately see. Our advice is to open up and let people know what's going on! If you kick this process off without any communication, there will be skepticism at best and general freaking out at worst.

Take the time to communicate what you're doing and ask them to work alongside you. Their support and encouragement will be critical. Your goal is better leadership! If they understand this, they will be much more understanding and tolerant of any awkward moments (like when you start listening instead of directing).

3. **Practice, practice, practice!** As we described earlier, habits change only if you practice the desired behavior again and again. The neuroscience doesn't lie! You must be intentional, and you must be diligent. Work on the new behaviors every single day. You'll be tempted—especially under stress—to revert to your bad habits. Don't let this happen!

Understanding the brain science actually prepares your brain for the changes. Change is difficult, and your brain may resist when your stress levels go up, but awareness works in your favor. Now you can identify *why* you're feeling the way you are and deal with it appropriately.

Yes, change will be hard, but a failure to change will be worse. And *expensive*.

Your Choice? Change or Irrelevance

Retired four-star U.S. Army general Eric Shinseki is a hero. Really, there isn't any other way to describe him.

A second-generation American born in Hawaii in 1942, Shinseki was highly educated, attending the U.S. Military Academy and earning a Master of Arts degree from Duke. During his military career of thirty-eight years, he earned two Purple Hearts, three Bronze Stars, multiple Distinguished Service Medals (from the army, navy, air force, and coast guard), and the Army Commendation Medal.

Shinseki is humble, heroic, and an incredible leader—but what does this have to do with you?

Rewind to 1999 when Shinseki became the thirty-fourth Chief of Staff of the Army (CSA). The CSA, a member of the Joint Chiefs, serves as the military adviser to the President, the Secretary of Defense, and the National Security Council. When Shinseki assumed the role, the army was generally tired, rigid, immobile, and ill-prepared to fight the war against global terrorism. Shinseki knew that a transformation was needed. The army needed to be nimble, mobile, flexible, and ready to strike quickly—something Shinseki referred to as Stryker Brigade Combat Teams.

To say his ideas were met with resistance is a lot like saying you're not looking forward to going to the DMV. #understatement

He was called before Congress to defend his "outrageous" proposal. Shinseki, cool and calm as ever, leaned forward in his chair and uttered the words that had become his mantra during his tenure as Chief of Staff, a phrase that we have adopted to the task of becoming a Counter Mentor Leader:

> If you don't like change, you're going to like irrelevance a lot less.[6]

As you all know, Shinseki was right.

In order to maintain our *relevance* in a war we'd never encountered, with an enemy we had never faced, we had to make changes. We had to *change* the most powerful army in the history of the world—even after having success for more than two hundred years.

The only real competitive advantage left in business is *people*. Those people are begging for leadership! They are begging for an opportunity to be a part of something special.

As a Counter Mentor Leader, you have the opportunity to have a dramatic impact—to *change people's lives*! You can make your team, in your organization, the BEST place that your people have ever worked!

You have a chance to create a legacy by developing a team of leaders to grow and develop others when you're gone!

Winston Churchill famously said, "To improve is to change, so to be perfect is to have changed often."[7] We suspect that was a phrase Shinseki studied and revered. It's even more relevant today than ever before.

Our advice?

You didn't get this far by making excuses. No need to start now. Start making changes!

Dump old-school Taylorian Management. Battle irrelevance. Take on Counter Mentor Leadership and revolutionize your workplace.

Remember: You get to choose your decisions.

You don't get to choose your consequences.

Endnotes

Introduction

1. Sinek, Simon. Conference presentation, Catalyst Conference, Atlanta, GA, October 2016.

Chapter 1

1. Orwell, George. *George Orwell (Volume 4) In Front of Your Nose: 1946–1950.* New York: Harcourt Brace & World, 1968. 51.
2. Taylor, Frederick Winslow. *The Principles of Scientific Management.* Harper & Brothers Publishers, 1911. Kindle edition, 2014.
3. Taylor, *The Principles of Scientific Management,* location 35.
4. Taylor, location 1078.
5. Taylor, location 485.

Chapter 2

1. Leonard, Elmore. Interviewed by John O'Connell. "Elmore Leonard: This Much I Know," *The Guardian,* December 11, 2010, https://www.theguardian.com/lifeandstyle/2010/dec/12/this-much-know-elmore-leonard.
2. Eyal, Nir. "Why Everyone Hates IT People," *Forbes,* April 13, 2012, https://www.forbes.com/sites/nireyal/2012/04/13/why-everyone-hates-it-people/#12cd65a438cb.
3. Tarafdar, Monideepa, John D'Arcy, Ofir Turel, and Ashish Gupta. "The Dark Side of Information Technology," *MIT Sloan Management Review,* Winter 2015 (December 16, 2014), http://sloanreview.mit.edu/article/the-dark-side-of-information-technology/.

4. "CareerBuilder Study Reveals Top Ten Productivity Killers at Work: Employers Share Most Unusual Things They Caught Employees Doing When They Should Have Been Working," *CareerBuilder*, June 12, 2014. http://www.careerbuilder.com/share/aboutus/pressreleasesdetail.aspx?sd=6/12/2014&id=pr827&ed=12/31/2014.

5. Gouveia, Aaron. "2014 Wasting Time at Work Survey: Workers Are Wasting More Time Than Ever in 2014." *Salary.com*, http://www.salary.com/2014-wasting-time-at-work/.

6. Gouveia, "2014 Wasting Time at Work Survey."

7. Gabbatt, Adam. "United Breaks Guitars singer reprises YouTube airline lament," *The Guardian*, August 19, 2009, https://www.theguardian.com/technology/blog/2009/aug/19/united-breaks-guitars-song-sequel.

8. Carroll, Dave. *United Breaks Guitars: The Power of One Voice in the Age of Social Media.* Carlsbad, CA: Hay House, 2012. See also "Dave Carroll," *Speakers' Spotlight*, 2017, http://www.speakers.ca/speakers/dave-carroll/.

9. Quoted in Hanna, Julia. "United Breaks Guitars," *HBS Alumni Bulletin*, November 29, 2010, http://hbswk.hbs.edu/item/united-breaks-guitars.

Chapter 3

1. de Bono, Edward. *Lateral Thinking for Management: A Handbook.* London: Penguin Books, 1990. 1.

2. "Millennials Check Their Phones More Than 157 Times Per Day," *Social Media Week*, May 31, 2016, https://socialmediaweek.org/newyork/2016/05/31/millennials-check-phones-157-times-per-day/.

3. "The Work Martyr's Cautionary Tale: How the Millennial Experience Will Define America's Vacation Culture," *Project: Time Off*, http://www.projecttimeoff.com/research/work-martyrs-cautionary-tale.

4. *Skyfall*, directed by Sam Mendes (2012; Eon Productions).

Chapter 4

1. Koulopoulos, Tom, and Dan Keldsen. *The Gen Z Effect: The Six Forces Shaping the Future of Business.* Brookline, MA: Bibliomotion, Inc., 2014. Kindle edition, locations 140–141.

2. This quote, commonly attributed to Socrates, was actually crafted by Kenneth John Freeman for his Cambridge dissertation published in 1907. For further details, visit http://quoteinvestigator.com/2010/05/01/misbehaving-children-in-ancient-times.

3. Ekins, Emily. "65% of Americans Say Millennials Are 'Entitled,' 58% of Millennials Agree," *Reason-Rupe Poll, Reason.com*, August 19, 2014, http://reason.com/poll/2014/08/19/65-of-americans-say-millennials-are-enti.

4. Stefania Corti, a Los Angeles-based fashion designer, is quoted in McDermott, John. "Why Gen X Is So Pissed at Millennials," *MEL Magazine*, January 3, 2017, https://melmagazine.com/why-gen-x-is-so-pissed-at-millennials-fdc1f2cc2e2c.

5. Williams, Ryan, interviewed by Robby Riggs in Washington, D.C., May 19, 2017.

6. Gottlieb, Lori. "How to Land Your Kid in Therapy," *The Atlantic*, July/August 2011, https://www.theatlantic.com/magazine/archive/2011/07/how-to-land-your-kid-in-therapy/308555/.

7. Gottlieb, "How to Land Your Kid in Therapy."

8. Gottlieb, "How to Land Your Kid in Therapy."

9. Gottlieb, "How to Land Your Kid in Therapy."

10. Gottlieb, "How to Land Your Kid in Therapy."

Chapter 5

1. Chemi, Eric. "Old-School Television Pros Talk about How Great Old-School Television Is," *MSN Money*, March 13, 2017, https://www.msn.com/en-us/money/other/old-school-television-pros-talk-about-how-great-old-school-television-is/ar-AAogdns.

2. Harter, Jim, and Amy Adkins. "Employees Want a Lot More from Their Managers," *Gallup Business Journal*, April 8, 2015, http://www.gallup.com/businessjournal/182321/employees-lot-managers.aspx.

3. Branham, Leigh. *The 7 Hidden Reasons Employees Leave* (New York: AMACOM, 2005).

4. Branham, *The 7 Hidden Reasons*, 3.

5. Boushey, Heather, and Sara Jane Glynn. "There Are Significant Business Costs to Replacing Employees," *Center for American Progress*, November 16, 2012, https://www.americanprogress.org/issues/economy/reports/2012/11/16/44464/there-are-significant-business-costs-to-replacing-employees/.

Chapter 6

1. Syrus, Publilius, quoted in Lyman, Darius Jr. *The Moral Sayings of Publilius Syrus, a Roman Slave: from the Latin*." L. E. Barnard & Company, 1856. Maxim 358, p. 37.

2. "U.S. Job Satisfaction Keeps Falling, the Conference Board Reports Today," *Conference Board*, February 28, 2005.

3. Lieberman, Matthew. "Should Leaders Focus on Results, or on People?" *Harvard Business Review*, December 27, 2013, https://hbr.org/2013/12/should-leaders-focus-on-results-or-on-people.

4. Lieberman, "Should Leaders Focus on Results," emphasis added.

5. Cited in Lieberman, "Should Leaders Focus on Results," emphasis added.

6. Beck, Randall, and Jim Harter. "Why Great Managers Are So Rare," *Gallup Business Journal*, March 25, 2014, http://www.gallup.com/businessjournal /167975/why-great-managers-rare.aspx.
7. Beck and Harter, "Why Great Managers Are So Rare."
8. "Famous Quotes by Vince Lombardi," http://www.vincelombardi.com/quotes .html.
9. De Neve, Jan-Emmanuel, et al. "Born to lead? A twin design and genetic association study of leadership role occupancy," *Leadership Quarterly* 24, Issue 1 (February 2013): 45–60. 46.
10. Myatt, Mike. "The #1 Reason Leadership Development Fails," *Forbes*, December 19, 2012, https://www.forbes.com/sites/mikemyatt/2012/12/19/the-1-reason -leadership-development-fails/#37cc917e6522.

Chapter 7

1. Maxwell, John. "Teamwork and Vision Go Hand in Hand," *John Maxwell Co.*, March 26, 2013, http://www.johnmaxwell.com/blog/teamwork-and -vision-go-hand-in-hand.
2. Adkins, Amy. "Employee Engagement in U.S. Stagnant in 2015," *Gallup: Employee Engagement*, January 13, 2016, http://www.gallup.com/poll/188144/employee -engagement-stagnant-2015.aspx.
3. Seppala, Emma, and Kim Cameron. "Proof that Positive Work Cultures Are More Productive," *Harvard Business Review*, December 1, 2015, https://hbr.org/ 2015/12/proof-that-positive-work-cultures-are-more-productive.
4. Branham, *The 7 Hidden Reasons*, 27.
5. Beck, Randall, and Jim Harter. "Managers Account for 70% of Variance in Employee Engagement," *Gallup Business Journal*, April 21, 2015, http://www.gallup .com/businessjournal/182792/managers-account-variance-employee -engagement.aspx.
6. Beck, Randall, and Jim Harter. "Why Great Managers Are So Rare," *Gallup Business Journal*, March 25, 2014, http://www.gallup.com/businessjournal/167975/ why-great-managers-rare.aspx.
7. Laurano, Madeline. *The True Cost of a Bad Hire*, August 2015, https://b2b-assets .glassdoor.com/the-true-cost-of-a-bad-hire.pdf.
8. Smart, Geoff, and Randy Street. *Who*. New York: Ballantine Books, 2008.
9. Ziglar, Zig. "Employees." *Ziglar.com*, https://www.ziglar.com/quotes/employees/.
10. Kohn, Art. "Brain Science: The Forgetting Curve—the Dirty Secret of Corporate Training," *Learning Solutions*, March 13, 2014, https://www. learningsolutionsmag.com/articles/1379/brain-science-the-forgetting -curvethe-dirty-secret-of-corporate-training.

Chapter 8

1. Van Gogh, Vincent, quoted in Stone, Irving, ed. *Dear Theo: An Autobiography of Vincent van Gogh*. 1937. New York: Plume, 1995. 115.
2. Carr, David. "How Obama Tapped into Social Networks' Power," *New York Times*, November 9, 2008, http://www.nytimes.com/2008/11/10/business/media /10carr.html.
3. "Political Fundraising in the Social Media Era," *MG Advertising Blog*, February 2012, http://www.mdgadvertising.com/blog/wp-content/uploads/2012/02/ political-fundraising-in-the-social-media-era.png.
4. Carr, "How Obama Tapped into Social Networks' Power."
5. Denning, Steve. "Peggy Noonan on Steve Jobs and Why Big Companies Die," *Forbes*, November 19, 2011, https://www.forbes.com/sites/stevedenning/2011/11/19/ peggy-noonan-on-steve-jobs-and-why-big-companies-die/#5e74eb89cc3a.
6. Deutsch, Claudia H. "At Kodak, Some Old Things Are New Again," *New York Times*, May 2, 2008, http://www.nytimes.com/2008/05/02/technology /02kodak.html.
7. Quoted in Deutsch, "At Kodak."
8. Sandoval, Greg. "Blockbuster laughed at Netflix partnership offer," *CNET. com*, December 9, 2010, https://www.cnet.com/news/blockbuster-laughed -at-netflix-partnership-offer/.
9. Thomas, Lauren. "Netflix shares rise after video streamer hits 100 million subscriber milestone," *CNBC*, April 24, 2017, http://www.cnbc.com/2017/04 /24/netflix-shares-rise-after-video-streamer-hits-100-million-subscriber- milestone.html.
10. *Jaws 2*, directed by Jeannot Szwarc (1978; Universal Pictures).

Chapter 9

1. Munro, Alice. "Go Ask Alice," *New Yorker*, February 19, 2011, http://www .newyorker.com/magazine/2001/02/19/go-ask-alice
2. Carroll, Dave. "The Full Story," *United Breaks Guitars*, http://www .davecarrollmusic.com/songwriting/united-breaks-guitars/.
3. Bullas, Jeff. "35 Mind Numbing YouTube Facts, Figures and Statistics— Infographic," *JeffBullas.com*, http://www.jeffbullas.com/35-mind-numbing -youtube-facts-figures-and-statistics-infographic/.
4. Ayres, Chris. Quoted in "'United Breaks Guitars': Did It Really Cost the Airline $180 Million?," *Huffington Post (Business)*, August 24, 2009, updated May 25, 2011, http://www.huffingtonpost.com/2009/07/24/united-breaks-guitars -did_n_244357.html.
5. Kottasova, Ivana. "United Loses $250 Million of Its Market Value," *CNN Money*, April 11, 2017, http://money.cnn.com/2017/04/11/investing/united -airlines-stock-passenger-flight-video/.

6. Sanders, Tim. *Dealstorming: The Secret Weapon that Can Solve Your Toughest Sales Challenges.* Penguin Publishing Group, 2016, Kindle Edition. 17–18.

7. Knowledge@Wharton. *Business Simplification 2015: The Unmet Strategic Imperative,* Wharton School of the University of Pennsylvania and SAP, 2015, http://d1c25a6gwz7q5e.cloudfront.net/reports/2015-03-03-Business -Simplification-2015-The-Unmet-Strategic-Imperative.pdf.

8. "Internet of Things (IoT) connected devices installed base worldwide from 2015 to 2025 (in billions)," *Statista,* https://www.statista.com/statistics/471264/ iot-number-of-connected-devices-worldwide/.

Chapter 10

1. Lord of Chesterfield, Philip Dormer Stanhope. *The Works of Lord Chesterfield, Including His Letters to His Son, Etc,* 153. Accessed at https://books.google .co.uk/books?id=l-c_AAAAYAAJ&printsec=frontcover&dq=the+works+ of+lord+chesterfield&hl=en&sa=X&ved=0ahUKEwjt4Jbg3qTVAhXhLc AKHUslCEUQuwUIKzAA#v=onepage&q=the%20works%20of%20lord% 20chesterfield&f=false on July 25, 2017.

2. Mark, Gloria. Interview, "Too Many Interruptions at Work?," *Gallup Business Journal,* June 8, 2006, http://www.gallup.com/businessjournal/23146/too-many -interruptions-work.aspx, emphasis added.

3. Mark, "Too Many Interruptions," emphasis added.

4. Mark, "Too Many Interruptions," emphasis added.

5. Cited in Boorer, Katie. "Productivity and the cost of distraction," *Human Resources Director Australia,* July 18, 2013, http://www.hcamag.com/opinion /productivity-and-the-cost-of-distraction-177342.aspx.

6. Boorer, "Productivity and the cost of distraction."

7. Steinhorst, Curt. "The Stats: Distractions at work are costing us all," *Curt Steinhorst.com,* http://www.curtsteinhorst.com/the-stats/.

8. Steinhorst, Curt. Interview, "CM125: 'Working While Distracted?'," *Counter Mentors* podcast, May 15, 2017, http://countermentors.com/cm125 -working-while-distracted/.

9. "The Work Martyr's Cautionary Tale: How the Millennial Experience Will Define America's Vacation Culture," *Project: Time Off,* http://www .projecttimeoff.com/research/work-martyrs-cautionary-tale.

10. Thomas, Maura. "Your Late-Night Emails Are Hurting Your Team," *Harvard Business Review,* March 16, 2015, https://hbr.org/2015/03/ your-late-night-emails-are-hurting-your-team.

11. Thomas, "Your Late-Night Emails."

12. Medina, John. Quoted from "The Brain Cannot Multitask," *Brain Rules Blog,* March 16, 2008, http://brainrules.blogspot.com/2008/03/brain-cannot -multitask_16.html.

13. Rubinstein, Joshua S., David E. Meyer, and Jeffrey E. Evans. "Executive Control of Cognitive Processes in Task Switching," *Journal of Experimental Psychology: Human Perception and Performance,* 2001, vol. 27, no. 4: 763–797. http://citeseerx .ist.psu.edu/viewdoc/download?doi=10.1.1.13.673&rep=rep1&type=pdf.

14. Quoted in Robertson, Porter. "Study: Multitasking is counterproductive," *CNN. com,* August 5, 2001, http://edition.cnn.com/2001/CAREER/trends/08/05 /multitasking.focus/.

15. "Drivers on Cell Phones Are as Bad as Drunks," *U News: The University of Utah,* June 29, 2006, https://archive.unews.utah.edu/news_releases /drivers-on-cell-phones-are-as-bad-as-drunks/.

16. "Up to 27 Seconds of Inattention After Talking to Your Car or Smartphone," *U News: The University of Utah,* October 22, 2015, https://unews.utah.edu /up-to-27-seconds-of-inattention-after-talking-to-your-car-or-smart-phone/.

17. "To Multitask or Not to Multitask," *University of Southern California Dornsife: Online Master of Science in Applied Psychology: Resources,* 2017, http://appliedpsychologydegree.usc.edu/resources/articles/to-multitask-or -not-to-multitask/.

Chapter 11

1. Kotter, John. "Accelerate," *Harvard Business Review,* November 2012, https:// hbr.org/2012/11/accelerate.

2. "The creed of speed," *The Economist,* December 5, 2015, http://www.economist. com/news/briefing/21679448-pace-business-really-getting-quicker-creed -speed.

3. Marsh, Peter. "The world struggles to keep up with the pace of change in science and technology," *Financial Times,* June 17, 2014, https://www.ft.com/content /b1da2ef0-eccd-11e3-a57e-00144feabdc0.

4. Carroll, Jim. "Keynote Feedback: Some Mind-Blowing Stats," *Jim Carroll.com,* October 2011, https://www.jimcarroll.com/2011/10/keynote-feedback-some -mind-blowing-stats/.

5. Carroll, "Keynote Feedback."

6. Stenovec, Tim. "More proof that Uber is killing the taxi industry," *Business Insider,* January 7, 2016, http://www.businessinsider.com/more-proof-that- uber-is-killing-the-taxi-industry-2016-1; Van Zuylen-Wood, Simon. "The Struggles of New York City's Taxi King," *Bloomberg Businessweek,* August 27, 2015, https://www.bloomberg.com/features/2015-taxi-medallion-king/.

7. Van Zuylen-Wood, "The Struggles of New York City's Taxi King."

8. Barro, Josh. "New York City Taxi Medallion Prices Keep Falling, Now Down about 25 Percent," *New York Times,* January 7, 2015, https://www.nytimes.com/ 2015/01/08/upshot/new-york-city-taxi-medallion-prices-keep-falling-now -down-about-25-percent.html?_r=0.

9. Rapp, Timothy. "Antonio Brown Fined for Posting Video of Mike Tomlin's Postgame Speech," *Bleacher Report*, January 17, 2017, http://bleacherreport.com/articles/2687432-antonio-brown-to-be-punished-for-posting-video-of-mike-tomlins-postgame-speech.

10 *Moneyball*, directed by Bennett Miller (2011; Sony Pictures).

Chapter 12

1. Maxwell, John. "John C. Maxwell: 5 Qualities of People Who Use Time Wisely," *Success.com*, June 2, 2015, http://www.success.com/article/john-c-maxwell-5-qualities-of-people-who-use-time-wisely.

2. Covey, Stephen R. *The 7 Habits of Highly Effective People: Powerful Lessons in Personal Change*. New York: Free Press, 1989. 23.

3. Covey, *The 7 Habits of Highly Effective People*, 23.

4. Gray, Albert E. N. "The Common Denominator of Success," Presentation to National Association of Life Underwriters, 1940, http://www.amnesta.net/mba/thecommondenominatorofsuccess-albertengray.pdf.

5. Gray, "Presentation."

6. Simester, Duncan. "The Lost Art of Thinking in Large Organizations," *MIT Sloan Management Review*, Summer 2016, http://sloanreview.mit.edu/article/the-lost-art-of-thinking-in-large-organizations/.

Chapter 13

1. De Pree, Max. *Leadership Is an Art*. 1987. New York: Crown Business, 2004. Kindle edition, 11.

2. Kruse, Kevin. "What Is Leadership?" *Forbes*, April 9, 2013, https://www.forbes.com/sites/kevinkruse/2013/04/09/what-is-leadership/#95177eb5b90c.

3. Kruse, "What Is Leadership?"

Chapter 14

1. Geneen, Harold S., and Alvin Moscow. *Management*. New York: Doubleday, 1984. 99.

2. Hollenbach, Dave. "The Firefighter's Creed," *Fire Engineering*, August 15, 2013, http://www.fireengineering.com/articles/fire_life/articles/2013/august/the-firefighters-creed.html.

3. *Remember the Titans*, directed by Boaz Yakin (2000; Walt Disney Pictures, Jerry Bruckheimer Films, Technical Black, Run It Up Productions Inc.).

Chapter 15

1. Beaton, Cecil. "The Secret of How to Startle," *Theater Arts*, vol. XLI, no. 5, May 1957.
2. Dorne, Eric, interviewed by Robby Riggs in Providence, RI, December 15, 2016.
3. Dorne, Eric, interview, 2016.

Chapter 16

1. Whyte, William Hollingsworth. "Is Anybody Listening" *Fortune*, September 1950: 174.
2. Riggs, Kelly. *1-on-1 Management: What Every Great Manager Knows That You Don't*. Dallas, TX: P3 Printing, 2008.
3. Definition from Merriam-Webster Dictionary, retrieved from https://www .merriam-webster.com/dictionary/influence.
4. Ziglar, Zig. Personal Facebook page, posted by Zig Ziglar on April 13, 2013, retrieved from https://www.facebook.com/ZigZiglar/posts/ 10151543396792863.
5. Conley, Randy. "3 Truths About Trust," *Leading with Trust*, February 5, 2017, https://leadingwithtrust.com/2017/02/05/3-truths-about-trust/.

Chapter 17

1. Wilson, Earl. "It Happened Last Night," *Morning News* (Wilmington, DE), October 30, 1961: 17.
2. Bohns, Vanessa K. "A Face-to-Face Request Is 34 Times More Successful than an Email," *Harvard Business Review*, April 11, 2017, https://hbr.org/2017/04/a -face-to-face-request-is-34-times-more-successful-than-an-email.
3. Green Peak Partners. "Research Results: Nice Guys Finish First When It Comes to Company Performance," *Market Wired*, June 15, 2010, http://www .marketwired.com/press-release/research-results-nice-guys-finish-first-when -it-comes-to-company-performance-1276170.htm.
4. Seppälä, Emma. "The Hard Data on Being a Nice Boss," *Harvard Business Review*, November 24, 2014, https://hbr.org/2014/11/the-hard -data-on-being-a-nice-boss.
5. Rigoni, Brandon, and Bailey Nelson. "Do Employees Really Know What's Expected of Them?" *Gallup Business Journal*, September 27, 2016, http://www .gallup.com/businessjournal/195803/employees-really-know-expected.aspx.
6. Fried, Jason. "The Danger of Keeping Your Team in the Dark," *Inc.com*, June 2015, https://www.inc.com/magazine/201506/jason-fried/lighting-the-way .html.

Chapter 18

1. Gladwell, Malcolm. *The Tipping Point: How Little Things Can Make a Big Difference*. Boston: Little, Brown and Company, 2000. 258.
2. Harter, Jim, and Amy Adkins. "Employees Want a Lot More From Their Managers," *Gallup Business Journal*, April 8, 2015, http://www.gallup.com /businessjournal/182321/employees-lot-managers.aspx, emphasis added.
3. Riggs, *1-on-1 Management*, 243.
4. Myatt, Mike. "Span of Control—5 Things Every Leader Should Know," *Forbes*, November 5, 2012, https://www.forbes.com/sites/mikemyatt/2012/11/05/ span-of-control-5-things-every-leader-should-know/#c3ad31b28c81.

Chapter 19

1. Dickens, Charles. "The Wreck of the Golden Mary," *Household Words*, December 6, 1856. 10. Accessed at https://books.google.com/books?id= jQ0HAQAAIAAJ&q=%22electric+telegraph%22#v=onepage&q&f=false.
2. Riggs, *1-on-1 Management*, 252–253.
3. Gribbons, Mary Kay, interviewed by Robby Riggs in Dallas, TX, April 3, 2017.

Chapter 20

1. Willink, Jocko, and Babin, Leif. *Extreme Ownership: How U.S. Navy SEALs Lead and Win*. New York: St. Martin's Press, 2015. 30.
2. Lencioni, Patrick. *The Five Dysfunctions of a Team: A Leadership Fable*. Hoboken, NJ: Jossey-Bass, 2002. vii.
3. Whipple, Mary. "About," *9th Seat.com*, http://www.9thseat.com/about/.
4. OED Online. Oxford University Press, June 2014, http://www.oed.com/view/ Entry/43546.
5. Macur, Juliet. "On Rowing Team, Smallest Body Has the Voice of Authority," *New York Times*, August 1, 2012, http://www.nytimes.com/2012/08/02/sports/ olympics/voice-of-authority-directs-us-womens-rowing-team.html.
6. Willink, Jocko, and Leif Babin. *Extreme Ownership: How U.S. Navy SEALs Lead and Win*. New York: St Martin's Press, 2015. Kindle edition, 8.
7. Willink and Babin, *Extreme Ownership*, 50.
8. "Geno Auriemma," *UConn Women's Basketball*, 2017, http://www.uconnhuskies .com/sports/w-baskbl/mtt/auriemma_geno00.html.
9. Altavilla, John. "UConn's Geno Auriemma On Importance of Practice," *Hartford Courant*, November 11, 2014, http://www.courant.com/sports/uconn- womens-basketball-blog/hc-geno-auriemma-love-practice-20141111-story .html.

10. Auriemma, Geno. Interview transcript, "When UConn's Geno Auriemma Talks Body Language, People Listen, Even Year Later," *Hartford Courant*, March 23, 2017, http://www.courant.com/sports/uconn-womens-basketball/hc-geno-auriemma-transcript-quote-0324-20170323-story.html.

Chapter 21

1. Connors, Roger, Tom Smith, and Craig Hickman. *The Oz Principle: Getting Results through Individual and Organizational Accountability*. 1994. Portfolio, 2004. 10.
2. Omara-Otunnu, Elizabeth. "The Big Four for the Big Four," *UConn*, April 2016, http://magazine.uconn.edu/2016/04/the-big-four-for-the-big-four/.
3. Blanchard, Ken, and Spencer Johnson. *The One Minute Manager*. New York: William Morrow, 1980. 31.
4. Townsend, Robert. *Up the Organization: How to Stop the Corporation from Stifling People and Strangling Profits*. New York: John Wiley & Sons, Inc., 1970. 33.

Chapter 22

1. Coolidge, Calvin. "Toleration and Liberalism," addressed to the American Legion Convention, Omaha, NE, October 6, 1925. Retrieved from http://www.presidency.ucsb.edu/ws/?pid=438.
2. *Dead Poets Society*, directed by Peter Weir (1989; Touchstone Pictures and Silver Screen Partners IV).
3. *Dead Poets Society*.
4. Quoted in Knight, Rebecca. "How to Make Your One-on-Ones with Employees More Productive," *Harvard Business Review*, August 8, 2016, https://hbr.org/2016/08/how-to-make-your-one-on-ones-with-employees-more-productive.
5. Koulopoulos, Thomas, and Dan Keldsen. *The Gen Z Effect: The Six Forces Shaping the Future of Business*. Brookline, MA: Bibliomotion, Inc., 2014. Kindle edition, location 3614.

Chapter 23

1. Drucker, Peter. *Classic Drucker: Essential Wisdom of Peter Drucker from the Pages of* Harvard Business Review. Boston: Harvard Business School Publishing Corporation, 2006. 83.
2. Himalayan Database, cited in "Everest by the Numbers: 2017 Edition," *The Blog on Alarnette.com*, December 30, 2016. http://www.alanarnette.com/blog/2016/12/30/everest-by-the-numbers-2017-edition/.

3. Leonhardt, David. "You're Too Busy. You Need a 'Shultz Hour,'" *New York Times*, April 18, 2017, https://www.nytimes.com/2017/04/18/opinion/youre-too-busy-you-need-a-shultz-hour.html, emphasis added.

4. Ford, Henry. Quoted by Don Soderquist, *The Wal-Mart Way: The Inside Story of the Success of the World's Largest Company*. New York: Harper Collins, 2005. 81.

5. Galagan, Pat, and Tony Bingham. "M'm M'm Good: Learning and Performance at Campbell Soup Company," *TD Magazine*, March 13, 2011, https://www.td.org/Publications/Magazines/TD/TD-Archive/2011/03/MM-MM-Good-Learning-and-Performance-at-Campbell-Soup-Company.

6. Schultz, Howard. Quoted in *Words of Wisdom: 1001 Quotes & Quotations*, volume 17. Kerala, India: Centre for Human Perfection, 2014. 80.

7. Ziglar, Zig. Quoted by Tom Ziglar in "Zig Ziglar talks about Twitter," *Ziglar Pure and Simple*, May 2, 2009, https://tziglar.wordpress.com/2009/05/02/zig-ziglar-twitter/.

8. Mayer, John D. 'Be Realistic" in "Leading by Feel," *Harvard Business Review*, January 2004, https://hbr.org/2004/01/leading-by-feel

9. Goleman, Daniel. *Emotional Intelligence: Why It Can Matter More than IQ*. London: Bloomsbury, 1996.

10. Goleman, foreword to McKee, Anne, and Richard E. Boyatzis, *Resonant Leadership: Renewing Yourself and Connecting with Others through Mindfulness, Hope, and Compassion*. Cambridge, MA: Harvard Business Review Press, 2005, x.

11. Bradberry, Travis, and Jean Greaves. *Emotional Intelligence 2.0*. TalentSmart, June 13, 2009, Kindle edition. Location 334.

12. Bradberry and Greaves, *Emotional Intelligence 2.0*, Location 353.

13. Lieberman, "Should Leaders Focus on Results?" emphasis added.

14. Ward, William Arthur. Quoted by Melissa C. Lott, "Photo Friday: The pessimist complains about the wind. . .the realist adjusts the sails," *Scientific American*, August 23, 2013, https://blogs.scientificamerican.com/plugged-in/photo-friday-the-pessimist-complains-about-the-windthe-realist-adjusts-the-sails/.

15. Collins, James C. *Good to Great: Why Some Companies Make the Leap . . . and Others Don't*. New York: HarperCollins, 2001. 1.

16. Raanan, Jordan. "Patriots coach Bill Belichick Getting Soft? That's What One of His Players Tells Him," *NJ.com*, January 28, 2015, http://www.nj.com/giants/index.ssf/2015/01/bill_belichick_getting_soft_thats_what_one_of_his.html.

Chapter 24

1. Barber, Benjamin. Quoted in Carole Hyatt and Linda Gottlieb, *When Smart People Fail*. New York: Penguin Books, 1987, 1993. 232.

2. Burkus, David. Interview, "CM112: 'The New, Millennial Approved Workplace," *Counter Mentors* podcast, July 20, 2016, http://countermentors .com/cm112-the-new-millennial-approved-workplace/.
3. Deloitte. *The 2016 Deloitte Millennial Survey: Winning over the next generation of leaders*, 2016. https://www2.deloitte.com/content/dam/Deloitte/global/ Documents/About-Deloitte/gx-millenial-survey-2016-exec-summary.pdf.
4. Mann, Annamarie, and Amy Adkins. "What Star Employees Want," *Gallup Business Journal*, March 8, 2017, http://www.gallup.com/businessjournal /205448/star-employees.aspx.
5. Quoted in Cameron, Christopher. Interview with Martha Stewart, "Martha Stewart Picks a New Path," *Luxury Listings NYC*, July 8, 2016, http://www.llnyc.com /stories/martha-stewart-picks-a-new-path.
6. "Paralympic gold medalist Kelly Gallagher is almost blind and can ski down slopes at 60mph, but says disabled people face uphill battle," *Belfast Telegraph*, April 18, 2016, http://www.belfasttelegraph.co.uk/life/features/paralympic -gold-medalist-kelly-gallagher-is-almost-blind-and-can-ski-down-slopes-at -60mph-but-says-disabled-people-face-uphill-battle-34666039.html.

Chapter 25

1. Burns, Robert. "To a Mouse." *Burns: Poems*. New York: Alfred A. Knopf, 2007. 25.
2. Tyson, Mike. Interviewed by Mike Berardino, "Mike Tyson explains one of his most famous quotes," *SunSentinel*, November 9, 2012, http://articles.sun -sentinel.com/2012-11-09/sports/sfl-mike-tyson-explains-one-of-his-most -famous-quotes-20121109_1_mike-tyson-undisputed-truth-famous-quotes.
3. Cunningham, Lillian. "In big move, Accenture will get rid of annual performance reviews and rankings," *Washington Post*, July 21, 2015, https:// www.washingtonpost.com/news/on-leadership/wp/2015/07/21/in-big-move -accenture-will-get-rid-of-annual-performance-reviews-and-rankings/?utm _term=.758700d274c7.
4. Cunningham, "In big move, Accenture."

Chapter 26

1. This quote appears to have originated with Carl Buehner. Quoted in Richard L. Evans, *Richard Evans' Quote Book*. Salt Lake City, UT: Publishers Press, 1971. 244, column 2.
2. Palmer, Anna, interviewed by Robby Riggs via FaceTime, April 5, 2017.
3. Steimle, Josh. "Reverse Mentoring—Investing in Tomorrow's Business Strategy," *Forbes*, May 5, 2015, https://www.forbes.com/sites/joshsteimle/2015/05/05/ reverse-mentoring-investing-in-tomorrows-business-strategy/#e89caaa67695.

4. Wadhwa, Tina. "Meet the 31-year-old who mentors the CEO of a $44 billion company," *Business Insider*, July 5, 2016, http://www.businessinsider.com/31 -year-old-employee-mentors-the-ceo-of-bny-mellon-in-reverse-mentoring -program-2016-7.

Chapter 27

1. Willink, Jocko, and Leif Babin. *Extreme Ownership: How U.S. Navy SEALs Lead and Win*. New York: St. Martin's Press, 2015. 61.
2. Regier, Nathan. Interview, "CM123: 'How Do You Conflict?'," *Counter Mentors* podcast, April 3, 2017, http://countermentors.com/cm-123-do-you-conflict/.
3. Namie, Gary. "2014 WBI U.S. Workplace Bullying Survey," *WorkplaceBullying .org*, February 2014, http://www.workplacebullying.org/wbiresearch/ wbi-2014-us-survey/.
4. Keenan, Jim. *Not Taught: What It Takes to Be Successful in the 21st Century that Nobody's Teaching You*. Denver, CO: A Sales Guy, 2015.
5. Keenan, Jim, interviewed by Robby Riggs and Kelly Riggs.
6. Guyton, Lizzy, interviewed by Robby Riggs in Boston, MA, April 15, 2017.

Chapter 28

1. Marshall, George C. Quoted in Walter Isaacson and Evan Thomas, *The Wise Men: Six Friends and the World They Made*. New York: Simon & Schuster, 1986. Kindle edition, 391.
2. Brock, David. "We Can't Ignore Poor Performers!," *Partners in Excellence Blog*, August 28, 2013, http://partnersinexcellenceblog.com/we-cant-ignore -poor-performers/.

Chapter 29

1. Mahoney, Rob. 2015. "Fine tuning: Coaching Stephen Curry, best shooter in the universe." Sports Illustrated, April 17. https://www.si.com/nba/2015/04/07/ stephen-curry-steve-kerr-warriors-coaching-staff-bruce-fraser.
2. Lombardi, Vince. "Will to Win," VinceLombardi.com, 2017, http://www .vincelombardi.com/quotes.html.
3. Kerr, Steve, as quoted by Rob Mahoney. "Fine tuning: Coaching Stephen Curry, best shooter in the universe," *Sports Illustrated*, April 17, 2015, https://www.si.com/nba /2015/04/07/stephen-curry-steve-kerr-warriors-coaching-staff-bruce-fraser.
4. "Coach," *Online Etymology Dictionary*, 2017, http://www.etymonline.com /index.php?term=coach.
5. Quoted in Kramer, Jerry. "Winning Wasn't Everything," *New York Times*, January 24, 1997, http://www.nytimes.com/ref/opinion/06opclassic.html.

6. Williams, Pat. *Vince Lombardi on Leadership: Life Lessons from a Five-Time NFL Championship Coach.* Charleston, SC: Advantage Media Group, 2015. 78.
7. Winfield, Kristian. "Gregg Popovich blasts Spurs for 'pathetic performance' in win against Mavericks," *SBNation*, November 22, 2016, https://www.sbnation.com/2016/11/22/13712152/gregg-popovich-spurs-angry-pathetic-mavs-video.
8. Lee, Michael. "San Antonio Spurs Coach Gregg Popovich dreads approaching end of Tim Duncan's career," *Washington Post*, October 4, 2014, https://www.washingtonpost.com/news/sports/wp/2014/10/04/san-antonio-spurs-coach-gregg-popovich-dreads-approaching-end-of-tim-duncans-career/?utm_term=.5a148c4ed43a.
9. McCarney, Dan. "The walking contradiction that is Gregg Popovich," MySanAntonio.com, April 19, 2013, http://blog.mysanantonio.com/spursnation/2013/04/19/the-contradiction-that-is-gregg-popovich/.

Chapter 30

1. Drucker, Peter. Quoted in Marshall Goldsmith, *What Got You Here Won't Get You There: How Successful People Become Even More Successful.* Hachette Books, 2007. 35.
2. Adkins, Amy, and Brandon Rigoni. "Managers: Millennials Want Feedback, but Won't Ask for It," *Gallup Business Journal*, June 2, 2016, http://www.gallup.com/businessjournal/192038/managers-millennials-feedback-won-ask.aspx.
3. Adkins and Rigoni, "Managers: Millennials Want Feedback."
4. Stosny, Steven. "What's Wrong with Criticism," *Psychology Today*, April 18, 2014, https://www.psychologytoday.com/blog/anger-in-the-age-entitlement/201404/whats-wrong-criticism.
5. Stosny, "What's Wrong with Criticism."
6. Patterson, Kerry, Joseph Grenny, Ron McMillan, and Al Switzler. *Crucial Confrontations: Tools for Resolving Broken Promises, Violated Expectations, and Bad Behavior.* New York: McGraw-Hill, 2004. 177.
7. Brock, David. "Dealing with Poor Performers," *Partners in Excellence Blog*, August 28, 2014, http://partnersinexcellenceblog.com/dealing-with-poor-performers/.
8. Patterson, Kerry, Joseph Grenny, Ron McMillan, and Al Switzler. *Crucial Confrontations: Tools for Resolving Broken Promises, Violated Expectations, and Bad Behavior.* New York: McGraw-Hill, 2004.

Chapter 31

1. Kennedy, John F. Speech in Raleigh, NC, September 17, 1960, retrieved from http://www.presidency.ucsb.edu/ws/?pid=74076.

2. Rigoni, Brandon, and Amy Adkins. "What Millennials Want from a New Job," *Harvard Business Review*, May 11, 2016, https://hbr.org/2016/05/what-millennials-want-from-a-new-job.

3. *Fight Club*, directed by David Fincher (1999; Fox 2000 Pictures).

4. Pink, Daniel H. *Drive: The Surprising Truth About What Motivates Us*. New York: Riverhead Books, 2009.

5. Pink, *Drive*, 203.

6. Sinek, Simon. "How Great Leaders Inspire Action," *TED Talk*, September 2009, https://www.ted.com/talks/simon_sinek_how_great_leaders_inspire_action.

7. Warren, Rick. *The Purpose Driven Life*. Grand Rapids, MI: Zondervan, 2002.

8. "Rick Warren's 'The Purpose Driven Life' Celebrates 10 Years," *Charisma News*, October 21, 2012, https://www.charismanews.com/us/34357-rick-warrens-the-purpose-driven-life-celebrates-10-years.

9. Mankins, Michael, and Eric Garton. "How Spotify Balances Employee Autonomy and Accountability," *Harvard Business Review*, February 9, 2017, https://hbr.org/2017/02/how-spotify-balances-employee-autonomy-and-accountability.

10. Branham, *The 7 Hidden Reasons*, 20.

11. Hollenbach, "The Firefighter's Creed."

Chapter 32

1. Commonly attributed to Robert Frost, this quote actually appears to have originated in *Hardware Age*, vol. 122, issues 10–17, 1928, 72. For more on this quotation and its attribution, see http://www.barrypopik.com/index.php/new_york_city/entry/the_brain_starts_working_when_you_get_up.

2. For our list of must-read leadership books, see p. 343 of this book.

3. Chabris, Christopher, and Daniel Simons. *The Invisible Gorilla: And Other Ways Our Intuitions Deceive Us*. Potter/TenSpeed/Harmony, 2010. Kindle edition. 7–8.

4. Scarlett, Hilary. *Neuroscience for Organizational Change: An Evidence-based Practical Guide to Managing Change*. London: Kogan Page, 2016. 86.

5. Duhigg, Charles. Interview with Terry Gross. "Habits: How They Form and How to Break Them," *Fresh Air*, NPR.org, March 5, 2012, http://www.npr.org/2012/03/05/147192599/habits-how-they-form-and-how-to-break-them.

6. Quoted in Owens, Mackubin Thomas. "Marines Turned Soldiers," *National Review Online*, December 10, 2001.

7. Churchill, Winston. *His Complete Speeches, 1897–1963*, ed. Robert Rhodes James, vol. 4 (1922–1928). London: Chelsea House, 1974, 3706.

Kelly & Robby's
Must Read List

1. *The 7 Habits of Highly Effective People: Powerful Lessons in Personal Change.* Stephen R. Covey. Free Press. 1989. (Personal Development)
2. *The Power of Habit: Why We Do What We Do in Life and Business.* Charles Duhigg. Random House. 2012. (Personal Development)
3. *Willpower: Rediscovering the Greatest Human Strength.* John Tierney and Roy Baumeister. Penguin Group (USA) LLC. 2006. (Personal Development)
4. *Grit: The Power of Passion and Perseverance.* Angela Duckworth. Scribner. 2016. (Personal Development)
5. *The 5 Dysfunctions of a Team: A Leadership Fable.* Patrick Lencioni. Jossey-Bass. 2002. (Leadership)
6. *Turn the Ship Around! A True Story of Turning Leaders into Followers.* L. David Marquet. Penguin Group (USA) LLC. 2013. (Leadership)
7. *1-on-1 Management: What Every Great Manager Knows that You Don't.* Kelly S. Riggs. 1-on-1 Media, Inc. 2008. (Leadership)
8. *The 7 Hidden Reasons Employees Leave: How to Recognize the Subtle Signs and Act Before It›s Too Late.* Leigh Branham. AMACOM. 2005. (Leadership)
9. *Crucial Confrontations: Tools for Resolving Broken Promises, Violated Expectations, and Bad Behavior.* Kerry Patterson, Joseph Grenny, Ron McMillan, Al Switzler. McGraw-Hill. 2004. (Communication)

10. *Made to Stick: Why Some Ideas Survive and Others Die.* Chip Heath and Dan Heath. Random House. 2007. (Communication)

11. *Switch: How to Change Things When Change is Hard.* Chip Heath and Dan Heath. Crown Business. 2010. (Change Management)

12. *Our Iceberg is Melting: Changing and Succeeding Under Any Conditions.* John Kotter and Holger Rathgeber. St. Martin's Press. 2005. (Change Management)

13. *Mindset: The New Psychology of Success.* Carol Dweck. Random House. 2006. (Psychology)

14. *Emotional Intelligence 2.0.* Travis Bradberry and Jean Greaves. TalentSmart. 2009. (Psychology)

15. *The Invisible Gorilla: How Our Intuitions Deceive Us.* Christopher F. Chabris and Daniel Simons. Harmony. 2010. (Psychology)

16. *Drive: The Surprising Truth About What Motivates Us.* Daniel H. Pink. Riverhead Books. 2009. (Psychology/Motivation)

17. *The ONE Thing: The Surprisingly Simple Truth Behind Extraordinary Results.* Gary W. Keller and Jay Papasan. Bard Press. 2013. (Motivation)

18. *The Gen Z Effect: The Six Forces Shaping the Future of Business.* Dan Keldsen and Tom Koulopoulos. Routledge. 2016. (Business Culture)

Author Biographies

Kelly Riggs is the founder of Business LockerRoom, Inc. (www .bizlockerroom.com), and co-founder of Counter Mentors (www .countermentors.com). He is an author, keynote speaker, and business performance coach for executives and companies throughout the United States and Canada, with revenues ranging from $3 million to the Fortune 500. His background as an executive and an entrepreneur has helped him to create a wildly successful track record of helping individuals and business owners dramatically improve their business performance.

Kelly has written two books: *1-on-1 Management: What Every Great Manager Knows That You Don't*, and *Quit Whining and Start SELLING! A Step-by-Step Guide to a Hall of Fame Career in Sales*.

Yes, Kelly is a Baby Boomer. And, yes, he takes his notes with a pen in his portfolio, and he thinks kids these days need to spend more time working and less time sending snaps.

Robby Riggs is the co-founder of Sana Sano Consulting (www .sanasanoconsulting.com) and Counter Mentors (www.countermentors .com). He is a high-performing transformation leader, working with companies ranging from start-up to Fortune 100, and is passionate about bringing people together to achieve more. Robby is an engaging, off-the-charts presenter and teacher who is highly sought after both in organizations and in the university setting.

Robby received his Master of Business Administration (MBA) from Boston University.

Yes, Robby is a Millennial. And, yes, he loves local coffee shops, enjoys working from home, and believes strongly that he should get a trophy.